AF333838

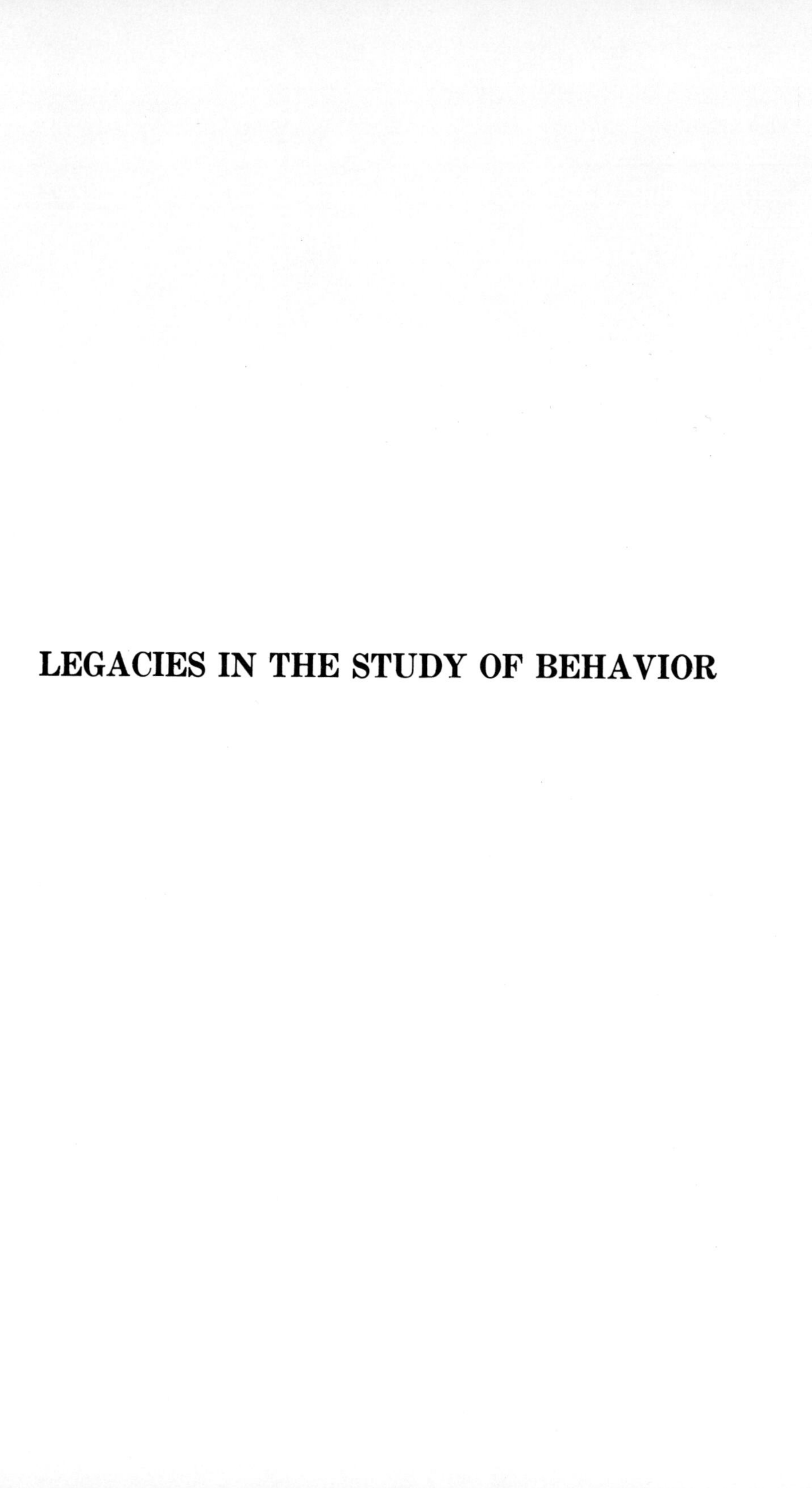

LEGACIES IN THE STUDY OF BEHAVIOR

Publication Number 951

AMERICAN LECTURE SERIES

A Publication in

The BANNERSTONE DIVISION of
AMERICAN LECTURES IN OBJECTIVE PSYCHIATRY

Editor

WILLIAM HORSLEY GANTT, M.D.
Pavlovian Laboratory
Veterans Administration Hospital
Perry Point, Maryland

Legacies in the Study of Behavior

<hr>

THE WISDOM AND
EXPERIENCE OF MANY

<hr>

By

JOSEPH WARREN CULLEN
Division of Research Grants
National Institutes of Health
Bethesda, Maryland

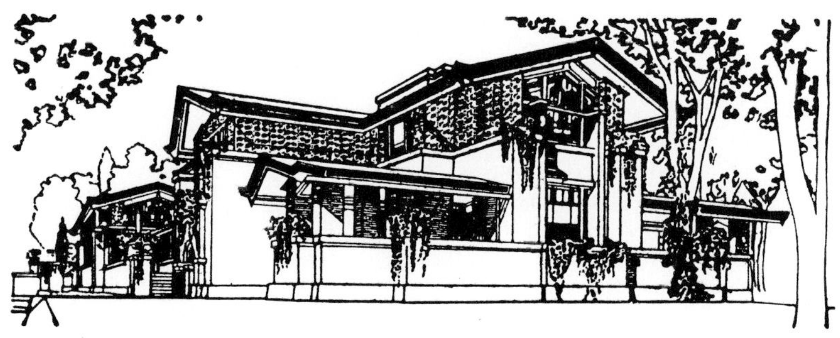

C H A R L E S   C   T H O M A S   ·   P U B L I S H E R
Springfield · Illinois · U.S.A.

Published and Distributed Throughout the World by
CHARLES C THOMAS • PUBLISHER
Bannerstone House
301-327 East Lawrence Avenue, Springfield, Illinois, U.S.A.

©*1974, by* CHARLES C THOMAS • PUBLISHER
ISBN 0-398-03147-9
Library of Congress Catalog Card Number: 74-1493

Printed in the United States of America
I-1

Library of Congress Cataloging in Publication Data

Cullen, Joseph Warren.
    Legacies in the study of behavior.

    American lecture series, publication no. 951. A publication in the Banner-
stone division of American lectures in objective psychiatry)
    1. Psychiatric research. I. Title.
[DNLM: 1. Behavior. BF121 C969L 1974]
RC337.C84   616.8'9   74-1493
ISBN 0-398-03147-9

To my wife Kay and my children, Neil and Jennie, who, more than all others, have taught me the importance of listening.

PREFACE

I BELIEVE THAT A SHORT INTRODUCTION is appropriate here, due to the unique nature of this book. Since the efforts presented herein are described as legacies, and since a legacy is a final document, each man can only provide one. On the other hand, the enclosed contributors could certainly provide us with volumes of observation, insight and advice. Would that we could be privy to all of it. The fact that they have taken the time to formulate that segment which they wish to bequeath as a legacy is, in our estimation, reason enough to listen.

All too often, men of science who have dedicated their lives to the pursuit of new knowledge retire from active research settings without a chance to freely express their latest conclusions, aspirations, concerns, and criticisms about science in general and their own discipline in particular. While the reasons for this oversight are myriad, the result is unfortunate. Their years of experience and intellectual maturity eminently qualify them as augurs of the future and exegetes of the past. Not to listen to them is tantamount to wasteful neglect, perhaps even arrogance. In fact, such an oversight is inconsistent with the intent of occidental pedagogy from the pre-Socratics to the present.

In early 1971, I wrote letters to twenty-six scientists whose contributions qualified them par excellence as candidates-at-large for such a legacy. There certainly were others who might have been approached. But it was not the intent of this editor to produce an encyclopedic college. In the initial missive soliciting their involvement, I appealed to these men to provide the scientific public with a document, the main impetus of which would address those scientific issues, which only they, as proven, mature and successful investigators, could provide. I noted that, after years of research, deliberation, and synthesis, they had accumulated a wealth of knowledge and dispositions which many would be interested in hearing. I stated that too many young scientists are destined to pursue perfunctory, or at times, even meaningless research interests perpetuated by an unripe scientific perspective. If these younger scientists could be provided with a compilation of legacies suggesting major research paths to be pursued, priorities to be considered, hunches to be followed, *caveats* to be aware of and philosophies to be cultivated, perhaps some of the detours which retard progress to creative and effective science could be avoided.

Let me not mislead the reader. This book is not an indictment of the uselessness of the young scientist, nor does it underestimate his potential. On the contrary, it is quite the opposite. While it is true that "the journey of a thousand miles begins with a single step" and the journey is necessarily long and tedious (and is perhaps a *sine qua non* in science for the neophyte), it is also true that a few appropriately chosen observations could be a catalyst for future scientific insight. It was particularly with the young scientist in mind, then, that this book was formulated. It is for him to read and weigh the advice and counsel of his scientific forebearers. The thoughts herein may temper his impulsivity and, at the same time, massage his enthusiasm. They may provide caveats or exhortations. This may even convince him to do nothing. But, if he reads these contents, he can never really be unaffected by them. The important thing is that he has read them and they issue forth from a cadre of men who have already proved that their intellects are to be reckoned with.

The book is a vehicle for intellectual stimulation and scientific arousal. As the British empiricists have insisted: *(Quidquid percipitur, per modem percipientis, percipitur)* Whatever is perceived, is perceived in the manner of the one perceiving. Why should we not enhance the probability of a successful career in science by sampling from a pool of ideas provided by those whose success is history?

Of the original twenty-six scientists approached, only eleven completed the task. In the first place, not all agreed to prepare a manuscript. This, however, was not due to a lack of interest; other priorities or failing health prevented their commitment. Many of them spontaneously offered encouragement, good will and advice about editing such a book. I am most grateful to these scholars for their nonvisible contribution.

It is with deep gratitude to the authors of this book that I present these legacies for the scrutiny and edification of anyone who reads them. Sincere gratitude is also expressed to Dale Van Hart for her enthusiastic energy in helping to put this book together.

While it is difficult to thank all those who provided the intellectual spark for this endeavor, there are two men who easily come to mind as great teachers, men who have provided sparks for many others as well. I thank them sincerely for all the wisdom and friendship they have provided. They are W. Horsley Gantt and Barron B. Scarborough.

Joseph Warren Cullen

CONTENTS

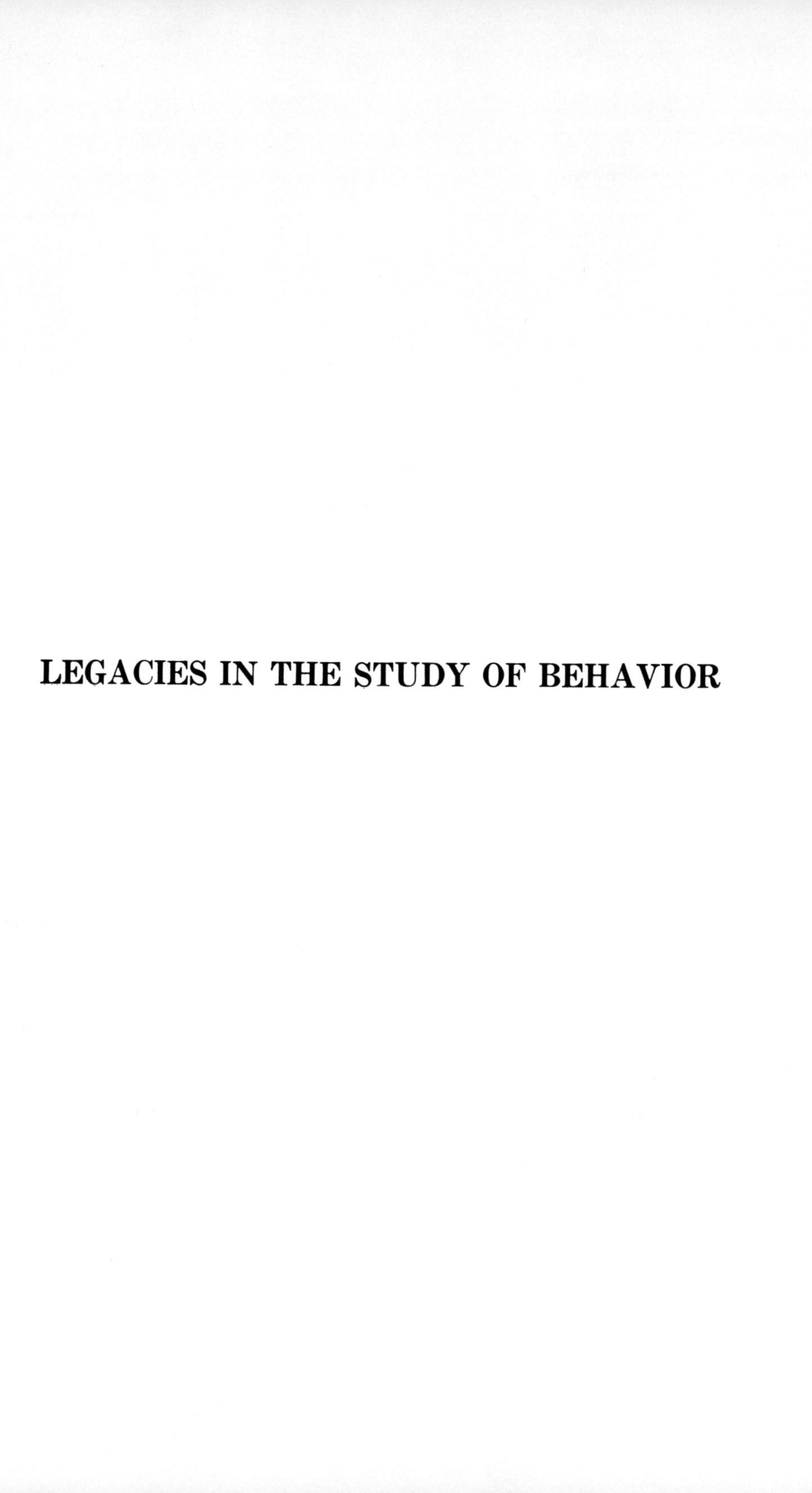

LEGACIES IN THE STUDY OF BEHAVIOR

Chapter I

PHYSIOLOGIST AT WORK

E. F. ADOLPH

Edward F. Adolph was born (1895) and reared in Philadelphia of south German ancestry. His father was a portrait engraver; his mother a school teacher. He had a classical education at Central High School in that city, which granted him its cusotmary A.B. degree in 1913. After three years in Harvard College he received a second A.B. degree (magna cum laude). There he did his first research work in zoology. At Yale University he pursued graduate study in chemical physiology and zoology. After a period of service in army hospital laboratories (World War I), he did a Ph.D. thesis at Harvard University. With the Ph.D. degree he received a traveling fellowship which enabled him to work in research at Oxford, to attend the tenth International Congress of Physiology in Paris (1920), and to visit cities and laboratories in western Europe.

On the return to the U.S. he married Mary Grace Bagg, an artist and school teacher. Three children were born (1923-1931). Dr. Adolph taught invertebrate zoology at Woods Hole in the summers of 1921-1924 and general physiology at the University of Pittsburgh in the corresponding academic years. After a period at Johns Hopkins University as a National Research Council fellow he joined the physiology faculty of the School of Medicine and Dentistry of the University of Rochester and has remained there ever since. He became Professor Emeritus in 1960 and is still actively involved in laboratory investigations.

Dr. Adolph was a fellow of the Guggenheim Memorial Foundation (at Berlin, 1927) and a Research Associate at Harvard University (1936).

He studied man in the warm desert in 1937, 1942 and 1943. The results were reported in a book published with associates in 1947. In recognition of these studies he received a Presidential Certificate of Merit. Dr. Adolph was president of the American Physiological Society in 1953. He was responsible for organizing the Society's committee on education. He was elected a fellow of the American Academy of Arts and Sciences.

Dr. Adolph was a consultant at various periods to the U.S. Bureau of Mines, the Committee on Medical Research, the Climatology Unit of the Quartermaster Department, the Subcommittee on Environmental Protection of the National Research Council, the Panel on Physiology of the Research and Development Board, the Aeromedical Laboratory and the Arctic Aeromedical Laboratory.

His journal articles have appeared in numerous biological periodicals, not the least of which are three classical monographs: on the regulation of size in unicellular organisms (1931), on physiological regulations (1943), and on the origins of physiological regulations (1968). He has served as referee editor of several journals, and at present continues as a member of the editorial boards of the American Physiological Society.

Introduction

WHAT KIND OF LEGACY can I bequeath? The legacy of a scientist consists largely in his reports of researchers. However, no legatee can readily ferret out what bits of wisdom lie hidden in those dated reports. For this reason I can be expected to gather some of my more comprehensive thoughts into an essay.

When I hesitate to write a legacy to physiologists, I face the question: is it better that I trace the development of my studies of physiological regulation and physiological adaptation than that some other person should do it? At one time my mentor L. J. Henderson considered it important to write down for posterity the mental processes and experiences through which he evolved his particular studies and concepts. How had he chosen and fulfilled his self-imposed tasks? During several summers he dictated his memories; but in the end he desisted from the effort. The record lies truncated in the Harvard University Library. My inference is that L. J. was continually frustrated in his attempts to identify the significant factors that steered his efforts. He was a person acutely aware of the difference between a determining influence and a rationalization, and nevertheless found that he repeatedly recorded rationalizations which later showed themselves for what they were.

The reader of a legacy probably imagines that the testator has an inflated regard for his own accomplishments, and plans to tell legatees how to conduct their lives. Disowning that plan, how shall I disillusion any who credit me with such an intention? I do not want to appear as the perfect experimenter who followed a logical pattern from a question to an answer. One recourse I have is to recount some pit-falling that should cut my image down to size; I could strive to make some shortcomings visible. But, who wants to read a record of aborted opportunities? Yet, an honest legacy will record false starts, thoughtless deeds, unfruitful decisions, failures of vision. Perhaps mercifully, those are the events that are soonest forgotten; in any case, I, too, fail to supply much self-critical material.

Every scientist has to be courageous enough to live with frailties, misdirected aims and fruitless endeavors. He can profit by recognizing them; though he has lost most of the candor that could do so.

Some citizens of the world think that a scholar-scientist should be able to state what he has contributed to the life of mankind, to show a measurable product from his existence. Indeed, students pay tuition fees to sample his guidance, libraries buy his publications, and occasionally news media attempt to describe what he does. Will I be able to state what I have done and how? I doubt it; but I can indicate some efforts that may arouse others to action and thought. For that is a reward of a teacher—after all the factual information he transmitted has entered limbo, the teacher's individuality still lives in his students.

REGULATORY PHYSIOLOGY

How did I come to study physiological regulations in a comprehensive manner? I was experimenting with the input and output of water. Frogs (or dogs) were given water through a stomach tube in varied amounts on different days. As urine formed it was collected without being allowed to accumulate in the urinary bladder. What significance to the organism lies in the ascertained fact that the amount of urine corresponded to the excess of water given? The answer was that the several speeds of elimination restore the water content of the body to a norm in equal times.

What happens in the converse situation, a deficit of body water? Frogs (or dogs) were made to lose body water through evaporation from the body surface when in a warm room. The fraction of the body water that was lost was measured by weighing them from hour to hour. At the end of the dehydration period frogs were allowed to sit in water, dogs were allowed to drink water. Both took water rapidly, frogs through the skin, dogs through the mouth. Soon they had taken up enough water to equal their deficit and no more.

In both water excess and water deficit the rate of water exchange proved to be proportional to the disturbance in body water content.

At this point I was told that drinking is a behavior; I was correlating a behavior with a measurable physiological state, water content. So far as I could see, there was no boundary between behavior and nonbehavior; water drinking filled a regulatory requirement of the dog exactly parallel to water absorption through the skin of the frog. Further, water drinking by neuromuscular alimentation was the converse of water elimination by renal filtration-reabsorption. All of these regulated processes together constituted the overall means of homeostasis of body water. From that conclusion I went on to realize that other bodily components such as heat, food and energy were similarly regulated in a pattern of intake and output, of gain and loss; in general, of metabolic exchanges (Adolph, 1943).

These physiological studies contributed to an understanding of homeostasis or homeokinesis only at the end of several years of experimentation with body water. At first I thought of movement of body water as a physicochemical process; maybe its study would help me to understand permeabilities (as, in frog skin) and excretion (as, in renal filtration). I was looking at tissue exchanges in the belief that cell volumes and body volumes (weights) would resemble sacks of solutions. Only when the factors that could influence these volumes were found to be too numerous for the application of extant physicochemical theory did I shift to another kind of view and admit that the body as a whole was profitting from the properties of its tissue exchanges. Data then in hand fitted this concept, and, so far as I was concerned, I had discovered regulatory physiology. In reality, of course, I had merely found my private path to grasping (albeit in a quantitative way) the concept of bodily maintenance that others had found by other approaches.

What deterred me from seeing that water exchanges of animals formed a homeostatic system in the years that elapsed from my first study of them (which already bore the title "regulation")?

(a) The doctrine prevailed that contributions to physiology had to reveal mechanisms.

(b) The time and place dictated to me an analysis in physico-chemical terms.

(c) The practice then pervaded physiology that physiology was studied at a laboratory bench and did not require imaginative thought. These were real road-blocks that had to be lived down before my efforts explored the notion that water exchanges accomplished something of significance to bodily maintenance.

One aspect of my new study of regulation was that the kinds of processes and tissues participating were of great variety. Excretion was the converse of drinking; nervous activities matched endocrine activities. This variety showed that one need not confine oneself to a single technical specialty, such as electro-physiology. It also suggested that if drinking was a behavior, then standard physiology had to include behavioral studies. One could not henceforth ignore the correlates that stood outside the standard repertoire of the physiology of that era. A long time was required to clear away doctrinaire rubbish, a fact that suggests there are today other unnecessary preconceptions blocking the minds of biologists.

THE INVESTIGATOR

What steers a nobody into his field of interest? Youthful experiences gave me an admiration for animal development (ontogeny). I saw chicks hatch. I collected frog eggs, put them in the goldfish aquarium, and saw the embryos form, feed, metamorphose into jumping frogs. In mature years I measured the growth and acquisition of actions of several species of amphibia, and recently, of mammals. Studies of development seemed to teach me to understand certain regulations of functions, as studies of maturity alone could not do. At birth, for instance, dogs failed to excrete excesses of body water, allowing it to accumulate; only after several days of development was the regulatory response to water excess established. Studies of several more kinds of functional development enabled me to grasp important features of the corresponding physiological regulations (Adolph, 1968).

How does developmental physiology illuminate function? The kinds of activities, such as movement, sensation and coordination, increase in number with age of the individual. As the embryo or infant self-differentiates, form and function change in unison. On the way, individuals of varied stages exist, and one can observe the stepwise installation of any activity. As the activity becomes available, the employment of it comes under control. For example, a heart beat can arise only in one region of one mesodermal tissue of the embryo (such as larval salamander or fetal rat). At first stereotyped, the beating later becomes susceptible to external influences such as nervous ones; in advanced stages the beating is modified in response to a host of coordinate activities in distant tissues. Regulations have accumulated, therefore, in a programmed manner that can be experimented with in varied partial combinations. Under limited circumstances the developing individual survives and acts without these regulations, whereas it becomes capable of more deeds with them. For me, such developmental studies have provided a powerful tool with which a physiologist's aims are pursued, both in thought and in experiment.

All scientists doubtless have rules or practices for scientific investigations. Most practices seem unformulated, unconscious; but their owner often defends them as the only suitable procedures. However, one finds that different researchers use unlike formulas. Therefore, an outsider can properly conclude that there are multiple ways to pursue scientific research; and that most of them are based on hunches and emotional preferences. I infer that every scientist grows up to follow examples of researches he observes around him. In the deeds of others he sees analogies to what he would like to do. He adopts some of their practices even without believing there are general features of research that can be formulated. He is using paradigms (see below) to guide his efforts.

The scientist, of all people, finds it hard to put into words what he thinks and does, because he spends his life trying to detach his emotions from the phenomena he studies. He has stuggled to make his reports sound as though the "law" behind the phenomena revealed itself without uncertainty or effort on his part. He poses as a logical person who took no blind paths, needed no guesses, saw no alternatives. What a stick of rectitude he was! The fact was that he had a hunch, he gave up a vacation to work on it, he made a half dozen false starts, he did last the experiment that logically came first, he rewrote his conclusions seven times. Actually he did not even start out to investigate the particular phenomena that he has now succeeded in analyzing. He pretends to eliminate all signs of motivation and doubt from his report! Does any reader believe the reporter knew the straight path to a scientific contribution? One may add the rhetorical questions: how did such self-misrepresentation on the part of scientists come to be practiced? What are its values? Is there any point in attempts to change the future style of reporting?

The scientist succeeds in his undertakings in spite of his pretenses. Even among scholars he is a privileged character. "The scientist differs from the nonscientist principally by the fact that problems are his daily fare, that he seeks them rather than deliberately avoids them" (Swanson, 1956). The advantage he enjoys was expressed many centuries ago: "He who is accustomed to research, seeks and penetrates everywhere mentally, passing constantly from one topic to another; nor does he ever give up his investigation" (Galen, 1929). Talents suitable for research can find their material in any discipline; but the scientist seems exposed to endless spurs that keep his mind in motion.

CONCEPTS

Where do ideas come from? Paradigms, one learned in the study of grammar, are examples that show one how to conjugate a hundred verbs one has not yet encountered. Their use enables one to work by analogy with better-known instances. For the scientist, a search for a mechanism is largely work by analogy; a search for biological regulations, evolutions, ontogenies is work by analogy. Some biologists will look for molecular components, others for thermodynamic patterns, still others for ecological relations. Yet, all of them will be contributing to an understanding by means of their skills and ingenuities. All will adopt procedures that have been used before, but adding more or less agility in the perception of the analogy or pattern (Kuhn, 1962).

Paradigms are not peculiar to sciences, nor to grammars; they are in use by everyone everyday. People solve many a dilemma by asking themselves: What did I decide last time I faced a comparable situation? What did I see my boss, teacher or parent do in such a difficulty? The skills they mobilize depend upon their recognition of similarities and differences between this occasion and previous situations. It is foolish to deny that the past is relevant to the present; everyone's behavior shows it is apropos whenever the elements of similarity can be traced.

Concepts are formed with examples and instances in mind. The first observation seems isolated; but sooner or later one realizes that it belongs to a group of observations. If the group is already well-defined, one now adds its whole weighty abstraction to one's new comprehension. If no similar phenomena have been heard of, one has to search for more of them firsthand. One thereby builds significance into the first and subsequent observations.

In illustration I revert to researches mentioned earlier. When I correlated rates of water excretion with body contents of water, the correlation stood as an interesting fact of physiology. After some weeks I saw that the correlation exists not only in frog but in dog, man and other familiar species. Next I discovered that such a correlation holds not only for water exchanges but for heat exchanges and some other components of organisms.

Finally I realized that such relations are the operative means of physiological regulations and of homeostasis. Each step eventually flashed into a concept, but the period between steps was long and its pregnancy obscure.

No two observations of phenomena are exactly alike. To see the resemblances in the midst of incidentals is the skill of the scholar. He builds for himself a frame (paradigm) of possible generalization. Now his attentions are sharpened, for he visualizes a pattern among phenomena. His mind is prepared for the next observation. If he can plan to see more of the specific phenomena, he can check the points of resemblance; if he has to wait for chance occurrences he can only hope to encounter them. In either case he broadens his generalization from the instances, and gradually enriches his concept beyond what another person's statement could supply to him. This and additional features of the biologist's occupation have been attractively presented by Arber (1954).

In the scientist's world only the positive accomplishment is mentioned. But I think one will also recognize that a contribution to the area of biology M is necessarily a deflection of effort from biology N. There is no way to estimate what riches have been missed in unexplored territories. Insofar as the sum of human efforts limits the total accomplishment in sciences, the likelihood may be entertained that equal effort in another direction would have yielded equal or greater results. To some persons, the specific choice of direction, the road taken, seemed obviously unique; to others, any alternative would likely have led to bright unknowns. Every day one by-passes whole realms of possible reward.

Like other scientists, I often hoped to hit upon an innovative idea that, when worked out, would constitute a breakthrough. The innovative idea usually proved either insubstantial or time-worn. However, to me each idea was creative in that it posed a question, and eventually I found an answer accompanied by an emotional thrill. The idea or notion furnished me with a private novelty of thought though not a public one. History shows that public revolutions are rare, and years of time may be required to demonstrate that the novel notion is superior to its predecessors. Nevertheless, small concepts or insights that enter the mind of everyone are not to be dismissed lightly; one has much to learn in testing whether they can be substantiated.

How do insights enter the mind? Of the accounts recorded by outstanding scientists I mention two. Helmholtz (1971), physiologist and physicist, wrote at his seventieth birthday:

> I have often found myself in the unpleasant position of having to wait for useful ideas. . . . They often steal into one's train of thought without their significance being at first understood. . . . Sometimes they are present without our knowing whence they came. . . I have always had to turn my problems about in my mind in all directions. . . Then, after the fatigue of the work had passed away, . . . the fruitful ideas . . . were most apt to come when I was leisurely climbing about on wooded hills in sunny weather.

Poincare (1946), mathematician, in major instances realized the significance of ideas with "suddenness and immediate certainty." Thus, when analysis of a certain problem had seemed stalled,

> travel made me forget my mathematical work . . . We entered an omnibus to go some place or other. At the moment when I put my foot on the step the idea came to me, without anything in my former thoughts seeming to have paved the way for it, that the transformations I had used to define the Fuchsian functions were identical with those of non-Euclidean geometry. . . I verified the result at my leisure.

Miscellaneous insights are present in any mind in latent form. If they would only surface! No amount of effort makes the majority of them visible. Yet external factors of unknown quality favor their unheralded appearance.

For me the laboratory does as much to bring notions to realization as do relaxations. Further, conversation with a fellow scientist promotes explorations into the known and the unknown, and compels expressions of belief that help to put inchoate questions into words. The colleague forces verbalizations or definitions or juxtapositions. He induces paradigms that I later either match or contradict.

Occasionally, scribbling or diagramming at random produces fruit. If the scribble does not seem fruitful today, it may find significance overnight. Whether or not "spontaneous" brainstorms can be channeled, often that which most recently occupies the mind is the question first solved. Apparently the mental product is nonrandom even if unpredictable.

Probably most important ideas start with the writing of a cryptic sentence on an old envelope. Some are lost, some die, and some develop. Without the old envelope and the stub pencil few would grow. The precarious growth is slow, delayed, misplaced; that is its curious quality. Why is the potential of the idea not at once apparent? Whose is the diapause and incubation—the idea or the idea-monger?

Most of the time I am unaware of myself as a physiologist and scholar. In the midst of reverie, however, I may suddenly realize that I contemplate a viewpoint or idea worth recording. I am experiencing the very sort of mental activity I earlier vainly hoped for. I am "stung by the splendor of a sudden thought" (R. Browning, 1872). Such an experience makes me suspect that the concept I brought to consciousness is only one out of many other nuggets that passed into oblivion.

A scientist, like other persons, spends most of his days, hours and minutes with trivial thoughts. They hardly deserve the name of thoughts; they are images and juxtapositions that pop up from nowhere. The stream of consciousness usually flows much too rapidly for connected reflection about its content. The stream is full of noise, and the span of time in which a pattern can be discovered after the noise has been filtered away is small indeed. This residue, however, is the wherewithal of the scholar; he is fortunate if one percent or even 0.1 percent of the flow yields a recognizable pattern. But, the scholar is not always a passive agent; he disciplines his mind to find connections among the images that float by. With practice he increases the yield of nontrivial concepts. That is his expertness; he becomes selective in the yield of ideas, he cultivates the art of having ideas.

A common supposition is that a science develops by accretion of facts, of generalizations and of concepts. But, it is also widely recognized that each of these generalizations and concepts becomes revised and susperseded. One often avoids use of notions that were universally accepted a decade or a century ago. He thereby admits that old observations come to stand in new contexts. Present climate determines present significance, under the scrutiny of new eyes and new minds and the aura of new times. That aura of thought makes the difference between outworn understanding and current understanding. It also implies that current views will be modified or superseded in their turn.

SCHOLARLY EFFORTS

I am struck with the query: how is it that, although I spent most of my working time in laboratories, appearing to be an empiricist, yet when I now come to write a legacy I speak as a builder of ideas and generalizations? For one thing, the laboratory investigations required attention to infinite details, whereas one cannot make an essay out of protocols and analyses. A diary may furnish materials for an intellectual history, but is not a legacy. The biographee probably had three meals every day, but no biographer finds it important to say so. Out of the activity in laboratories arose comprehensive motions; yet daily spade work was indispensable to the extended mental horizon. Therefore my legacy emphasizes certain summits generated from a seemingly plodding career.

Above, I mentioned my studies of physiological regulations as one summit of my effort; they evolved from measurements of specific relations in body water exchanges. I also mentioned studies of development in ontogeny; they furnished a method for analysis of regulations. Now I will describe studies of physiological adaptation that have repeatedly appeared in my repertory.

A physiological adaptation is a process of modification whereby the individual responds differently when repeatedly exposed to a given environmental influence. Often the modification favors both action and survival in the new environment, for example, increase in capacity for work by a man or a rat placed in high altitudes. Many investigators have described adaptations they observed in varied kinds of organisms; I felt driven to ascertain what the numerous adaptations have in common. And I now conclude that the capacities for specific forms of physiological adaptations develop in each individual during ontogeny, according to programs furnished by inherited factors as prescribed by ancient natural selection. In later life an item in the capacities may be aroused by a particular trigger, for example, by liberation of erythropoietin during altitude exposure (Adolph, 1972).

For more than forty years, I infer, a feeling of imprecision about adaptations stayed in my subconscious. At decade intervals in that period, partial comprehensions erupted. Some eruptions came with specific laboratory observations, others with information derived from the publications of fellow scientists. What a slow development of ideas and of their matching with extant data! Hindsight emphasizes the snail's pace at which these studies progressed. In the end it now seems to me only "natural" that physiological regulations should be flexible enough (adaptable) to change with persisting circumstances; only "natural" that there be a molecular basis for triggering the change; only "natural" that the direction of change will usually favor adequate operation in the new circumstances. Today biologists design experiments on adaptation in the expectation that subjection of individuals to factor A will result in modifications in some property that enhances operation in the presence of factor A, and extant details reveal that such a rule prevails.

Apparently some block to comprehension limits the speed with which one can develop and test a realistic concept such as "physiological adaptation." Abundant information showed that adaptations regularly occurred when triggered; the time I required for concentrated thought about them was available. Still, insight can progress only by steps. A small step is easier to accept in one's thinking than a big step. One would like to take a big step, but cannot grasp enough of its implications to justify it. Few are the Darwins who have the patience to check enough details by which they may convince themselves and others that there is a rule, while aware of the great odds for error.

The scholarly effort, once consummated, needs clear presentation. Writers subconsciously aim what they express at particular individuals. Usually they are unaware of an abstract person that could be called a general reader. But the particular individual serves as the central recipient of the communication; if it gets across to him, the aim was accurate. Speakers likewise select someone in an audience to serve as the representative listener. They keep such an individual in view; if the individual shows incomprehension or disinterest the speaker modulates his diction. An emotionally involved audience reacts upon the speaker and may help him to express himself superbly.

The general environment of a scholar may definitely limit the breadth and depth of the work he does. But also, another environment may induce him to exert initiative and to accomplish deeds and thoughts that otherwise he would not produce. The expectancies of his job, his colleagues, his students force him to a degree of effort or a plane of sophistication that would be unattained elsewhere. That is a way in which one university or one department does more than select talent; it may induce it. "Men habitually use only a small part of the powers which they actually possess and which they might use under appropriate conditions." (Wm. James, 1911).

Scholars interact strongly even when they see one another rarely. My experience is that a colleague at work in the next corridor or in another university unknowingly monitors my work. I have him in mind, I imagine what moves he would think important, I seem to know what steps he will approve. When it is stated that persons A and B "had little to do with one another," the inference cannot be drawn that they did not interact. Scholars I have never even seen exert an influence in my thought and deed. But those I have once known will continue to exert most influence. Their thinking furnishes paradigms and critiques for my thinking and doing. Each colleague is part of my alter ego who argues my decisions and aims.

One may lead a progressive life once he has noted that he can learn from each mistake or each wise decision. Instead of blaming his lot in life, he resolves to profit from experience. This lesson is no novelty; all persons day after day revise their lives, perhaps without realizing that they do so. But in addition, one may be glad of experience, even of adverse experience, for what it brings to the experiencer. Foresight would be impossible if past events added nothing to one's pool of case histories, for from those case histories one continually revises action.

Summary

What am I saying? No two scientists meet the same problems or think the same thoughts, but they use similar tactics, whatever their professed philosophies. Each, at last, traces the path he has travelled in terms of the specific studies in which he found nonobvious results. Though each rationalizes differently what he did and how he did it, in reality he reasoned in analogies and paradigms that enabled him to fit his results into the great body of insights called science. At the same time, his experience was unique, and the questions that he raised in his problem-solving are bequeathed to his legatees. Membership in the great company of problem-solvers, mind-users and concept-makers is the common reward of scientists.

REFERENCES

Adolph, E. F.: *Physiological Regulations.* Lancaster, Cattell, 1943.

Adolph, E. F.: *Origins of Physiological Regulations.* New York, Academic Press, 1968.

Adolph, E. F.: Physiological adaptations: Hypertrophies and superfunctions. *Am Sci, 60:*608, 1972.

Arber, A.: *The Mind and the Eye.* Cambridge, University Press, 1954.

Browning, R.: A death in the desert. In *Selections from the Poetical Works.* New York, Crowell, 1872.

Galen, C.: On habits. *Greek Medicine,* trans. by A. J. Brock, London, Dent, 1929.

Helmholtz, H.: An autobiographical sketch. In *Selected Writings of Hermann von Helmholtz,* trans. by R. Kahl. Middletown, Wesleyan, 1971.

Henderson, L. J.: Memories. Manuscript in Harvard University Library Archives, 1939.

James, W.: The energies of men. In *Memories and Studies.* New York, Longmans, 1911.

Kuhn, T. S.: *The Structure of Scientific Revolutions.* Chicago, University Press, 1962.

Poincare, H.: Science and method. In *The Foundations of Science,* trans. by
G. B. Halsted. Lancaster, Science Press, 1946.
Swanson, C. P.: [Book Review], *Q Rev Biol, 31*:36-37, 1956.

Chapter II

PERSONALITY AS AN INTEGRATIVE CONCEPT IN PSYCHOLOGY

HANS J. EYSENCK

Hans J. Eysenck was born in Berlin in 1916. He left Germany in 1934 to study French and English History and Literature at the Universities of Dijon and Exeter. He received his B.A. degree from the University of London in 1938 and a Ph.D in Psychology from that same institution in 1940. He was appointed Research Psychologist at the Mill Hill Emergency Hospital in 1942 and carried out research there which formed the basis of "Dimensions of Personality." At the end of the war he was appointed Psychologist to the Maudsley Hospital. Research carried out there formed the basis of "The Scientific Study of Personality." Dr. Eysenck was appointed Reader and Director to the Psychological Department at the Institute of Psychiatry (University of London) in 1950 and received a full professorship in Psychology in 1955. During these years he wrote "The Structure of Human Personality" and "Psychology of Politics." He has held Visiting Professorships at the University of Philadelphia in 1949 and at the University of California in 1954. Professor Eysenck's bibliography is extremely comprehensive. It includes 22 authored books, 6 edited volumes as well as over 300 published scientific papers.

I**T IS IMPOSSIBLE** to understand a man's work unless you understand what it is that he is trying to achieve, and why he is trying to achieve it. My experimental work has been governed by certain general assumptions, biases, points of view, hypotheses, principles — call it what you like; unless these are understood, the reader holding different points of view (consciously or unconsciously) is likely to misunderstand the problems posed, and criticize for the wrong reasons the solutions offered. I believe that the principles on which I have based my work are important; more important probably than the detailed research findings which I have published. My specific theories may be quite erroneous, but even though this should turn out to be so, I would still maintain that something of the kind I tried to accomplish is necessary if psychology is to be a science, and that someone else better equipped than myself will have to take up the torch and try again.

There are many different ways of introducing these principles, but in a volume of this kind the autobiographical may be the best. I was pitchforked into psychology by historical accident, not by design; my primary interests had always been in the "hard" science, particularly physics and astronomy, and I had intended to become a research physicist.[1] However, when Hitler

[1]It is interesting to note that those psychologists with whom I have always felt the greatest affinity (Spearman, Thurstone, Cattell) all came from a similar background as did Clark Hull. In my own Department, I have always found students with a background of "hard" sciences much more congenial than those with a background in the humanities. Fleming (1969) has given a fascinating description of "émigré physicists and the biological revolution" in which he demonstrates convincingly how the thought processes and intellectual habits of physicists led them to revolutionize biology when they brought these to bear on biological problems. He contrasts the "formalism" of many biologists, which finds an interesting duplicate in the attitude of many experimental psychologists, with the simplistic attitude of the physicists. "For a physicist there are *fewer* things in heaven and earth than are dreamt of in a biologist's philosophy." Leo Silard, for instance, was well aware that what he had brought to biology was "not any skills acquired in physics, but rather an attitude: the conviction which few biologists had at the time, that mysteries can be solved. . . They lacked the faith that things are explainable — and it is this faith . . . which leads to major advances in biology." To many biologists the physicists seemed brash, arrogant, and full of *hubris*; nevertheless, their methods suc-

ceeded where others' had failed. I often feel that the formalism of many experimental psychologists is derived from a worm's eye view of what scientific method really is; this view bears little relation to what physicists actually do. Take the notion that a theory is "disconfirmed" by a negative result, and hence discarded; this is wide-spread in psychology, but obvious nonsense to anyone familiar with the history of science, let alone its present practice. The absence of parallax was a severe blow to Copernicus's heliocentric theory, and his explanation (that the stars were so far away that parallax could not be measured) so obviously *ad hoc* that according to this maxim his theory should have been given up; yet by the time parallax was observed several hundred years later, the theory was firmly established. All scientific theories are full of anomalies; only psychologists believe in the immaculate conception (see Lakatos and Musgrave, 1970, for a good discussion of what is now regarded as good philosophy of science in this respect.)

came to power I decided to leave my native Germany; the University of London required that I should pass their matriculation examination, which I did in subjects which seemed the easiest at the time. When I then presented myself for registration as a student, I was told that I had taken the wrong subjects; I would have to wait another year before being allowed to take the right subjects and register. This I could not do, lacking the financial resources; I asked, "Is there no scientific subject I could take?" and was told, "Oh yes, there is always psychology." "What is that?" I exclaimed in my ignorance, only to be told, "It's very nice; you'll like it."

This interesting prediction was not entirely fulfilled; although I was lucky in having as my professor Sir Cyril Burt, probably one of the most mathematically-minded psychologists of his generation, and a very able man; the subject itself, regarded as a science, left much to be desired. In particular, there seemed no kind of unity about it; different textbook chapter headings were quite unrelated, and could be taken in any order whatever. Where chemistry has the atom as its unifying concept, biology the cell, genetics the gene, psychology seemed to have nothing except a plethora of terms, the very meaning and applicability of which were doubtful and restricted. More than that: different chapters made quite different and even contradictory assumptions which could not all be true. The chapters on learning, perception and other areas of what was generally labelled "experimental psychology" seemed to assume that all men are exactly equal in their abilities, their performance, and their reactions; how otherwise could one justify the universal habit of averaging results obtained from groups of subjects, or the equally universal habit of trying to obtain universal laws from groups of sophomores? The general quest seemed to be for functional relationships of the kind: $a = (f)b$, the assumption being that this is what the "hard" sciences do, and that what is good for physics is also good for psychology.

The chapters on individual differences, on personality, and on abnormal psychology, however, obviously denied this basic premise. Here we were told that people differed profoundly one from the other, in abilities, personality traits, attitudes, physique, and in every conceivable way; it was even made clear that the whole bodily constitution, including its biochemistry, was highly individual. Having postulated such very important differences, members of this group might have been thought likely to attempt to link these with the concepts elaborated by their experimental colleagues, but no such thing. Instead they postulated *ad hoc* concepts and theories in rich profusion; so rich indeed that the whole field resembled nothing more than a jungle full of exotic plants which unfortunately provided little nourishment. Between these two groups there was little friendship lost; the experimental psychologists only spoke to the physiologists (and not always even that), and the personality theorists only spoke to the psychoanalysts; never would one group as much as acknowledge the existence of the other.

To me this seemed an absurd situation, and one which inevitably led to a very fundamental failure on the part of psychology to achieve the minimum degree of scientific respectability: replication of research findings. If individual differences are as powerful and universal as the personality theorists taught, then how could universal laws, applicable to everyone, ever be produced by the experimentalists? The search for a general functional law $a = (f)\,b$ looks rather less appealing when we have to confront the possibility that the (f) in this formula may be different for every person in the world! How could we expect to find our "laws" replicated when the individuals taking part in the "replication" were in fact fundamentally different from those on whom the original law was based? The general disregard for replication experiments, and their frequent failure when performed, seemed to lend substance to my misgivings.

Here we semed to have an impasse which admitted of no solution. Experimentalists held a conception of human nature which emphasized essential identity from one person to another; without this assumption the whole procedure of experimental psychology made no sense. Personality theorists tended towards an idiographic point of view according to which individuality was supreme, and no two organisms were identical; on this assumption, psychology as a science was not a feasible proposition! This confrontation, one would have thought, might have given rise to a great deal of thinking and debate; nothing of the kind. Both sides proceeded as if the other did not exist, and no theorist seemed concerned to discuss this problem.

Clearly some compromise had to be found, and naturally I gravitated towards the sort of solution which had become widely accepted in physics and chemistry. Here too it is true, as Spinoza had pointed out, that "everything that exists is unique"; even two electrons, seemingly identical, differ in their temperospatial coordinates. But many of the differences are irrelevant to a particular problem; a man differs from a pig, but both obey the law of gravitation when thrown from the top of a tower. It becomes necessary to discover the dimensions of variability which are relevant to a particular problem, or set of problems; having done that, we are free to disregard those which are not so relevant.

The physicist would never dream of imitating the psychologist who derives his laws from any random group of subjects he can gather together in his laboratory: it is really inconceivable that any schoolboy would even attempt to derive physical constants or laws from random bits of rubbish carelessly thrown together! The chemist specifies very clearly what elements or mixtures of elements go into his experiment, and he does not generalize his results to other elements or mixtures of elements. The table of the elements is fundamental to all his thinking, but even before Mendeléeff's time the notion of different substances having different properties was fundamental to all experimental work in the "hard" sciences. Thus we are led to a compromise position; we may not have one law $a = (f)a$, and we may not have an infinity of such laws, but we might add to the law a constant or constants referring to the particular personality variables concerned. Take as an example Hooke's law of elasticity: *Stress* = k × *Strain,* where k is a constant (the modulus of elasticity) which depends upon the nature of the material and the type of stress used to produce the strain. This constant k, i.e. the ratio $\dfrac{\text{Stress}}{\text{Strain}}$, is called Young's modulus, and is illustrated in Figure II-1a (Savage and Eysenck, 1964.) A and B are two metals differing in elasticity; they are stressed by increasing loads, and the elongation corresponding to each load plotted on the abscissa. It will be seen that identical loads θ give rise to quite different elongations, α and β. Without k there is no meaningful law of any kind; individual differences are an explicit feature of the law. We also talk about stress and strain in psychology, referring to environmental or experimental stresses and emotional and other strains produced in this way; discussion and meaningful prediction is impossible unless we recognize individual differences, corresponding to k, which modify the strain produced by identical stresses in different people. We will return to this point later, when we shall discuss part b of Figure II-1.

In psychology, there are two ways along which we might arrive at a solution to our problem. The first would be to take any particular law, $a = (f)b$, test a large number of individuals, and then sort these out into groups according to the form of the (f) function. As an example, consider a study of the effects of massed practice on the Muller-Lyer illusion. Köhler had predicted that practice would cause the illusion to decline, due to "satisfaction." I had formulated a contrary hypothesis, namely that as some kind of mental effort was required to restrain the illusionary effect, and as fatigue would set in over time and cause this effort to become less effective, the illusion would increase. We thus have

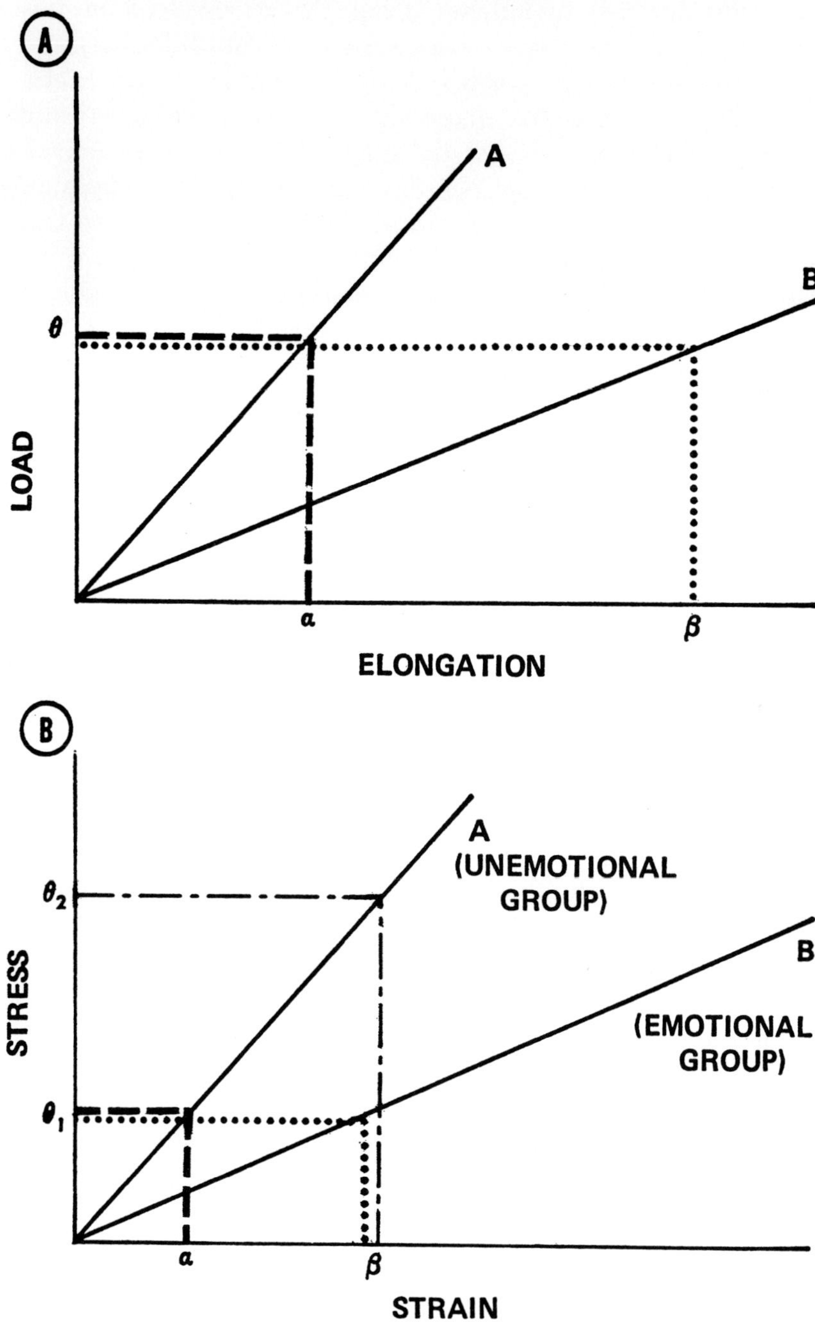

Figure II-1. Illustration of Hooke's Law (1a) as applied to the measurement of emotionality (1b).

two quite opposed hypotheses about the *(f)* involved in this particular functional relation between *a* (amount of illusion) and *b* (duration of massed practice.) An experiment (Eysenck and Slater, 1958) settled the question: There was no statistically significant effect one way or the other! (There was an overall trend towards an increase, but this was not significant because of the very large variances observed.) More important than this negative finding, however, was a positive one: There were three main types of subjects, showing respectively (a) a consistent trend upwards, (b) a consistent trend downwards, or (c) a consistent trend maintaining their original position. Note that trial results were not dotted randomly all over the place; there were consistent trends in nearly every subject, but these trends were dissimilar. Disregard of these individual differences would mean disregard for over 99 percent of all the sources of variance in this experiment!

It would not be possible to make a rough grouping of our subjects, as into a, b and c above, in accordance with their consistent patterns of reaction; we could write a formula in which response decrement or increment would be a meaningful function of duration of practice, different for each group. This would render behavior lawful for each group, and it would get us over the worst excesses of averaging over clearly dissimilar individuals. But the thought of constructing a whole science out of fractionating the subjects of each and every experiment in this fashion is not appealing; the Baconian approach might appeal to someone with infinite time on his hands, and an incapacity for being bored, but it is not in line with modern scientific methodology. We could, indeed, do something of the kind for some 10,000 different experiments, and then correlate the composition of the various groups formed; in this way we would find out whether the person who improves with repetition on the Muller-Lyer illusion experiment is also the person who over time shows less evidence of tridimensionality on the Pulfrich phenomenon. In this way, supposing there were groupings linking certain experimental findings together, we would achieve some kind of typology, based on an empirical foundation, and clearly relevant to experimental psychology. This would clearly be desirable; is there not a better method of achieving the same result?

The alternative I proposed was based on certain basic premises which may perhaps be briefiy summarized in the following form. Behavior, including in this term both everyday conduct and performance in an experimental situation, is in part governed by such factors as the amount of cortical arousal, the degree of emotional (autonomic) activation, etc. If one could identify and measure some of these factors, assuming them to be permanently characteristic of a given person, i.e. "trait" rather than "state" characteristics, then we might have here a way of short-circuiting the impossibly long and circuitous Baconian method outlined above. Assuming that some people are characterized by a habitually low level of cortical arousal, while others are characterized by a habitually high level, it would seem likely that these two "types" of people would differ consistently in their everyday behavior, and also in experimental investigations to which degree of arousal was relevant (conditioning, vigilance, thresholds, etc.). The term "type" in this context does not of course mean a categorical separation into water-tight compartments, as in the ancient typology of Galen (cholerics, melancholics, phlegmatics, sanguinics); these two "types" are conceived merely as the extremes of a continuum, with most people having an average amount of arousal. Such a theory possesses one clear advantage: it is falsifiable. We can make some clear-cut predictions from it and test these predictions experimentally and/or observationally. Verification of a reasonably large number of predictions would suggest that we were approaching a meaningful "typology" which would present us with the looked-for compromise between the extreme views of the "everyone is alike" and the "everyone is different" schools. We would in fact end up with a dimensional view of personal differences, having taken care to isolate those dimensions which would be most relevant to our purpose. There are obvious difficulties in doing this, but a knowledge of relevant theories in the fields of experimental psychology, and physiology would presumably be of help in formulating reasonable hypotheses.

My own efforts to look for appropriate dimensions began with work described in my book *Dimensions of Personality* (Eysenck, 1947); I emerged from a large number of descriptive and factor-analytic studies with two orthogonal dimensions, which I called E (extraversion-introversion) and N (neuroticism-stability.) I have traced these conceptions back through some 2,000 years of medical-philosophical-psychological writing (Eysenck, 1970), and have shown that large numbers of modern studies done since my book appeared have given rise to two factors very closely resembling E and N, although often under different names (Eysenck and Eysenck, 1969). I think there is really very little doubt now that in the personality realm these factors are important and replicable; they have been replicated even in countries like Japan, India, Israel and Egypt where one might have expected social and cultural differences to mask them at least to some extent. The material on which most of this work has been based is observational (ratings) or introspective (self-ratings), and the excellent agreement between these two disparate methods suggests a certain amount of validity as far as the resulting factors are concerned. Note that it is not suggested that these two factors are the only ones which make up the concept of personality; to state this would be as unreasonable as to suggest that two elements were all that was needed. We obviously cannot at this early moment state just how many different dimensions are likely to be involved in determining conduct and behavior; my concentration on these two is dictated entirely by the need to restrict one's experimental work within manageable compass. It is, perhaps, worth while mentioning at this point that these two dimensions are clearly relevant to social problems of various kinds; neurotics for instance tend to be found predominantly in the high N-low E quadrant, while criminals are found predominantly in the high N-high E quadrant (Eysenck, 1965.) Burt (1965) has shown that when children are rated on these two dimensions, and are then followed up over thirty-five years, those who later become hospitalized neurotics or habitual criminals tend to come predominantly from the appropriate quadrants, and other follow-up studies have given similar results.

Contrary to the American *Zeitgeist* with its largely environmentalistic bias, I had always conceived of these major dimensions of personality as being the result of an interaction between genotype and environment; without ever wishing to deny the importance of the environment, I thought it foolish to disregard the fact that human beings are biological organisms, inheriting certain structures and connections within the central nervous system, and the autonomic system. Consequently the very fact that E and N seemed to be basic to personality and conduct suggested to me that they probably had a firm biological foundation in physiology, neurology and anatomy, and above all that heredity probably played a very large part in the causation of the observed individual differences. This now seems beyond question; a number of studies on MZ and DZ twins, brought up together and apart, demonstrates that heredity produces more than 50 percent of the variance as far as differences between individuals on E and N are concerned (Eysenck and Prell, 1951; Eysenck, 1967.) This immediately leads us to the question of just what are the underlying structures which are responsible for the genotype; clearly it cannot be behavior which is inherited, but only this supposititious physiological-neurological-anatomical complex underlying behavior.

My own hypotheses have been published in detail elsewhere (Eysenck, 1967); I have suggested that cortical arousal, mediated by the reticular formation, lies at the root of the E dimension, and the visceral brain and the autonomic system at the root of N. Extraverts are conceived as having a habitual low degree of arousal, introverts as having a habitual high degree of arousal, with ambiverts at various stages intermediate. High N scorers are conceived as having low thresholds for emotional reactions, low N scorers as having high thresholds. There are many complications to this simple scheme; these I cannot, of course, deal with here. However, there is now good physiological evidence in favor of some of these hypotheses; we have recently found, for instance, that EEG potentials evoked to sound differ considerably in extraverts and introverts, those of the latter having shorter latencies and greater amplitude, very much as called for by our theory.

There is also a large body of experimental evidence from psychological (as opposed to physiological) studies, most of which supports the theory; evidence has been summarized and presented elsewhere (Eysenck, 1967, 1971.)

Let me now return to the problem of accounting for the disparate results often obtained from experimental studies in psychology, and demonstrate how recourse to the personality concepts of E and N can overcome these difficulties. As an example, I shall take reminiscence in verbal learning—if for no other reason than because it has become almost the prototype of the non-replicable kind of experiment. One eminent reviewer named it the "now-you-see-it-now-you-don't" phenomenon. Essentially, when a list of words, or paired associates has been learned to some kind of criterion, and a rest is given after the massed learning, reminiscence is shown by the fact that performance is better than it was immediately after learning. Sometimes this is indeed found, but sometimes we get forgetting instead, and sometimes there seems to be no change at all. Can our personality theory throw some light on this problem?

Howarth and Eysenck (1968) have published an experiment in which they verified a theory according to which we would expect reproduction of learned material to be characterized by forgetting in extraverts, reminiscence in introverts (and presumably by little change in ambiverts—this last prediction was not tested, however.) The argument is based on Walker's well known extension of some widely accepted laws of remembering circuits, and long-term memory, mediated by chemical traces in the cell; a process of consolidation (through protein synthesis, probably involving R.N.A.) is required to transform the former into the latter, and such consolidation takes place essentially during a period of rest. Furthermore, the length and strength of consolidation are conceived of as depending crucially on the degree of arousal in the cortex—high arousal = strong, long-continued consolidation. This would suggest that introverts would have better memories, being in a state of high arousal, and this would indeed be so but for one exception: According to Walker, during consolidation the cells involved in the process are not free to reproduce the material learned, and consequently retrieval during that time is impeded. Thus extraverts, having a short and weak consolidation period, would be better able to reproduce the material learned shortly after learning has finished, because during that time the introverts would be handicapped by having their strong, long-continued consolidation interfere with reproduction. After a lengthy period of rest, however, when consolidation had ceased even in the most introverted, introverts should be superior in their reproduction, having assimilated the material so much better. Thus if different groups of extraverts and introverts are made to learn the verbal material to an equal extent before rest, and are then given different periods of rest before reproduction, we would expect a cross-over to result, with extraverts superior shortly after learning, and introverts superior a long time after learning. Figure II-2 shows the results of the experiment; it will be seen that the predicted cross-over does in fact take place, and that introverts show reminiscence, extraverts forgetting.

The experiment is quoted, not because it verifies the theory, but because it demonstrates beautifully the imperative need for experimental psychologists to use the concepts of personality theory in their work. Clearly it is possible to obtain any kind of result if we carry out our experiment on some random group of subjects; if the majority are extraverted, we will get forgetting; if introverted, reminiscence; and if ambivert, neither. The experiment would only be replicable if the E scores of the subjects are known, and can be duplicated in the selection of the replication sample. Furthermore, the addition of personality theory clarifies considerably the general theory of reminiscence, and verifies certain propositions, such as Walker's theorem. What happens when there is no control over personality variables is only too well known: All the variance due to these variables is thrown into the error term, which as a consequence becomes huge, and often outweighs the contribution of the main effects. This is not the way of science; an experiment is only well controlled when all the variables which are likely to contribute to the observed effects are neither manipulated, or at least measured,

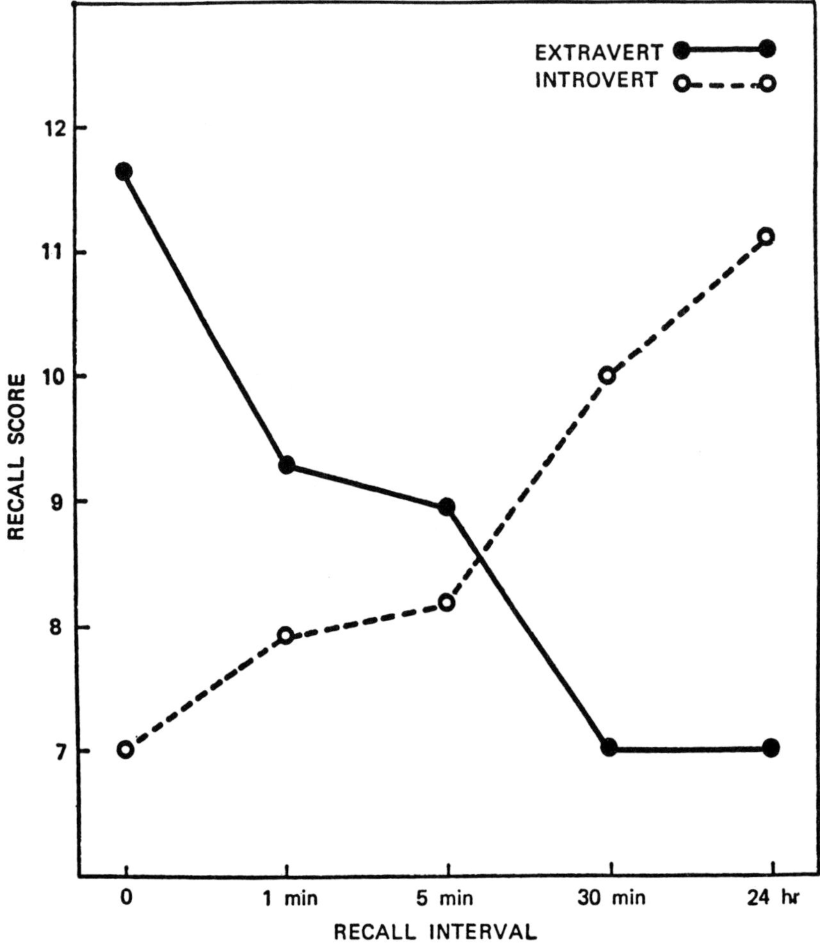

Figure II-2. Recall scores of different groups of extraverts and introverts after varying recall intervals.

so that their effects can be estimated. The failure of experimental psychologists to take personality into account is thus a major fault in their designs, and one which cannot be excused by appeal to any rule of scientific procedure. I would say that of all the faults which are apparent in psychological experimentation, the disregard of personality variables is the most serious; it bids fair to render nugatory many of the achievements of the experimentalists. My point is thus not that the inclusion of personality variables in the experimental design is a useful, or even a desirable addition; I am suggesting that it is mandatory.

If the experimentalists, then, are guilty of leaving out of account a fundamentally important variable, social psychologists, educationists, industrial psychologists, and clinicians do not fare any better. Quite typically they ask questions which in the nature of the case are meaningless and impossible to answer. Such questions as: Does streaming promote better learning in the classroom? Do teaching machines produce better examination results than lectures? Is client-centered therapy more effective than desensitization in curing neurotic patients? What are the effects of cognitive dissonance? Is praise or blame more effective in motivating school children? In learning an industrial skill, is it better to go for speed first, and then improve accuracy, or vice versa?—all of these are supposed to be answerable, and have been investigated by experts in these various fields. Yet apart from the obvious difficulties attending the definition of "better," it is implicitly assumed that there is some universal answer, that all children, all neurotics, all apprentices react uniformly to a given procedure. Nothing could be farther from the truth. As I have pointed out, introverts seem to benefit more from machine teaching, extraverts from live teaching (Eysenck, 1967). Praise motivates introverted children, blame extraverted ones (Thompson and Hunnicut, 1944.) Holden (1969) has shown that the effects of streaming (both social and educational) are quite different for introverted and extraverted children. It seems likely that the contradictory results which experiments on cognitive dissonance have produced are due to the facts that introverts and extraverts differ in their reactions to the defining experiment. Speed and accuracy can be traded off against each other, and extraverts usually go for speed, introverts for accuracy (Eysenck, 1947); this must modify one's training programme profoundly.

Clinical work, in particular, has neglected the important field of personality assessment for the purpose of choice and evaluation of therapy, although one might have thought that clinicians, being almost by definition concerned with personality change, would be sensitive to the personality patterns in their clients, and possibly also in themselves. Yet only one study has been published in this field which makes the personality of the patient a major variable (DiLoreto, 1971.) He explicitly stated as one of his major hypotheses that *different therapies would be differentially effective with different types of patients.* The therapies employed, each using two therapists familiar with the method, were systematic desensitization (Wolpe), client-centered therapy (Rogers), and rational-emotional therapy (Ellis.) The personality types contrasted were extraverts and introverts; the target symptom was social anxiety, and batteries of tests and highly reliable observational analyses were used to measure pre- and post-status of the subjects. The outcome showed desensitization to be the most effective treatment, being equally applicable to extraverts and introverts. Client-centered therapy was about $2\frac{1}{2}$ times more effective in reducing anxiety with extraverts than with introverts. Rational-emotional therapy was nearly three times more effective in reducing anxiety with introverts than with extraverts. On the whole, treatments produced better effects than placebo or no treatment, but extraverts showed about five times more spontaneous remission than introverts! These results show what could be done in this field if researchers took seriously not only the outcome problem but also the interaction between outcome, personality of the patient, and personality of the clinician; Truax and Carkhuff (1967) have begun a study of the latter variable, with promising results. So far, however, not one single researcher has taken both these personality variables into account in spite of the obvious fact that results are crucially dependent upon their proper control and measurement. I find it difficult to understand this failure or the similar failure to use personality differences to predict outcome of therapy; Martin et al. (1969) have shown in our laboratories that simple speed of eye-blink conditioning predicts outcome of both psychotherapy and behavior therapy with considerable success, those who condition better showing better prognosis—as they should (Eysenck and Rachman, 1965).

Psychopharmacology is another field which has left out personality variables to its own great disadvantage; as I have shown in *Experiments with Drugs* (Eysenck, 1963), personality interacts with drug effects in predictable ways, and efforts to predict or explain the drug effects without reference to the personality of the subject, or the strain of the rat involved, are doomed to failure. The same drug, in identical concentration, can have opposite effects on people at different positions of one or other of the dimensions of personality discussed above; I have given several examples of this (both for human beings and for rats) in the *Biological Basis of Personality* (Eysenck, 1967.)

Even the sacred realms of theory are not safe from the incursions of personality and individual differences. For many years the followers of Tolman, on the one hand, and of Hull and Spence, on the other, have argued over fundamental laws of learning and conditioning; whole libraries of books and journal articles have been written on this subject, and students have spent countless hours soaking up this mass of contradictory experimental material, trying to make sense out of it all. Yet as Jones has pointed out (see discussion in Eysenck, 1967), the protagonists in fact used different strains of rats in their experiments—Tolman used an emotional strain, Spence and Hull an unemotional strain! Many, if not all, of the differences in the behavior of these rats could be explained on the grounds of strain differences; there may be no theoretical conflicts to discuss at all! I am not here saying that this is in fact so; obviously the suggestion needs careful working through, and many experiments require to be done, replicating each side's work using both strains and comparing results. Yet what is so interesting, and so sad, is that all these years have gone by without a single person pointing out this fundamental difference, and suggesting that possibly it might lie at the basis of the theoretical conflict. Imagine one set of physicists working on superconductivity with one metal which does show this phenomenon, while another set of physicists worked on superconductivity with another metal which did not; would they be inclined to argue for thirty years over theories set up to "explain" their respective phenomena, without ever suspecting that perhaps what caused their different results was the use of a different metal by the other fellow?

My first item of advice to young research workers, therefore, would be that in whatever field they were working—experimental, social, clinical, educational, industrial, subnormal, pharmacological, or environmental—they should be very much concerned, in designing their studies, to consider the possible role that personality differences might play. If cortical arousal, motivation, emotion and autonomic activation could be suspected of playing an important role in their work (and it is difficult to think offhand of areas where this would not be so), then knowledge of the subjects' E and N scores must be considered mandatory. This is so particularly when the regression of the main effects is nonlinear, as it so often is according to the Yerkes-Dodson Law (now often referred to as the inverted-U relation between drive and performance.) Even apparently obvious predictions can come to grief when attention is not paid to these complexities. Thus it seems indisputable that easier verbal associations should be learned better than difficult ones; yet McLaughlin and Eysenck (1967) have shown that while this is true of most groups, it is not true of stable extraverts! The low arousal of this group, multiplied by the low arousal-producing properties of very easy tasks, produces poor performance; when more difficult problems produce greater arousal, performance improves to such an extent that it is actually better for the difficult than the easy problems! There are many such complications in all these fields, and this is not the place to go into them; I have done so in great detail elsewhere (Eysenck, 1967.)

There are other ways in which personality concepts can play an important part in psychology; I will only have space to consider one. Consider the following problem. There are many experiments in the literature using "emotion" or "autonomic activation" as the independent variable, manipulating it in various ways, and measuring the effects, i.e. the particular dependent variable in which the experimenter is interested. Equally, there is in personality theory the concept of "emotionality" or neuroticism, i.e. the hypothesis that there exists a dimension of personality along which subjects can be geared from most reactive emotionally to least reactive. How can we tie these two quite divergent sets of experiments and theories together? Look back at Figure II-1a; it shows Hooke's law of elasticity, bringing together a concept taken from general physics (strain.) The dependent variable is thus a ratio, stress/k, depending on both. Exactly the same type of formula can be applied in the psychological field, as shown in Figure II-1b. Again the stress (independent variable) is plotted on the ordinate, and the brain (dependent variable) on the abscissa. We now represent the dimension corresponding to k, i.e. emotionality, by taking one group of low-emotionality subjects (persons or animals), A, and a group of high-emotionality subjects, B. Identical stress θ_1, gives rise to quite different strains α and β. It would require stress θ_2 to make the strain in A animals or persons equal to that produced by θ_1, in B animals or persons. Differences between θ_1 and θ_2 are the kinds of differences traditionally studied by experimental psychologists; differences between A and B are the kinds of differences traditionally studied by personality psychologists, believers in the importance of constitutional factors, and clinical psychologists. Physicists have never attempted to make a choice between these two sets of variables, or to study them in isolation; it seems equally futile for psychologists to do so. Provided the modulus employed is even moderately correct, and more than a mere analogy, the experimental possibilities suggested by this method of approach seem promising.

Two sets of studies may serve to illustrate the general schema here outlined. Rosenbaum, working with human subjects (1953, 1956), found that threat of a strong shock led to greater generalization of a voluntary response than did threat of a weak shock; degree of generalization is here the measure of strain adopted, and the independent variable is the stress imposed by the experimental situation. He also discovered in another experiment that anxious subjects showed greater generalization to identical threat than did nonanxious subjects; again degree of generalization is the measure of strain, but this time the independent variable is k, or individual differences in emotionality. The experiment shows that the emotional reaction studied by the experimental psychologist (as in the first experiment) is similar to, or identical with, the emotionality studied by the personality psychologist (as in the second experiment.) This provides us with an important metholdological tool for studying the precise nature of the personality variable measured by our ratings, or our questionnaire; it enables us to test accurately the truth or falsity of our hypotheses about the nature of the personality dimensions measured. It has often been pointed out that the naming of factors derived statistically from matrices of intercorrelations between ratings, or self-ratings, or tests is subjective; here we have an objective method of testing the accuracy of the factor interpretation. (It is not, of course, suggested that a single experiment of this kind is sufficient to settle a problem of this magnitude. The experiment was merely used to illustrate the method in question; many diverse experiments would be required to come to any acceptable conclusion).

Our second example is taken from experiments with rats reported by Savage and Eysenck (1964). We have bred two strains of rats (emotionally reactive and emotionally nonreactive) which are relatively pure; the basis of selection for inbreeding was performance on the open field test. In this test, the 100-day-old rat is exposed to a round enclosure which is brightly lit and which is exposed to white noise of a certain loudness; this is the stress, and the measure of strain adopted is defecation. The number of fecal boluses deposited over unit time is taken as the measure of emotionality. At first sight this performance criterion [about the heritability of which much is now known (Eysenck, 1964)] may strike the reader as unrealistic and improbable; perhaps it measures nothing but the ease of defecation of the animal! We can now use the same methodology as in the Rosenbaum experiment to show that what we are measuring is indeed a general trait of emotionality in these animals. To do this we require an experimental set-up which is widely agreed to produce an increase in emotion in rats; we used frustrative nonreward. In the experiment, the rat is taught to run a double runway; he goes from starting box S to goal-box 1 (G1), where he is given some food. He then goes from G1 to goal-box 2 (G2), where he is again given food. His speed in going from S to G1, and from G1 to G2 is carefully measured, and constitutes the strain measure. If we now omit placing food in G1 this frustrative nonreward will produce an increase in emotion in the animal, and he will run from G1 to G2 more quickly than he did previously; this increase in speed of running is the measure of his emotional upset. Following our previous paradigm, we can now say that if our emotional rats are truly emotional in the same sense of the word operationally defined in our experiment with frustrative nonreward, then the emotional animals should increase their speed in traversing the distance from G1 to G2 more than the nonemotional rats. The results bore out this prediction; the reactive strain showed a greater increase in running speed than did the nonreactive strain.

Again, it must of course be borne in mind that one experiment is not sufficient to establish an important point like the precise nature of a scientific variable; there are by now some 50 experiments on our two strains, using the same paradigm as above, and supporting our use of the term "emotional" and "nonemotional" to designate the two strains. The great majority of these experiments support our use, and verify deductions made from the hypothesis that we are here dealing with a general factor of "emotionality." Thus we would seem to have a method which enables us to make more precise our conceptualizations of important variables in the personality field; this is a great advance on the previously available methods which relied essentially on subjective judgment. Furthermore—and this too is a very important contribution—we can attempt to specify more precisely the degree to which a concept like "neuroticism" (in humans) resembles, or is identical with, a concept like "emotionality" (in rats.) It has often been pointed out that rat analogues of human behavior throw only very uncertain light on the problems posed by humans, and a more precise method of pointing these analogies was clearly desirable. It would seem that the paradigm outlined above can be used with great effect to create a proper nomological network in which to accommodate our concepts; if the two terms are in fact referring to identical underlying realities, then emotional rats should show greater generalization than nonemotional rats, and high N persons should show greater frustrative non-reward than low N persons. (Again, of course, these two suggestions are only representative of a much larger number which would be required to be made the subject of experiment before any confident decisions could be made on this point.)

This, then, would be my second suggestion to young investigators in psychology. When you are concerned with personality variables, do not rest content with subjective "naming" procedures which may appeal to you, and may indeed have some persuasive charm even for other investigators; consider your factor, trait or other concept merely as a hypothesis, and investigate this hypothesis as you would any other—by recourse to an experiment. The method outlined on the last few pages gives you a paradigm which can be adapted in many different ways, and to many different problems; its virtue is that it renders amenable to experiment vague notions like "similarity," "analogous," and the like. It is my considered opinion that one of the main reasons why factor analysis has not been received with open arms by many experimental psychologists, and why it is still considered somewhat outside the charmed circle of methods of analysis approved by experimentalists, is precisely the subjectivity of the "naming" procedures, as well as the lack of rigor involved in carrying out rotations purely to statistical criteria such as simple structure, or hyperplane maximization. The method here suggested provides us with an experimental alternative, and I believe that the widespread use of this alternative will considerably strengthen experimental research into personality.

It may not have escaped the reader that the two ideas and suggestions I have discussed in this chapter may be regarded as mutually complementary. The first point stressed was that experimental psychology could not really get on without paying some attention to individual differences, and that personality dimensions such as E and N played a tremendously important part in most if not all psychological experiments. One might say that in offering this advice, and making available these concepts and the measuring devices developed in order to give them a proper operational definition, personality theory has put experimental psychology into its debt; this is a genuine contribution by personality theory to experimental psychology. The second point stressed above somewhat redresses the balance; now it is experimental psychology which helps personality theorists define their concepts more clearly, and link them with the much more thoroughly explored fields of the experimentalist. What I am trying to say, in fact, is simply that both sides have something to gain and nothing to lose by getting to know each other better, and by becoming better acquainted with each other's problems and successes. Indeed, what each side can gain by this interchange seems to be quite considerable; the main weaknesses of experimental psychology and of personality theory could in this manner be eliminated (at least in principle). This is not a small advantage, and to it should be added another one—the unification of psychology. Where we now have two quite divergent and even hostile camps, we would have instead one group of co-operating and mutually helpful psychologists. Both sides would use identical concepts, to the everlasting advantage of both. Changes and improvements on the one side would immediately and automatically benefit the other. We would have one psychology rather than the present position of *quot homines tot sententiae.* This indeed is what to me would be the most outstanding advantage of accepting the general principles I have here discussed—the creation of a unitary science, instead of a schizophrenic split separating one group of workers from another.

There is one further advantage which I think the student can gain by adopting some such "personalistic" point of view as I have outlined. I have already mentioned the help it can give him in research, whether experimental or personality oriented; there is also a great advantage in what for want of a better word I may perhaps call "understanding." In dealing with people, in trying to see "what makes them tick," in ordering one's life, psychology has been notoriously less useful than one might perhaps have had a right to expect. Similarly, our ability to create a psychological technology has been badly limping behind the impressive facade of our metatheoretical discussions, statistical sophistication, and experimental rigor. Both these very real disadvantages, in my view, have been due to neglect of a proper typology, such as that outlined here. It is difficult to understand people's sexual behavior, for instance, unless one realizes the degree to which E and N govern both their actions and their feelings. I have shown elsewhere how closely personality variables determine a person's sexual adjustment (Eysenck, 1970, 1971); it will always remain a mystery to me why every other investigator of this important and interesting field has been content to deal with averages and variances, rather than with subgroups identified in terms of personality theory. The interest of a finding such as that the average person has intercourse 2.46 times a week is sadly reduced when we discover that this average covers an enormous range of reactivity, from people who have intercourse once a month or even once a year, to others who have intercourse several times each night. I would argue that the average adds very little to our understanding, but that it does help us to know that extraverts have intercourse much more frequently than introverts, that they begin to have intercourse earlier in life, with more different partners, in more different positions, etc. The fact that these findings are predictable from our general theory adds to their interest, but even simply from the descriptive and predictive point of view I would venture to argue that facts of this kind are in a different class from simple averages and variances; if this is so, why has psychology restricted itself so sternly to these nonrevealing types of statistics—unless it be because they are so much easier to collect.

In a similar way, I find my understanding aided by a realization that criminals and neurotics are both characterized by a high degree of emotionality (N), but that the former are extraverted, the latter introverted. Given also that there is a strong degree of predetermination in this (because of the largely heritable nature of these personality dimensions), I feel that now we are in a position to advance methods which might cure the neurotic and rehabilitate the criminal. I have discussed these methods in some detail in my books on behavior therapy (Eysenck, 1960, 1964) and criminality (Eysenck, 1964), and will not do so here; to my mind the creation of a behavioristic technology is inextricably bound up with a proper understanding of human typology.[2] The

[2]When we turn from the pure to the applied in science, there is often an inevitable incursion of specific factors which necessitates the use of subjective evaluation. Thus no two bridges are alike; they differ in width, length, type of support, exposure to wind, rain, snow and other natural hazards, use by trains, cars, trucks and pedestrians, and in a thousand and one different ways. This does not reduce bridge building to guess-work, but it does mean that the application of such scientific knowledge as there is, is less precise than in the typical laboratory situation. Consider, for example, the frequently and widely advocated use of atomic energy for peaceful purposes, such as creating craters for canal building, etc. Much accurate knowledge is available about the atomic process, but practical application suffers from uncertainty as to predictability of cavity radius, fracture radius, permeability, chimney heights and crater dimensions; moreover, each individual application depends on the idiosyncratic nature of the physical materials directly affected by the explosion. Conditions of individual application are always unique, and hence there is always a greater margin of uncertainty than in laboratory investigations. The same must inevitably be true when we are dealing with a behavioristic technology. Yet critics often make the unfair and meaningless comparison between such behavioristic applications of psychological principles, and laboratory work in physics; the proper comparison would be with such applied uses of physics as those mentioned above.

neurotic (or the criminal) is not for the most part just an ordinary, average sort of person who happens to have gone wrong somewhere, or to have encountered some odd and unusual quirk of fate; he is fundamentally different from the ordinary, average sort of person—the neurotic by being too easily conditionable, the criminal by not being sufficiently conditionable, and both by having too strong and lasting autonomic reactions. Any attempt to improve their lot by arguing from the hypothesis that they are exactly like everyone else is, I would suggest, bound to lead to failure—and the fact that for several thousand years failure has indeed been the inevitable result of everything we tried to do strengthens my belief in the truth of this observation. Already behavior therapy has considerably improved the probability of neurotic recovery, as compared with traditional methods of psychotherapy; even with respect to criminals the outlook seems promising, although much less empirical work unfortunately has been done in this field. Better understanding, and greater opportunities for improving the world we live in, are two important consequences of the introduction of a proper typology into psychology; I often wish that some such theory had been available when I started out in psychology as a young student. Had there been, I doubt if I would have been so dissatisfied with the state of the art as it then was!

REFERENCES

Burt, C.: Factorial studies of personality and their bearing on the work of the leader. *Br J Educ Psychol,* 35:368-378, 1965.

Di Loreto, A. O.: *Comparative Psychotherapy:* An Experimental Analysis. Chicago, Aldine Press, 1972.

Eysenck, H. J.: *Dimensions of Personality.* London, Routledge & Kegan Paul, 1947.

Eysenck, H. J.: *Behaviour Therapy and the Neuroses.* Oxford, Pergamon Press, 1960.

Eysenck, H. J. (Ed.): *Experiments With Drugs.* Oxford, Pergamon Press, 1963.

Eysenck, H. J.: *Experiments in Behaviour Therapy.* Oxford, Pergamon Press, 1964.

Eysenck, H. J.: *Experiments in Motivation.* Oxford, Pergamon Press, 1964.

Eysenck, H. J.: *Crime and Personality.* New York, Houghton Mifflin, 1965.

Eysenck, H. J.: *The Biological Basis of Personality.* Springfield, C. C. Thomas, 1967.

Eysenck, H. J.: *The Structure of Human Personality,* 3rd ed. London, Methuen, 1970.

Eysenck, H. J.: Personality and attitudes to sex: a factorial study. *Personality,* 1:355-376, 1970.

Eysenck, H. J.: Personality and sexual adjustment. *Br J Psychiat, 118:* 593-608, 1971.

Eysenck, H. J.(Ed.): *Readings in Extraversion-Introversion.* London, Staples, 1971.

Eysenck, H. J.: *Psychology Is About People.* London, Alan Lane and the Pelican Press, 1972.

Eysenck, H. J. and Eysenck, S. B. G.: *Personality Structure and Measurement.* London, Routledge & Kegan Paul, 1969.

Eysenck, H. J. and Prell, D.: The inheritance of neuroticism: an experimental study. *J Ment Sci,* 93:441-465, 1951.

Eysenck, H. J. and Rachman, S.: *Causes and Cures of Neurosis.* London, Routledge & Kegan Paul, 1965.

Eysenck, H. J. and Slater, P.: Effects of practice and rest on fluctuations in the Muller-Lyer illusion. *Br J Psychol,* 49:246-256, 1958.

Fleming, D.: Émigré physicists and the biological revolution. In Fleming, D. and Fleming, B. (Eds.): *The Intellectural Migration.* Cambridge, The Press of Harvard University, 1969, pp. 152-189.

Holden, L. A.: The effects of personality type and of changes in Junior School streaming policies on goal-setting, social relations, and symbolic learning. London, Unpubl. Ph.D. thesis, 1969.

Howarth, E. and Eysenck, H. J.: Extraversion, arousal, and paired-associates recall. *J Exp Res Personal,* 3:114-116, 1968.

Lakatos, I. and Musgrave, A.: *Criticism and the Growth of Knowledge.* Cambridge, University Press, 1970.

McLaughlin, R. J. and Eysenck, H. J.: Extraversion, neuroticism and paired-associates leanring. *J Exp Res Personal,* 2:128-132, 1967.

Martin, I., Marks, I.M., and Gelder, M. G.: Conditioned eyelid responses in phobic patients. *Behav Res Ther,* 7:115-124, 1969.

Rosenbaum, G.: Stimulus generalization as a function of level of experimentally induced anxiety. *J Exp Psychol,* 45:35-43, 1953.

Rosenbaum, G.: Stimulus generalization as a function of clinical anxiety. *J Abnorm Soc Psychol,* 53:281-285. 1956.

Savage, R. D. and Eysenck, H. J.: The definition and measurement of emotionality. In: Eysenck, H. J. (Ed.): *Experiments in Motivation.* Oxford, Pergamon Press, 1964.

Thompson, G. C. and Hunnicutt, C. W.: The effect of repeated praise or blame on the work achievement of "introverts" and "extraverts." *J Educ Psychol,* 35:257-266, 1944.

Truax, C. B. and Carkhuff, R. R.: *Towards Effective Counseling and Psychotherapy.* Chicago, Aldine, 1967.

Chapter III

A SCIENTIST'S LAST WORDS

W. HORSLEY GANTT

W. Horsley Gantt was born on October 24, 1893, at Wingina, Virginia. Following his primary and secondary education, much of which was provided through his mother, he matriculated at the University of North Carolina, where he received a B.S. in 1917 with a major in Psychology. Three years later, he received the M.D. degree at the University of Virginia Medical School. After two years of research on the liver at University Hospital in Baltimore, he left the United States to go to Russia with the American Relief Foundation under Herbert Hoover. There, he assumed the Directorship of the Medical Division of the American Relief unit in Petrograd. In that same year, he met Professor Ivan P. Pavlov and joined his laboratory as an apprentice scientist. When the American Relief effort was terminated, Dr. Gantt left Russia and spent an interim year carrying out research on liver pathology at the University College Medical School in London. He then rejoined Pavlov in Petrograd at the Institute of Experimental Medicine, where he spent the next half decade (1924-1929) collaborating with the man who truly inspired his education in the "art of science."

When Dr. Gantt returned to the States in 1929, he was invited by Professor Adolf Meyer, the father of biological psychiatry, to institute a Pavlovian Laboratory at Johns Hopkins Medical School, the principles and protocols of which would become an evolution of those already elaborated in the Russian tradition. Dr. Gantt directed this opus for four decades and, to this day, actively participates at Johns Hopkins as Professor Emeritus. Professor Meyer's choice of Dr. Gantt was hardly unsolicited. It was due to the recommendation of men like John Dewey, a founding father of American psychology, and Alan Gregg, the Director of the European Division of the Rockefeller Foundation.

In his writings, Gantt has proposed and developed many scientific principles, most of which have not only stood the test of time, but have aided the clinician on both the medical and psychiatric fronts. Indeed, in his half century of research effort, he has been bedfellow to no less than the neurophysiologist, the neuropharmacologist, the psychopathologist, the psychologist, the physiologist, and the psychiatrist.

Dr Gantt's scientific papers number in excess of two hundred. In addition, he has written and translated seven books and has edited fifteen others. For the work recorded in one of these volumes, Experimental Basis for Neurotic Behavior,[1] he received the Lasker Award. This work truly established him as a bona fide founder of the so-called psychosomatic approach in medicine.

In his career, Dr. Gantt has been an active member of many professional societies, the most noted of which included the Purkinje Medical Society (Prague, honorary member), the American Neurological Association, the American Physiological Society, the Collegium Internationale Activitatis Nervousae Superioris (president), the Royal Society of Medicine (London), the International Brain Research (IBRO), the American College of Psychiatrists, and the International Collegium of Psychosomatic Medicine, and is honorary member of the Argentina Psychosomatic Society. He held the president's chair in the Society of Biological Psychiatry (1959), the Pavlovian Society of North America (1955-1965), a society which he personally co-founded in 1955, the Collegium Internationale Activitatis Nervosae Superioris (1966 - -) and the American Psychopathological Association (1961).

Honors and awards have not been infrequent in Dr. Gantt's career. He was given the Lasker Award in 1946 for his research on nervous diseases and the American Heart Association Award in 1950 for investigations into the etiology of hypertension; he was elected to the Medico advisory board of CARE in 1957 and the American College of Psychiatrists in 1971. In 1950, he was granted the American Heart Association Award and in 1971, his scholarly work earned him the Gold Medal Award from the Society of Biological Psychiatry.

Amidst all these activities and achievements, Dr. Gantt has still found time to be the Editor-in-Chief of two scientific journals: Conditional Reflex, and Soviet Neurology and Psychiatry. Since 1956, he has also been the Editor of the American Lectures in Psychiatry Series, published by Charles C Thomas Publishing Company. Added to this, and additional support for his international stature, are the various solicitations made by leading national encyclopedias to have Gantt author those sections related to reflexology. The most noteworthy examples include his section on the "Conditional Reflex" in the British Medical Psychology Handbook (1972), his treatise on "Reflexology" in the German Encyclopedia of Medicine (1968), and his bibliographic essay on "Pavlov" to be published this year in the Encyclopedia Britannica.

In addition to his life's dedication to basic science, Dr. Gantt has also been a physician. As early as 1925, he spent what leisure time he had in Russia traveling through the countryside compiling as much epidemiological information as possible. With these data, he wrote his first book, a Medical Review of Soviet Russia,[2] an undertaking later to be labelled by the medical historian, F. H.

---

[1] W. H. Gantt, *Experimental Basis for Neurotic Behavior.* New York, Hoeber, 1944.

Garrison, as an opening chapter in geomedicine. Even more so, however, has Gantt contributed to psychiatry. By using the principles of the conditional reflex, he has facilitated diagnostic evaluations of mental illness, including differential diagnosis between organic and functional psychoses and has provided a scheme for a prophylactic psychiatry based on a conditional reflex examination.

Dr. Gantt is still engaged in biomedical research as Senior Scientist of the Pavlovian Research Laboratory at the V.A. Hospital, Perry Point, Maryland, a laboratory he founded in 1958, Psychiatrist at the Johns Hopkins Hospital and professor of psychiatry at the Univ. of Maryland.

[2]W. H. Gantt, *A Medical Review of Soviet Russia.* London, British Medical Association Press, 1928.

I

OUR LAST WORDS are usually uttered when we are in a morbid state and they therefore are not representative of the best that we have to bequeath as a legacy to those who have considered it worthwhile to listen to us. For this reason, Dr. Cullen affords us a rare opportunity to join together with other fellow scientists to recite our *opus magnum* while in possession of our faculties. To be on the stage with those whom Dr. Cullen has selected as important scientists makes this a special privilege.

These "last words" constitute a kind of Will and Testament. They are not so much original in the sense that I may never have said some of them before, as being what I consider important to say now.

Pavlov wrote a model "Last Will and Testament" to scientists everywhere, which cannot be equalled for its brevity, clarity, and substance. Though not plagiarizing it, I am nevertheless strongly under its influence.

What I have to say is the result of a life now exceeding fourscore years, dominated by the seeking for the answers posed by the universe around and within me. The universe of my life has never been limited to that environment within the confines of the laboratory.

Working in the atmosphere of medicine as a young clinical physician two years out of medical school, I had become frustrated with the methods of clinical science as I saw, heard and read about them until I saw Pavlov demonstrate his experiment on the conditional reflex to me on 29 October, 1922. From that time, I have been convinced of the capability of the scientific method to answer *certain* questions in psychobiology when these questions are clearly stated. Some of these questions have been partially solved by Pavlov and others, but, as the scientist knows, when he solves one question, the solution poses another.

II

I like to think of myself as a scion of an old Virginia ancestry, taught by my mother, with my feet in the soil, a follower of the ideals of Hippocrates. But I almost foundered on the rocks of despair from the crass materialism and conventionality of 20th Century America, until rescued by Pavlov with his ideals of truth and his courage to support the right, who showed me how to explore the secrets of nature through scientific research. He launched me on a threshold where I have felt a firm footing. To him I owe a large part of whatever I have achieved in science. Although the interruption of seven years of my life devoted to him and his science may have delayed my institutional advancement, I think that he enabled me to contribute more to the science of medicine than I would have otherwise.

My father having died before I was three, my mother was left penniless to care for my brother, Henry, and me. She supported us on her teacher's salary of $35 a month until we entered college. Also, she was my best teacher, with the exception of Pavlov. At her death, she left us each $500 and land valued at $1,000. Her religious principles have been a beacon throughout my life. She allowed us the freedom to climb 80-foot trees when we were six and eight years old and to spend a large part of the day exploring the James River, having taught us to swim without knowing how herself. Though impoverished and having to work our way through school, I have looked back on our childhood as a happy period.

Until age thirteen, I was taught by my mother. Then I

entered Miller School in Virginia, and thence to the University of Virginia for three years. By taking extra courses during my first two years of medical school at the University of North Carolina, I obtained my B.S. with this three years of college. Teaching school for two years at $85 per month enabled me to pay my way through medical school for two years and with the generous loan from a cousin for the last two years.

As I look back on this period I cannot recall knowing where I would get the money for more than a year. For a large part of my life, certainly until I got my first regular paying position in the Johns Hopkins University at age 38, I never knew where I would get money for the succeeding year. My chief regret at my pecuniary situation was that I had to delay marriage and a family until age 41; I did not finish repaying the money I had borrowed for my education and sojourn with Pavlov until I was about 45 years old. I did not accept a (meager) salary offered me by the Soviet government for my last two years in Russia, because I did not want to be under this obligation to a Marxist government.

After two years in college, I gave up the idea of making high grades; instead, I devoted my energy to try to understand. This resulted in my grades falling to about one-third from the top. My desire to learn and to probe to get the answers often brought me into conflict with the instructors: one professor of surgery told me, "You ask too many questions!" There were some welcome exceptions: Professor Halstead and Adolf Meyer of the Johns Hopkins Medical School, who welcomed questions and discussions.

When I left Baltimore for Russia to work under Herbert Hoover with the American Relief Administration (ARA), I took one suitcase and a small box of laboratory data to complete an article in the three months I intended to stay. But when Pavlov showed me his work with the conditional reflex on October 29, 1922, I decided to extend my sojourn to learn what he could teach me. We in the ARA had to leave Russia at the expiration of the relief work, reporting to the headquarters in London. As the Soviet authorities did not honor their promise of a return visa to work in Pavlov's laboratory, I had to wait one year before I could obtain this permission. This time was spent in research on liver function at the University College Medical School, London.

Reentering Russia in January 1924, I remained another five years without leaving for fear I would not be readmitted.

During these five years, I had to live pretty much as a Russian with all their privations. Though I did not actually suffer from obvious malnutrition, I knew the sensation of hunger pangs at times, sometimes going several days without food. For a period of about two years after having pneumonia in 1924 followed by poor nutrition, I was coughing blood and probably had tuberculosis. As exercise seemed to me a cardinal part of therapy, I forced myself to walk one and one-half hours daily whether in rain, fog, snow or subzero weather. Everything in Russia was in short supply; in 1927-28, I had to stand in line two hours to buy four sheets of paper to record experiments and about as long for a pound of bread. From 1924 to 1929, when the U.S. had no official representation in Russia, I was considered by some an unofficial diplomat.

The purpose of my sojourn in Russia was not only to learn from Pavlov but to learn about life. I worked with his assistants, both with animals and with humans, translated his book on conditional reflexes into English, wrote my own *Medical Review of Soviet Russia*, first published as a series of articles in the *British Medical Journal*.

Perhaps my most important and original contribution while in Europe was the assessment of the effects of war, famine, revolution and national influence on disease incidence. This was later referred to as "geomedicine" by the medical historian, F. H. Garrison. While I was painstakingly collecting these data, as there were no published data in Russia, the head of the ARA in Petrograd said to me in 1923, "Gantt, you are wasting your time; there will never be six people in the world who will read this." But I thought it was important and I persisted. My data for 1920-1933 constitute most of the facts on disease and famine published outside of Russia during this era.

In Russia, I followed Pavlov like a dog to find out his thoughts and science because I thought then, and still do, that he was one of the greatest geniuses of science and one of the great men of all time.

In 1927, I met John Dos Passos in Russia. We walked through the Caucasian Mountains together, discussing the pros and cons of Marxism, free will, etc. The subject of free will has occupied my thoughts for many years. I find precise notes on this subject in my writings of 1924. Briefly, I feel that as it can not be definitely clarified any more than the sensations and states of consciousness can be expressed objectively that we must take a pragmatic view. Pragmatism requires acting as if there were free will. To do otherwise, we stand to lose everything if there be free will, and if there be not, we have lost nothing. While we seldom, then or later, agreed on politics, Dos Passos remained until his death in 1970, one of my staunchest friends. With his statement that he saw no reason why differences of opinion should impinge on friendship, I agree.

III

When I returned to the United States, although I had no definite plans for my future career, Adolf Meyer gave me the opportunity to found a Pavlovian laboratory at the Johns Hopkins Medical School. This laboratory was supported by the Rockefeller Foundation for fifteen years. I am grateful to Alan Gregg, the director, for his faith in me during the years when my publications were few, saying to Dr. Lewis Weed, then vice president for the Medical School, who wanted to drop me because of paucity of publications, "Gantt is a long distance runner." (I held the two-mile record in the South for many years). I mention this for the benefit of those who think the necessity to publish is a recent phenomenon. Adolf Meyer and the ex-Dean, Dr. Thomas Turner, and Dr. E. C. Andrus, are those to whom I owe much for support during the forty-three years I have been connected with the Johns Hopkins University.

The Pavlovian Laboratory at the Johns Hopkins Medical School was supported until about 1950 on a budget of $6,000 to $15,000, including my own salary, that of a technician, a secretary, and all running expenses. A visitor from the press at that time expressed surprise that "so much good work could come out of a slum laboratory."

When I became emeritus in 1959, at the invitation of Drs. Middleton and Casey of the Veterans Administration in Washington, I founded the Pavlovian Laboratory at Perry Point, Maryland. I continued as director of the Johns Hopkins Pavlovian Laboratory without pay until 1964, when I was succeeded by Dr. Joseph V. Brady.

Before 1939, my major work in the laboratory was with experimental neurosis and the application to the psychiatric patients.

Since my publications record my work in the U.S. after 1929, I shall give only a brief account of those years. Briefly, my contributions as I see them to science have been: new factors at the origin of experimental neurosis, the comparison of the role of the center and periphery in the conditional reflex, establishment of the laws of the cardiac conditional reflex, a project for prophylactic psychiatry started experimentally in 1943, laws for conditioning expressed by the phenomena of schizokinesis, autokinesis, organ-system responsibility, the separation of the *sensation* of pain from the objective signs in the conditional reflex (schizokinesis), some laws of psychopharmacology. In 1939, with Hoffman, a co-worker from Norway, I established the cardiac conditional reflex, and have continued until the present to elaborate the laws of cardiovascular conditioning.

IV

In what follows, I shall say what I would like to see investigated in the future, as a result of my own work and experience, the view from Mt. Pisgah into the Promised Land which I have not time to explore. To these visions of a frontier I shall add some thoughts and what I consider useful rules for the scientist. My early work was with experimental neurosis. Using the conditional reflex method to determine the status of psychiatric patients in 1943, I based my idea for a prophylactic psychiatry. In the discussion of areas for investigation, I omit those that are too limited or self-evident to deserve mention here, and those I have mainly completed. Among these are the relation of peripherally- and centrally-acting agents in the formation of the conditional reflex, schizokinesis, etc. I fix my attention to what are the most significant areas arising out of my work to be explored in the future. The areas I would like to see developed are those of autokinesis, organ-system responsibility, and prophylactic psychiatry.

AUTOKINESIS. The study of the conditional reflex has, in my opinion, made grave errors, and indeed its whole future is threatened by the unbalanced emphasis on the external environment to the neglect of the internal environment. A look at genetics is one example of this internal environment, but I have in mind something else, *viz.*, not the static inherited constitution, but the *developments* that occur *within* the nervous system and possibly those elsewhere within the organism. Evident examples are accretions of habits, allergies, immunities, etc. But, there are substantial changes seen in laboratory dogs that occur among the *traces* of former conditional reflex excitations while nothing in the external environment is happening, indicating there are progressive interactions continually occurring. These may be in the direction of improvement, such as we see in the behavior of a patient after *one* visit to the therapist, or *one* episode in his life. It is like a seed planted, growing. It needs soil, air and water, but it has within itself the potentiality for growth, an interchange between roots and leaves. In higher organisms, there is the capacity for continual internal interaction. There is a well-defined internal universe as well as an external universe, and there is continuous internal interaction among its members as well as action between the organism and the external universe. Furthermore, there are internal adaptations, internal conditional reflexes formed totally within, as well as between the subjective and the external universe. This interchange I call *positive autokinesis,* when it is in the nature of anabolism. We also know of the opposite—which happens in life carrying the patient downward— *negative autokinesis,* catabolism. At present, we have no method of studying the mechanism of autokinesis, and this is what I would like to see developed. It may be through the EEG; it may be through biochemical means yet undiscovered, combined with behavioral. This is perhaps the most important concept that has come from my laboratory.

ORGAN-SYSTEM RESPONSIBILITY. Another area important in the advance of the understanding of behavior is the recognition of a particular physiological system being studied, e.g., whether it is a system involved in speedy acts, such as the cardiovascular, the gastrointestinal, or the motor, or whether the system is one requiring a slow act of maintaining a homeostatic balance for which a conditional response would *never* be of value, but would often result in wasteful imbalance. Space does not permit a more detailed discussion. But it should be emphasized that gross errors have been made recently, due to the assumption that all physiological systems will form conditional reflexes just as those involved in defense or gastrointestinal secretions. This is an example of stereotyped, rigid, encrusted thinking. The principle to investigate is what I term *Organ-System Responsibility,* where each system has a function to perform in the body economy.

PROPHYLACTIC PSYCHIATRY. Another vast undeveloped area, arising out of my work and ideas is that of the prevention of mental disease. This means the *development of a rational prophylactic psychiatry.* This would involve the examination of large numbers of the population, beginning with children, by many methods including the conditional reflex, biochemical, genetic, and following them for perhaps thirty years, with significant and detailed resumes at the end of each decade. In this way, we would obtain knowledge that would enable us to establish a prophylactic psychiatry which does not exist today. The study of dogs as well as of patients by the method that I and some others have carried out indicates that we can predict to some extent by an examination of motor, cardiovascular, respiratory conditional reflexes which individuals are susceptible to stress. Biochemical assays and complete medical examinations should be completed. In this way, we could look forward to protecting the susceptible individuals *before* they become psychotic and we may possibly develop preventive drugs for this purpose.

V

Pavlov, in his last Will to young scientists, emphasized the emotional devotion to science to which he added certain rules of work and attitude, one of which was humility. Every searcher for truth should heed this advice of Pavlov, as well as Plato's exhortations on humility. I recommend I. P. Pavlov, "Last Will and Testament" which can be found in *Conditioned Reflexes and Psychiatry*, by I. P. Pavlov (Translated by W. H. Gantt), International Publisher, New York, 1941.

The scientist is like the ancient priest in that he should be a missionary of truth. More than others, he should feel this responsibility, a *noblesse oblige*. There is often the temptation to poach in the field of others, to claim for himself as originator of what another has devised. The temptation is great, especially because it is so difficult to define who is the creator of an idea. If one is conscientious, this can be avoided. Free discussion is the *sine qua non* for scientific progress. Open discussion is one of the best ways to foster ideas.

> Science rests on experiments; its results are attained through talks among those who work in it and who consult one another about their interpretation of these experiments. Such talks form the main content of this book. Through them, the author hopes to demonstrate that science is rooted in conversations.[3]

But if one is afraid of having his ideas stolen, free discussion is inhibited. When, in discussion, a new idea comes to light, those involved should agree to share the work and the idea. A note should be made of the preceding conversation leading to it, the evolution and birth of the idea. Though few ideas are completely

---

[3]Werner Heisenberg, *Physics and Beyond: Encounters and Conversations*, trans. by A. J. Pomerans. New York, Harper and Row, 1971, p. xvii.

new, the exact formulation and the method can be original. This means teamwork which makes science more interesting. Nothing is more stifling and obnoxious than to be in a laboratory where the workers abhor discussion from fear of revealing their thoughts. The head of a laboratory can abolish this anxiety by giving priority to the first to produce an idea and encouraging teamwork among those in his laboratory.

I should like to emphasize here the extreme importance of ideas in science. Most "scientific" works repeat in a slightly modified form the idea of the creator. Thus, thousands of articles, many of them worthless, some significant, are published on the same original theme, slightly modified or reworded, (e.g., salivary conditional reflexes, cardiovascular conditional reflexes, hormonal control, lipids, etc.) often with the assumption that investigators are rated on the mere number of publications—regretfully sometimes true. The elaboration of an idea is essential, but it is only the genius who makes a discovery which, as Szent Gyorgi says, "is seeing what everyone sees and thinking what no one has thought."

Many scientists are reluctant to give credit to those who may have done important work in the same field. A scientist loses nothing by giving credit; on the other hand, I believe generosity often benefits him. Sooner or later the scientist who fails to give credit where it is due is detected and rightfully condemned.

Scientists should learn to think in facts and concepts, rather than in words and cliches. For example, not simply to say that the conditional reflex is ringing a bell and getting a flow of saliva, but to think of the auditory stimulation to the ear, the brain connections, the outflow over the sympathetic and parasympathetic nerves to the various salivary glands, possibly participation of the other activities. Thus, he keeps before him facts instead of becoming a tinkling cymbal, repeating a concatenation of syllables like a nursery rhyme—a sort of autohypnosis which prevents thinking.

VI

I have found science more exciting as the years of work

accumulate. It is like finding the missing pieces of a puzzle, the plan of which becomes clearer with time. Each year brings some additional fragment of knowledge. And if one has played the game honestly, he not only finds it exciting, but he can walk erect and face the world without fear. He has an inner satisfaction that not only comes from having faithfully completed a task, but of enjoying each step and contributing some truth. There are no failures because each movement must be made before the next can be executed.

Although the work of the scientist is absorbing, exciting, thrilling, there are, of course, many disappointments, obstructions, reversals. These are of many kinds. The investigator may find that he has not asked the relevant question of Nature, or his question may be what Planck calls a phantom question. Or perhaps there is no available method or apparatus. Nearly all scientists think they need more space and money. I have found that too much money and too many people can be a disadvantage. Nothing is ever perfect in life, and, as H. G. Wells says, "What fun would life be if there were no obstacles to overcome"? The game of science is its own reward. The more one sets his eye on prizes, position and power, the more likely he is to be disappointed and the less he is of a scientist.

In a life one must know that science is not the whole of life. It is one of the joys to the true seeker of knowledge. Its place in life should not be exaggerated. One should understand what it can do and what it cannot.

The scientist is everlastingly crying for the light of truth, but he is also a human who recognizes that he has a responsibility and a duty to perform in the universe, in the immediate uinverse of time and place, and as the prophet says, to God and to his neighbors. Pavlov sees science lifting man from his present gloom of bestial interhuman relations.

> Only science, the exact science about the human himself, and the most sincere approach to it from the side of Omnipotent Nature, will deliver him from his present gloom, and will purge him from his contemporary shame in the sphere of inter-human relations.[4]

4W. H. Gantt, *A Medical Review of Soviet Russia.* London, British Medical Association, 1928.

Life is perhaps easier for the scientist and the prophet because they seek less of material goods for themselves.

Although the scientist does not perform his experiments for any reason of "use," he nevertheless has the hope, a very strong hope, that they will lead to some beneficial effect in life. His position is that of the poet:

> Behold we know not anything,
> We can but hope that good will fall,
> At last far off, at last to all,
> And every winter change to spring.
>
> —TENNYSON

The young scientist is in the position of being inspired by the sense of wonder, the zeal for the search for truth, and the excitement of looking for what is not evident. It is of great value to a young scientist to keep himself in touch with the ideals of the great ones in past and current history. He may do this by reading of the methods and achievements of those whom he holds high, or if he is fortunate, by working as an apprentice with such a person. Here, humility to learn is of value, to say to himself, quoting Pavlov, "I am ignorant."

The older scientist drawing to the close of his career has the satisfaction not only of the same spirit that animated him in searching for the truth when young, but in viewing his own life and achievements from a distant perspective of many years, joys, tears, dreams; he sees himself humbly, as so well expressed by Tennyson in a verse from *In Memoriam:*

> So runs my dream, but what am I?
> An infant crying in the night,
> An infant crying for the light,
> And with no language by a cry.

Faith, the "substance of things hoped for, the evidence of things not seen," is the process involved in scientific work as well as in religious belief. A scientist frequently begins some research with the intuitive belief, a hunch that something is true without any clearly defined reason; it is this faith which guides him to formulate a plan and to perform experiments.

It may be of value to young scientists to emphasize the role of faith in science in comparison with faith as a quality of relegion. Many scientists think of their subject as divorced from faith, all of its tenets as provable. On the other hand, we have beliefs in science, which, though often obscure, are as inviolable a part of science as the Ten Commandments are in religion. In religion, we accept as unquestionable the rules of the Commandments. But in order to establish that one should not murder his wife and eat his children, steal and invade, he must go to the accepted beliefs for which there is no proof. One can go back only two or three steps* until he comes to an article of faith established by experience for which there is no proof, but these are the principles that we live and die for. In geometry, we recognize similarly the necessity of axioms. In science, these are not overtly expressed, but they are just as fundamental, equally as unprovable. For example, there can never be more than a conviction, faith, that the speed of light, the constitution of matter is the same in one part of the universe under the same conditions as in another part. In science, we accept, take for granted, more than we do in most other subjects. It is fallacious not to recognize both the relativity of science as dependent on conditions, but also that the basic rules are unprovable except by reference to unprovable axioms, established only by experience as are the axioms of geometry, of religion. In science, the basis for this faith is chiefly the data brought to use by the external sense organs; in religion, it is a more experiential, inner intuition, not verifiable by experimentation.

Science, unlike religion, can never stop for long on any threshold. With current methods and concepts, it forges new connections and relations, and not to continue to do so would mean a cessation of progress. Religion, on the other hand, concerned with certain ways of acting toward man and God, needs stability on the foundation of faith.

To me, the universe still presents the thrill for the explora-

---

*This is strikingly illustrated when a child questions an order from a parent by asking, "Why"? The answer can be given only in about two statements before the parent comes to an unanswerable query and has to resort to the statement, "Because I say so."

tion of the unknown. This allurement increases with age. And the warmth of true friends, the companionship of family and children continue to make life more worthwhile with the years.

In my psyche, I do not feel inclined to say *l'envoi* either to the spirit or to the actuality of science, i.e., to its daily work. The time will come when my soma refuses to support my psyche in its quest for the unexplored—or perhaps my psyche will sink with my soma, and the days to this time are steadily waning—but until then, I expect to pursue the search with continued joy.

With Time the child is impatient, for the lover it is eternity, with riper years, it is a matter of indifference, but for the octogenarian Time brings nostalgia and a realization that the ticks of the clock are numbered. From Mt. Pisgah, he looks backward and forward. He throbs with the remembered thrills of the climb, and with wonder and with awe he looks into the promised land of the unexplored. From this altitude, the scientist who has lived a full life can say, with Browning:

> What I aspired to be
> And was not comforts me,
> A brute I might have been
> But would not sink in the scale
> . . . .
> Youth shows but half; trust God,
> See all nor be afraid.

VII

At some instant in his own time and by the clock of the universe the curtain will drop, he must shuffle from the stage, and face resolutely the Angel of the Darker Drink, who

> At last shall find you waiting by the river brink,
> And offering his cup, invite your soul,
> Forth to your lips to quaff, you shall not shrink.

—OMAR KHAYAM

At the fourscore year mark without disabling infirmities, and, as I feel, in the prime of my mental function, I have now said what I think. When the Dark Ferrash strikes to prepare my tent for another guest, may I be as resolute!

Chapter IV

ON LIFE AND WORK

E. Gellhorn

Ernst Gellhorn was born on January 7, 1893, in Breslau, Germany. Following an earlier classical education he received the M.D. and Ph.D. degrees respectively from the Universities of Heidelberg and Muenster in 1919. He joined the medical faculty of the University of Halle, received the venia legendi in 1921, and became an Associate Professor of Physiology in 1925. Four years later he was invited by Dr. A. R. Moore to join the Department of Animal Biology at the University of Oregon as Associate Professor. In 1932 he went to the University of Illinois School of Medicine as Professor of Physiology. In 1943 he went to the University of Minnesota as Professor of Neurophysiology and retired from this position in 1960.

In his scientific career he received several prizes: from the University in Berlin in 1917; from the New York Academy of Sciences, the A. Crossy Morrison Prize in 1930; from the College of Physicians, the Alvarenga Prize in 1935; and a medal from the Carbon Dioxide Research Association in 1957.

Before coming to the United States he published an extensive series of investigations on sensory and general physiology. Part of these experiments were summarized in Neuere Ergebnisse der Physiologie in 1926, in Allgemeine Physiologie, 1931, which he edited and for which he wrote the physicochemical section, and in Das Permeabilitaetsproblem in 1929.

In the United States he published the following books:

I. The Vasomotor System in Anoxia and Asphyxia (in collaboration with E. H. Lambert), 1939.

II. Autonomic Regulations, 1943.

III. Physiological Foundations of Neurology and Psychiatry, 1953.

IV. Autonomic Imbalance and the Hypothalamus, 1957.
V. Emotions and Emotional Disorders (in collaboration with G. N. Loofbourrow), 1963.
VI. Autonomic-Somatic Integrations, 1967.
VII. Biological Foundations of Emotion, 1968.

The majority of the papers which Professor Gellhorn published since 1929 dealt with neurophysiological problems, such as the physiological basis of shock therapy, functions of the motor cortex, hypothalamic-cortical relations, physiological factors altering convulsions, the tuning of the central nervous system, homeostasis, partial discharges of the sympathetic and the role of the ergo- and trophotropic systems under physiological and clinical conditions.

Professor Gellhorn has died since the writing of this legacy, on April 20, 1973.

> . . . like all great ends, singleness of mind is not an end but a beginning. . . A countryman has it who, being himself very old and without hope of the event, goes upon his knees to plant an acorn in the ground.
>
> CHARLES MORGAN.

THIS LITTLE CONTRIBUTION falls short of being a strictly scientific paper. It confines itself to comments on the professional life of a physiologist in the past fifty years and certain phases of his work. It also reports personal experiences of the writer which, as he approaches his eightieth year are admittedly influenced by the weakening of the neocortex and release of the emotional hypothalamic system. It is hoped, however, that they do not lack general interest as a longitudinal study and make a small contribution to the philosophy of living.

ON TEACHING AND RESEARCH

It has been noted that our University administrators appreciate teaching less than research. The termination of staff appointments due to inadequate publications is not uncommon in our Universities whereas research, i.e. published papers or books, compensates easily for poor teaching. At a number of institutions it has become a more or less accepted practice to reduce the teaching obligations of the "great" scientists, particularly at the undergraduate level.

Having not studied these matters in detail I can judge them

only on the basis of my own experience. Although more than sixty years have passed, I still remember the deep impression great academic teachers made on me as a young student. I had the good fortune of listening to the great classical scholar, U. von Willamowitz-Moellendorf, who in the crowded auditorium maximum of the University of Berlin lectured before undergraduate and professional students on Plato in an atmosphere of awe and respect. He was old, spoke like a philosopher and poet and looked like a Greek seer. I had read some of the Latin and Greek classics in high school in their original language, but was entirely unprepared for this experience. I felt the indelible influence of a dedicated man. I witnessed an act of creation at the highest level; it was an unforgettable experience. There are, of course, dedicated men and women active in areas unrelated to teaching and research, but the deep-rooted enthusiasm which maintains dedication to one's life work, regardless of intrusions of fate is a *conditio sine qua non* of the great teacher. Other academic teachers supplemented and reinforced these impressions. The philosopher Georg Simmel whose books show his analytical power revealed in his lectures his mind at work, and the lectures of Friedrich Krauss on thyroid dysfunctions provided similar intellectual stimuli.

There are several conclusions I like to draw from these observations:

1. The lecture should not be replaced by television regardless of how good the T.V. speaker is.

2. The contact between lecturer and student should be increased. Lecturer-student conferences would enhance the former's teaching ability and the latter's understanding and appreciation of the science involved. The conferences now in use in which each staff member meets a fraction of the lecture audience each week are useful to keep the staff alert but they fail to give the lecturer the opportunity to further his teaching aims and direct the student's attention to books, implications of research results, etc. Moreover, enthusiasm and involvement so important for the student's career and success are more easily generated by the lecturer. The staff member who is a specialist in gastrointestinal

physiology may be pretty poor in arousing the student's interest in the intricacies of the cerebellum. If the classes are too large to permit an adequate discussion, the type of conference I advocate may be held with graduate students only.

3. The double obligation to teach and do research should be retained or even expanded. The awareness of having given good lectures at a time when his research failed him, is important for the scientist's morale.

4. The lectures even of good speakers who are inexperienced or unsuccessful in research are stale when compared with those of a productive scientist. The smooth speaker will satisfy the multitude and use all techniques which will make it easy for the students to take notes and pass examinations with a minimum of effort, but he will not stir their imagination. Information is available through books; the lecture system stands and falls with the personality of the teacher.

I mentioned the influence of some outstanding representatives of the humanities on students of natural and biological sciences, theoretical and applied. This suggests that the curriculum of students of science, medicine, etc., should be broad. The esthetic arousal through literature and the arts, for instance, enriches the students' minds and enhances their humanness. An interdisciplinary education even on a modest scale but not confined to the undergraduate years might do wonders in advancing human understanding of the problems man is facing today. Is there a problem more worthy of the labors of the best?

It is, of course, impossible to discuss this problem here in detail. Suffice it to say that even the professional schools, in spite of their crowded schedules, should make one hour available for a weekly lecture-discussion period in which leading authorities of the University would deal with those aspects of their disciplines that are important for modern man.

Psychologists and psychiatrists have been much interested in recent years in the phenomenon that rodents which had been handled a few times during a limited period of their early lives show changes in growth and emotional behavior when compared to their litter mates which had not been handled. It is possible that the influence which man's formative years have on his later life is related to these observations. Alert educators should take advantage of these phenomena.

SOME REMARKS ON MY PHYSIOLOGICAL STUDIES

A large part of my work was summarized and evaluated in books and critical papers published since 1926 and deals with borderline problems involving physiology, psychology, psychosomatic medicine and neuropsychiatry.[1] It was preceded—among other studies—by experimental work on the effects of hypoxia, hyper- and hypocapnia on the vascular and sensory systems, the EEG and complex psychological processes such as word association, etc. These studies convinced me that complex physiological processes depend on the same physiological factors as the simple sensory reaction to optical flicker (fusion frequency). It is, therefore, expected that psychological processes of varying degrees of complexity can be altered by physiological means regardless of whether one considers the physiological cerebral changes as the *cause* of the psychological effects or not. For the all-important question of the *control* of the psychic events and particularly of the emotions this nature of the psychophysiological relations is relatively irrelevant.

I had planned to review some of my life's work which, from an analysis of the physiological basis of shock therapy, leads through the application of Hess' concepts of the ergotropic and trophotropic systems, to the theory that the ergotropic-trophotropic quotient plays an essential role in maintaining emotional balance and restoring it in psychosomatic and neuropsychiatric disorders. I feel, however, that I am no longer able to do so and restrict myself to the following remarks.

I. The results of the analysis of shock therapy based on the effects of hypoglycemia, coma, electrically or chemically-induced convulsions and the action of carbon dioxide were expressed in my early work in terms of excitability of autonomic centers but

---

[1]The references selected below were chosen from this work to aid the reader in finding the original literature. They do not necessarily reflect the most significant work (Gellhorn, 1943, 1953a, b, 1954, 1964, 1965, 1967b, 1968a, b, 1969a, b, 1970; Gellhorn & Kessler, 1943).

more recently in terms of the activity of the ergotropic and trophotropic systems and the ergotropic-trophotropic quotient. The linkage between autonomic and somatic processes was stressed. It includes the role of the gamma system and its effect on the proprioceptive feedback to the diencephalon, and the dependence of the state of activity of the cortex on the ergotropic-trophotropic quotient. The beneficial effect of shock therapy seems to be related to a shift in the ergotropic-trophotropic balance to the ergotropic side. These procedures should, therefore, be applied to patients with a low ergotropic reactivity (Hoskin's schizophrenics with sluggish sympathetic reactivity) (Cf. Shakow, 1971). On the other hand, patients with a high ergotropic-trophotropic ratio should be benefited by procedures reducing this quotient. Experimental and clinical studies of psychosomatic disorders (narcolepsy, hypertension, neurosis) and some psychoses seem to be in fair agreement with this statement (Gellhorn and Kiely, 1972).

Hypoglycemia was shown in man and animal to greatly increase the blood pressure rise induced by anoxia. This effect is due to the enhanced reactivity of the autonomic (ergotropic) centers to chemo-receptor stimulation. The enhanced pressor reaction to small concentrations of carbon dioxide and also to increased intracranial pressure persists after sinoaortic denervation showing that the ergotropic centers themselves are in a state of heightened excitability in hypoglycemia.

The central interaction between electroshock and hypoglycemia is dramatically demonstrated in *adrenodemedullated* rats which, kept at a comatose blood sugar level after insulin never recover spontaneously; but they show arousal,[2] restitution of righting reflexes and normal EEG when an electroshock was applied in the comatose state although *the blood sugar remained unchanged.* It is suggested that increased discharges from the hypothalamus and reticular formation to the cortex are responsible for the effect. The heightened ergotropic reactivity after

---

[2]This was shown by Gellhorn and Kessler in 1943, six years before Moruzzi and Magoun discovered the ascending reticular formation and its diffuse action on cortical potentials and arousal.

repeated electroshocks, and the persistence of this effect for weeks was likewise shown (Gellhorn and Safford, 1948).

II. The importance for the state of the cerebral cortex of changes in the ergotropic-trophotropic balance[3] at hypothalamic

1. The ergotropic and trophotropic systems are characterized by integrated autonomic and somatic action. Ergotropic excitation (ergotropic-tuning) is induced by procedures leading to sympathetic and diffuse cortical excitation, increased activity and tone of striated muscles and behavioral arousal and even rage. Conversely, trophotropic excitation is characterized by increased parasympathetic discharges, sleep-like potentials in the EEG, lessened muscle tone and drowsiness or sleep.

2. Three degrees of tuning induced by increasing intensities of stimulation are distinguished. At the first stage of ergotropic tuning the tone and reactivity of the ergotropic system is increased while that of the trophotropic system is reciprocally inhibited. Corresponding changes in reactivity occur during the tuning of the trophotropic system. At the second stage reversal phenomena occur: a stimulus which under control conditions evokes a trophotropic response, elicits an ergotropic response in the tuned state. The third stage shows loss of reciprocity and appearance of pathological states of consciousness.

and reticular levels can only be pointed at. Physiological procedures (involving stimulation of peripheral receptors and central structures, or lesions in limbic areas, hypothalamus, and reticular formation) and drug action may alter the state of the whole organism as indicated by the state of wakefulness, emotional responsiveness and conditional reactions. Changes may range from deep coma to maximal emotional excitation and convulsions. Reciprocity between ergotropic and trophotropic reactions may, under conditions of strong stimulation be converted into simultaneous discharges of both systems while anxiety, hallucination and other pathological mental states occur. To take care of this bewildering variety of normal mental states which are associated with alterations of the ergotropic-trophotropic quotient it must be assumed that several states of heightened ergotropic and trophotropic "tuning" exist. Thus, intensive joy and rage, psychologically so different, involve increased muscle tone and, therefore, enhanced ergotropic discharges. Similarly, postprandial happiness as well as depressive conditions (worry, etc.) lead to

[3]For those not familiar with the ergotropic and trophotropic systems and their behavior, I add:

increased trophotropic discharges (sleepiness, spindles in the EEG and muscular relaxation). The elaboration of multiple ergotropic (or trophotropic) emotions may be based in part on differences in the proprioceptive patterns that are transmitted to hypothalamus and cortex when different facial expression patterns are evoked. It must also be taken into consideration that hormones liberated from different parts of the hypothalamus are bound to alter the character of the hypothalamic-cortical discharges.

III. It is well established that motor functions are enhanced by emotional excitement. The activation of the sympathetic system (including the increased secretion from the adrenal medulla) has been held responsible for this effect. With the recognition that the ergotropic system evokes not only peripheral (sympathetic) but also central (cortical) discharges, the question arises as to whether the latter affect the motor cortex. This is indeed the case: cortically induced contractions are magnified by minimal stimulation of the ergotropic division of the hypothalamus. In view of the diffuse action of the ergotropic system on the cortex, a similar enhancement of sensory functions was to be expected. Acoustic and optic responsiveness of the specific sensory projection areas was increased when the hypothalamus was stimulated, and even subthreshold stimuli were effective. Similar effects were obtained from reticular stimuli. The lowering of the threshold of perception through arousal and emotional excitement seems to be related to these findings.

The important observation that cortical projection areas retain their responsiveness to specific sensory stimuli in deep barbiturate anesthesia or during inhalation of carbon dioxide in high concentrations supports the assumption that perception is not the result of activation of lemniscal paths and specific projection areas, but is due to the interaction of two ascending systems, the diffuse reticular and hypothalamic system and the specific systems confined to the projection areas. Since the diffuse systems are present in the cortex outside the projection areas, one should know whether different electrographic patterns are elicited by hypothalamic and reticular stimuli which possibly correspond to different psychological states (perception and arousal respectively), but one should also bear in mind that discrepancies exist between electrographic and behavioral indicators of arousal and related processes.[4]

Changes in ergotropic-trophotropic balance may result in changes in autonomic reflexes, emotional reactivity and perception. This statement holds not only for the inborn reactions just discussed, but also for the individually acquired experiences the physiological model of which is Pavlovian conditioning. This is not surprising since numerous experiments involving hypothalamic stimulation and lesions, the action of spreading depression, etc., suggest that conditioning is accelerated when the ergotropic-trophotropic quotient increases, but is delayed or abolished as the quotient decreases. Under these circumstances changes in perception paralleling changes in autonomic reactions occur as conditioning is reinforced through repetition of the conditional reflexes or other procedures. It is thought that acquired reactions (such as responses to a severe emotional trauma that changes the ergotropic-trophotropic balance) may ultimately lead to alterations and disturbances in perception.[5] Obviously, restitution of the ergotropic-trophotropic balance should be the therapeutic goal. Physiologists, psychologists and philosophers should be interested in the fact that perception in its quantitative and qualitative aspects depends on such volatile factors as the ergotropic-trophotropic balance.

Since emotional and perceptual disturbances are common in early phrases of psychoses, the fundamental change in perception associated with alterations in ergotropic-trophotropic balance is of great psychiatric interest.

[4]See Gellhorn (1967a) pp. 164, 241, 242 for the literature.

[5]Just one example may suffice (Pschonik, 1956). If heat (63°C) is applied to the dorsal and warmth (43°C) to the volar surface of the forearm, the former evokes vasoconstriction and pain and the latter vasodilation and warmth. After many repetitions it can be shown that vasomotor and also sensory reactions are determined by the site of stimulation. Then the 43° stimulus (warmth under control conditions) elicits vasoconstriction and pain from the dorsal surface and the 63° stimulus (pain under control conditions) elicits vasodilatation and warmth from the volar surface. Through tuning of the ergotropic and trophotropic systems vasomotor reflexes *and* perceptual responses have been completely reversed.

IV. There are two important aspects of the functions of the ergotropic and trophotropic systems which have a significance even beyond the reach of physiology. One has to do with the hierarchical organization of the central nervous system. Jackson elaborated this concept by pointing out that movements are represented at several levels of the nervous system. At the spinal level the most primitive reflexes are elicitable whereas animals with sections of the brain stem at pontine and diencephalic levels show increasingly complex reflex movements. They are further refined in the intact organism by contribution from the neocortex. Similarly, temperature-regulating reflexes are demonstrable in the spinal animal refined at the hypothalamic level, and modified by the cortex. The ergotropic and trophotropic systems share the hierarchical organization with the somatic nervous system.

Secondly, it should be stressed that the ergotropic and trophotropic systems serve not only autonomic-somatic reflexes but a wide variety of organismic reactions. Changes in ergotropic-trophotropic balance involving the hypothalamus or the limbic system may convert the rage into the pleasure syndrome and vice versa. Innate and acquired reactions follow the same rules of tuning. Social factors such as crowding or prolonged isolation are likewise determinants of behavior and related to the ergotropic-trophotropic balance.[6]

High degrees of tuning lead to ergotropic plus trophotropic discharges and altered states of consciousness. They comprise the dream stage of sleep, Zen meditation, states of anxiety, delirium, etc. Similarly, a great variety of emotions can be induced in persons who had received a large dose of Adrenaline and were then subjected to different emotional situations. These and other experiments suggest at least two things:

1. That the trophotropic plus ergotropic discharges do not determine the specific character of the psychological disturbance although normal perception is interfered with in every instance. The pathophysiology of the central nervous system has been advanced by showing that alterations in the ergotropic-trophotropic

---

[6]Ethologists have made pertinent observations on lower animals which probably involve the same mechanisms (Eibl-Eibesfeldt, 1967).

quotient may impair or restore mental functions and alter mood and emotions in normal subjects.

2. The ergotropic and trophotropic systems may discharge partially as well as completely. This makes it possible for the ergotropic system to produce a variety of ergotropic emotions. This is the reason why Schachter was able to evoke, through administration of adrenaline, an ergotropic state in which happiness as well as anger could be elicited by suitable stimuli (situations) in his experimental subjects. He would have found it difficult or impossible to produce a depressed state under these or similar circumstances which Bull had already studied in hypnosis.[7]

Although the importance of neurophysiological procedures for the alteration of psychological states is emphasized in this paper, it is realized that psychological guidance (empathy) probably contributes to the stability of the therapeutic results.

V. Cannon's experimental study of the sympathectomized animal has greatly influenced the thinking of physiologists, psychologists and physicians concerning the role which the autonomic nervous system plays in organismic reactions. He showed that changes in the internal environment (hypoxia, hypoglycemia, hemorrhage, severe emotional excitement, excessive exercise and exposure to cold) elicit diffuse sympathetico-adrenal discharges which tend to counteract changes of the blood and, thereby, prevent damage to heart and brain. The sympathetic system as a whole seemed to be involved and showed little if any differentiation. Some remarks seem to be in order to indicate the present state of these problems.

Considerable retention of sympathetic-like action in exercising sympathectomized dogs suggests that somatic reactions play an important role under these and related circumstances. Thus, as hypoxia increases, carbon dioxide begins to accumulate and enhances muscle tone and, thereby, venous return and minute volume of the heart. Since exposure to cold increased shivering even in animals with denervated adrenals, ergotropic discharges account better than sympathetic discharges alone for these adjustment reactions. In addition, limited (partial) sympathetic

[7]For further details see Gellhorn (1970, pp. 84, 85).

discharges have been observed on stimulation of spinal cord and hypothalamus (Gellhorn, Cortell and Murphy, 1946) and have recently been demonstrated in man in learning experiments (DiCara and Miller, 1969). From these observations it may be concluded that diffuse sympathetic discharges as established in Cannon's emergency reactions are just one form of activation of the ergotropic system under physiological conditions. Others consist of a great variety of restricted ergotropic patterns.

Utilizing the excretion of noradrenaline as indicator of the neurogenic phase and the excretion of adrenaline as that of the hormonal (adrenomedullary) phase of the ergotropic system, it has been shown that under certain experimental conditions (exposure of chronic cold-adapted animals to cold) noradrenaline excretion is enhanced while that of adrenaline is unchanged. On the other hand, insulin hypoglycemia may evoke increased adrenomedullary excretion without producing a change in noradrenaline. Even intraergotropic changes of a highly adaptive character may occur. Thus, in the unacclimated rat adrenaline and shivering counteract, on exposure to cold, the fall in body temperature, but after weeks of cold acclimatization the adrenaline in the cold test remains virtually unchanged, but that of noradrenaline is increased and its effectiveness on the heat production of the muscles is likewise enhanced. Shivering is no longer necessary.

The homeostatic reactions described thus far are based on the enhancement of circulation, metabolism (blood sugar) and heat production through increased ergotropic reactions; but there is still another fundamentally different adjustment mechanism available. When it is no longer possible to meet the oxygen demands of the organism and particularly of the brain through increased ergotropic action, the trophotropic system is activated with the consequence that the oxygen needs of the organism are reduced. This is accomplished to a large extent by a fall in body temperature. Thus, life is preserved, although cerebral excitability is greatly reduced. A closely related phenomenon is this: Characteristic behavioral syndromes suggesting trophotropic dominance may follow unsuccessful ergotropic adjustment reactions

in man and animals (Ploog, 1964). These reactions may preserve
life since giving up fight by the weaker partner may inhibit ag-
gressiveness of the strong.

EMOTION AND EDUCATION

*Man konnte den Menschen zum halben Gott bilden wenn man ihm
durch Erziehung suchte alle Furcht zu nehmen.*[8]

Recent investigations on the physiology of the ergotropic and
trophotropic systems seem to have broadened our understanding
of integrated processes in the normal organism and shown the
applicability of this work to problems of psychology, medicine
(especially psychosomatic medicine), and psychiatry. Knowledge
of the basic physiology of the emotions may also be of value to
the layman and might be taught to high school students or fresh-
men in college in courses of biology or psychology. Some of the
material which may be presented in such a course is outlined in
the following pages.

Since emotional disturbances lead frequently to various forms
of psychosomatic diseases, emotional involvement seems to be
undesirable. This notion is held particularly by young men in the
belief that emotionality tends to counteract the attainment of
male virtues such as hardiness and strength. In emotional situations a conflict may, therefore, arise which leads to peculiar behavioral phenomena. One can commonly observe in a movie or
legitimate theater that at moments of serious emotional tension
some men in the audience suddenly begin to laugh rather noisily.[9]
The following mechanism seems to be involved.

An environmental stimulus coming from screen or stage tends
to create a trophotropic state manifesting itself in crying and/or
secretion of tears. This effect is lessened or prevented by will-
induced laughter which is accompanied by increased action of
the facial muscles and probably also by enhanced tension of the
skeletal muscles. Both effects lead to increased proprioceptive

[8]"Man could approach God-like stature if one could eliminate all fear through
education." Friedrich Schiller.

[9]This is not a phenomenon peculiar to the U.S. as one prominent psychologist
(Koffka) thought. I have seen it in Germany in the 1920s and since this time
in this country in performances attended by high school and college students.

discharges which impinge upon the hypothalamus. As a consequence the state of tuning of the ergotropic division of the hypothalamus is increased and that of the trophotropic division inhibited. The depressing effects of trophotropic dominance are prevented and the emotional balance is restored.

The following observations illustrate further that a change in muscle tone by voluntary action, through learning or via reflexes induces a change in the emotional state:

1. Expressing vituperation in a loud voice leads to a psychogalvanic reflex. Repetition of this experiment while the subject is relaxed lessens this effect subjectively and objectively: emotion and vocal intensity are greatly diminished and the psychogalvanic reflex becomes minimal.

2. An increase in baroreceptor discharges causes a decrease in muscle tone and emotional excitation whereas a lessening of these discharges has the opposite effect.

3. Muscle tension and oxygen consumption are increased when the subject is harassed during mental work. Mental work as such does not exert ergotropic effects.

4. Severe muscular work leads to enhanced proprioceptive discharges and ergotropic excitation. The syndrome thus evoked is similar to that induced by stimulation of the ergotropic division of the hypothalamus (elevation of the blood sugar, improved circulation through the activated muscles, mobilization of noradrenaline and adrenaline, etc.). Obviously, marked muscle activity leads always to peripheral *and* central activation of the ergotropic system as in an emotional situation.

5. An ergotropic emotion tends to be inhibited in the relaxed state but facilitated when the muscle tone is increased.

The problem of dealing with human emotions must take into consideration the fact that emotions are, at least to a certain extent, controllable by will. Moreover, changes in muscle tone, induced voluntarily or reflexively, tend to alter the trophotropic-ergotropic balance in the same direction. The emotional responsiveness is lessened in the relaxed state because hypothalamus and hypothalamic-cortical projections receive fewer proprioceptor discharges. This mechanism could be utilized not only in the therapy of the neuroses but also as a preventive measure in persons who have learned to relax their skeleton muscles in situations arousing emotions. Conversely, in acute fear, when trophotropic discharges become dominant, blood pressure and heart rate may fall and cause circulatory collapse. The willed tensing of the muscles may lessen this effect and prevent loss of consciousness under these circumstances. Reflex adjustment via the sino-aortic baro-receptors may likewise contribute to the restitution of the trophotropic-ergotropic balance and circulatory homeostasis.

It seems to me that the temporal course of homeostasis and its importance for the control of the emotions should not be neglected. From Sherrington's studies on somatic reflexes it is known that inhibition is followed by "a rebound to superactivity" before the normal excitability is restored. Similar rebound phenomena are seen when the ergotropic system is activated while the autonomic effect is recorded. Then the pressor effect seen during stimulation is followed by a period of hypotension *after* stimulation before the control level is restored. But the rebound is not confined to the autonomic part of the ergotropic and trophotropic systems: behavioral changes may likewise occur. Repetitive stimulation of the midbrain reticular formation leads first to increased arousal but later to a state of trophotropic dominance. The cat yawns, curls up and finally falls asleep. One would, therefore, expect that in man too an intensive but brief excitation of the ergotropic system is followed by increased trophotropic discharges. This may account for the seemingly paradoxical result that certain persons react to a pistol shot with a small galvanic reflex and extensive general movements whereas others show that a prolonged duration of this reflex is associated with minimal motor responses.

It is suggested that massive proprioceptive discharges reinforce the ergotropic excitation and create ideal conditions for a trophotropic rebound. On the contrary, in the absence of these massive discharges the ergotropic excitation is built up more gradually and followed, at the end of the stimulation period, by ergotropic after-discharges which prevent the development of a trophotropic rebound.

If one remembers that under natural conditions this rebound takes place *after* a brief but intensive ergotropic discharge (during the killing of the prey) and is associated with the consumption of the prey, one realizes that this biphasic reaction is highly adaptive: Phase I enhances muscular strength and alertness and, therefore, aids the overcoming of the enemy; Phase II induces a state of trophotropic tuning in which digestive processes are optimal. Obviously, civilized life gives little opportunity to use this mechanism—and this is the reason why the excitation of the ergotropic system and the liberation of its associated neurohumors (adrenaline and noradrenaline) may lead to unpleasant symptoms in conditions in which flight or fight are taboo for social reasons.[10]

SOME PERSONAL EXPERIENCES

I believe that every young man and woman should know that emotional sensitivity of the adult is not a sign of weakness. The successful attempt to reduce it below a certain level would be dearly paid for by the subsequent sterility of their lives. Writers and poets agree that the richness of one's life and its productivity are, to a large extent, determined by one's responsiveness to emotion-arousing stimuli. Heine expresses this directly in his poem, "Out of my great pains do I make my little songs." Nietzsche's statement, "Great pain is the final liberator of the spirit," and Hölderlin's words, "He who steps on his suffering stands higher," imply that through tragic and painful experiences hidden spiritual resources are liberated.

The physiologist may call attention to the fact that the sensory and motor cortex show an increased reactivity to various forms of excitation when the hypothalamus is activated at the same time and that this phenomenon is observed even with subthreshold hypothalamic stimuli. Moreover, cortical areas which do not react to a certain (acoustic or optic) stimulus may do so under the influence of hypothalamic stimulation. The psychological experience that a profound emotional shake-up may bring into being new cortical (intellectual or artistic) abilities is thought to be related to the facilitation of cortical processes through hypothalamic activity.

[10]For further implications of this work, see Gellhorn (1967a, 1970).

I explored these matters objectively nearly twenty years ago in physiological experiments without any presentiment that some day I would experience the subjective side of this phenomenon: It appeared in my 76th year after the passing of my good wife and weeks of agonizing readjustment. Although I never carried out literary activities previously, I began to write little stories, satires, essays, etc., of which two examples are recorded below.[11]

I wish to add that this tragic experience has greatly enriched my life. It makes me wonder whether scientists and other intellectual workers dedicating themselves completely to their professional tasks would not do well to pay more attention to their emotional life.[12]

CONCERT

A little while ago I was in the garden. Something unusual was happening. A rather noisy concert was going on. It was not contrapuntal but loud and apparently expressed happiness. I could easily distinguish soloists and chorus. The intensity of the singing and the endurance of the performing artists suggested that they were competing with one another like the Meistersinger of old. Listening closely I heard what sounded like eager, eager, — Ernie, Ernie, — and Vincent, Vincent. — I wondered, do the birds know that I am going on a trip to see my children and grandchildren?

To my disappointment I did not hear any names of the girls. Then I realized that their names were hidden in the beauty of the coloratura arias which the soloists presented with enthusiasm from tree tops and telephone wires, reminding anybody who wishes to hear that life is beautiful.

[11]These two stories were taken from my recently published book, *The Time Concertina—Meditations of a Humanist*. Copies can be obtained for a nominal fee by writing: Dr. Ernst Gellhorn, 15 Wendover Drive, Charlottesville, Virginia 22901.

[12]After the manuscript for this article had been completed I found this idea confirmed in an essay of Broch (see Hermann Broch der Dichter Zürich, Rhein Verlag 1964, p. 23). He raises the question *"ob ein solch ausschliessilch auf wissenschaftliche Erkenntnis gerichtetes Leben—es ist das alte Mönchsideal in moderner Verwandlung—nicht doch genötigt ist, an tiefsten Lebenserkenntnissen vorbeizugehen. Er stellt neben jene 'rationale Erkenntnis' die 'Erkenntnis des Gefühls.'"* ("whether a life exclusively directed toward scientific understanding—it is the old monks ideal in modern form—does not compel one to pass by the deepest comprehension of life. He places the emotional comprehension in juxtaposition to the rational comprehension").

And remember: Whether we believe in the existence of a heavenly conductor or consider beauty a by-product of evolution is not of primary importance. What really counts is that we hear the music.

AFTER THE STORM

I have lived in Santa Barbara for a good many years and see the beach and the ocean almost daily. You might think I have seen all that is to be seen but this is far from true as this little story shows. During the last 48 hours we have had a severe storm with rainfall of about twelve inches. I was anxious to see the beach after the storm and went as soon as the clouds lifted. I saw an angry ocean of heavy waves following each other in quick succession, preventing our most courageous surfers from riding them. But I saw something else. All along the beach there were innumerable "soap" bubbles, small and large and all a little dirty. I pondered what this all meant. Then an inner light appeared and I knew: It was washday for the fish. Although they don't get very dirty in the sea they need a real cleaning once in a while and nature cooperates. The winds hit the waves very hard and small bubbles appear providing a bubble bath for the fish.

To verify my explanation I asked a fisherman who had just caught a fish whether it looked particularly clean. He looked at me in a funny way. Apparently, he was so eager to catch fish that he remained unaware that this was wash day for the fish. Of course, to notice this you need more than the outer eye. Fortunately, the inner eye is right behind it. It is good not only for dreaming. It makes you see beauty where before you had seen colors. When you see in the mountains a double rainbow on which many fairies are running and dancing, you are seeing with that inner eye of yours about which I have been talking.

REFERENCES

DiCara, L. V. & Miller, N. E.: Heart-rate learning in the noncurarized state, transfer to the curarized state, and subsequent retraining in the noncurarized state. *Phys Behav*, 4:621-624, 1969.

Eibl-Eibesfeldt, I.: Ontogenetic and maturational studies of aggressive behavior. In Clemente, C. D. and Lindsley, D. B. (Eds.): *Aggression and Defense*. Los Angeles, University of California, 1967.

Gellhorn, E.: *Autonomic Regulations.* New York, Interscience, 1943.

Gellhorn, E.: *Physiological Foundations of Neurology and Psychiatry.* Minneapolis, University of Minnesota Press, 1953.

Gellhorn, E.: Physiological processes related to consiousness and perception. *Brain*, 77:401-415, 1954.

Gellhorn, E.: *Autonomic Imbalance and the Hypothalamus.* Minnneapolis, University of Minnesota Press, 1957.

Gellhorn, E.: Motion and emotion. *Psychol Rev, 71:*457-472, 1964.

Gellhorn, E.: The neurophysiological basis of anxiety: An hypothesis. *Perspect Biol Med, 8:*488-515, 1965.

Gellhorn, E.: *Principles of Autonomic-Somatic Integrations.* Minneapolis, University of Minnesota Press, 1967a.

Gellhorn, E.: The tuning of the nervous system: Physiological foundations and implications for behavior. *Perspect Biol Med, 10:*559-591, 1967b.

Gellhorn, E.: Central nervous system tuning and its implications for neuropsychiatry. *J Nerv Ment Dis, 147:*148-192, 1968a.

Gellhorn, E.: The neurophysiological basis of homeostasis. *Confin Neurol, 30:*217-238, 1968b.

Gellhorn, E.: The consequences of the suppression of overt movements in emotional stress: a neurophysiological interpretation. *Confin Neurol,* (Basel), *31:*289-299, 1969a.

Gellhorn, E.: Further studies on the physiology and pathophysiology of the tuning of the central nervous system. *Psychosomatics, 10:*94-104, 1969b.

Gellhorn, E.: The emotions and the ergotropic and trophotropic systems. *Psychol Forsch, 34:*48-94, 1970.

Gellhorn, E.: *The Time Concertina: Meditations of a Humanist.* Charlottesville, E. Gellhorn, 1972.

Gellhorn, E., Cortell, R. and Murphy, J. P.: Are mass discharges characteristic of central autonomic structures? *Am J Physiol, 146:*376-385, 1946.

Gellhorn, E. and Kiely, W. F.: Autonomic nervous system in psychiatric disorders, In Mendel, J. (Ed.): *Biological Psychiatry.* New York, Wiley, 1972a.

Gellhorn, E. and Kiely, W. F.: Mystical states of consciousness: Neurophysiological and clinical aspects. *J Nerv Ment Dis, 154:*399-405, 1972b.

Gellhorn, E. and Kessler, M.: Interaction of electric shock and insulin hypoglycemia. *Arch Neurol Psychiat, 49:*808-819, 1943.

Gellhorn, E., Koella, W. P. and Ballin, H.: Interaction on cerebral cortex of acoustic or optic with nociceptive impulses: the problem of consciousness. *J Neurophysiol, 17:*14-21, 1954.

Gellhorn, E. and Safford, H.: Influence of repeated anoxia, electroshock and insulin hypoglycemia on reactivity of the sympatheticoadrenal system. *Proc Soc Biol Med, 68:*74-79, 1948.

Ploog, D.: Verhaltungsforshung und Psychiatrie. In Gruhle, H. (Ed.): *Psychiatrie der Gegenwart,* vol. I/IB. Berlin, Springer, 1964.

Pschonik, A. T.: *Die Hirnrinde und die rezeptorische Funktion des Organismus.* Berlin, VEB Verlag, 1956.

Shakow, D.: Some observations on the psychology (and some fewer on the biology) of schizophrenia. *J Nerv Ment Dis, 153:*300-316, 1971.

Chapter V

STUDY OF BEHAVIOR: SCIENCE OR PSEUDOSCIENCE

Jerzy Konorski

Jerzy Konorski was born in Lodz (Poland) in 1903, the son of a lawyer. While still in high school (finished in 1920), he decided to be a scientist, although his scientific interests were then not well defined. Gradually they crystallized around the problem of how the brain controls behavior. For this reason he started to study first psychology (1921-1923) and then medicine at the University of Warsaw. He received the MD degree in 1929.

While a student in 1927 Dr. Konorski came across the recently edited fundamental book of Pavlov on conditioned reflexes and began to study it together with a colleague Stefan Miller. Soon the two realized that Pavlovian conditional reflexes did not cover all acquired animal behavior. Thus they arrived at the concept of Type II conditional reflexes based on award-punishment principle. In a self-made laboratory Konorski and Miller began to study these reflexes. They got in touch with Pavlov and described their results to him. He was interested in them and invited the men to Leningrad to work in his laboratory. Konorski stayed in Leningrad for two years (1931-1933). That period of his life settled his scientific career.

For the rest of his life, Dr. Konorski continued to work almost incessantly in this domain: from 1934 till 1939 in the Nencki Institute of Experimental Biology in Warsaw; from 1940 till 1944 (the war years) in the Subtropical Biological Station in Sukhumi (Caucassus), and from 1945 to the present again in the Nencki Institute. Since the Institute's building had been badly destroyed

*during the war, Dr Konorski, together with a group of its former workers, trans-
ferred it temporarily to Lodz, where he obtained a chair of neurophysiology in
the newly established University of Lodz. About 1955 a new building for the
Nencki Institute was erected in Warsaw where he is presently.*

*When the Institute was resuscitated after the war, Konorski became its
Deputy Director and Head of the Department of Neurophysiology. And from
1968 until now he has been Director of the Institute.*

*Dr Konorski is a member of the Polish Academy of Sciences, Foreign Asso-
ciate of the National Academy of Sciences, foreign member of the American
Academy of Arts and Sciences and honorary member of the Roumanian Academy
of Sciences.*

*Professor Konorski has died since the writing of this legacy, on September
14, 1973.*

Introduction

BEFORE STARTING TO WRITE this paper I decided to be certain of
the precise meaning of the word "legacy." In the *Concise
Oxford Dictionary* I found that it is "a material or immaterial
thing handed down by predecessors." Thus, I understand that
I am here in a role of a predecessor, expected to hand over my
thoughts about the field of science I have been concerned with
throughout my life to the present generation of scientific workers.
Analyzing these thoughts now, I realize that they are shaped
by my past. This means that although my views concerning particular problems of brain functions and brain-behavior relations
have drastically changed with the development of my own
research work and that conducted by other authors, my general
ideas have remained amazingly similar to, although not identical
with those I held forty-five years ago at the beginning of my scientific career. Accordingly, my scientific "legacy" requires explanation of the origin and development of my scientific "Weltanschauung." This calls for some autobiographical facts which
have been dealt with in detail elsewhere (Konorski, 1973).

Pavlov claimed that experiments on brain functions, executed in anesthetized animals are not a "true" physiology of this
organ for the following reasons. The brain is *the* organ developed for the highest control and integration of animal behavior on the basis of messages arriving to it from receptors.

This is its real and unique function. Therefore studying its activity in a situation in which this function is strongly reduced and simplified by anesthetic drugs is unreasonable and cannot teach us anything about how the brain works in normal conditions. The only way to approach the normally functioning brain is to make experiments on wakeful animals presenting them with various types of natural stimuli and observing their responses.

It should be recalled that the concept of a "reflex," denoting simple inborn responses to particular stimuli, was already well established in physiology by the end of the 19th century. Therefore Pavlov also resorted to this concept as the basis of his investigations by introducing the term "conditional" reflex, in contradiction to the "unconditional" reflex as dealt with in neurophysiology up to that time. In his writings Pavlov stressed very strongly that all *essential* properties of conditional reflexes were exactly the same as those of unconditional reflexes, except that the latter were inborn, while the former were acquired during the animal's life as a result of his individual experiences. Thus, it was thought that the careful study of conditional reflexes and their properties should pave the way for an understanding of their physiological mechanisms within the brain. In this way a new important branch of science was originated and called by Pavlov the "physiology of higher nervous activity."

I became a full adherent and a strong advocate of this approach, and was even proud to belong to a small group of people who took part in this noble enterprise. My own main contribution to this enterprise shared with my colleague and coworker Stefan Miller, was the discovery of Type II conditional reflexes, based on a different paradigm than the Pavlovian reflexes, and a thorough description of their properties and categories (Miller and Konorski, 1928, 1969; Konorski and Miller, 1933, 1936). These reflexes were subsequently called operant responses by Skinner (1938) and instrumental responses by Hilgard and Marquis (1940).

In the late thirties, when I became better acquainted with

the physiology of the central nervous system, I became much more critical towards the Pavlovian theory of cerebral processes, since I had realized that this theory is in complete discord with the general principles of neurophysiology. In order to understand this discord one must take into account that before Pavlov began his research work on conditioned reflexes, he spent about twenty years on a different subject — the physiology of the digestive tract. In this domain Pavlov won a worldwide reputation, crowned by the Nobel prize in 1903. When he later drastically changed the line of his investigation, he was not properly acquainted with the achievements of modern neurophysiology, which were founded on Ramon y Cajal's studies on the histology of the nervous system (1909, 1911) and developed by Sherrington in his studies on the activity of the spinal cord (1906). Therefore, he did not try to adjust his concepts of the activity of the cerebral cortex to the general principles of functioning of the central nervous system. Rather he attempted to build his theory of cortical processes on the basis of his own ideas which had emerged from experiments on conditioned reflexes.

The main difference between the two lines of ideas, that of Ramon y Cajal and Sherrington on the one hand, and that of Pavlov, on the other, was briefly this. According to the first two authors the central nervous system is a huge nerve-net in which the nervous processes (impulses) are traveling from one neuron to the others by nerve fibers (axons), and transmit either excitation or inhibition by synaptic contacts. This transmission, being strictly unidirectional, conveys information either from reception to the brain, or from the brain to effectors, or between various structures of the brain. On the other hand, Pavlov claimed that the excitatory or inhibitory processes originating in the given points of the cerebral cortex by the operation of corresponding conditional stimuli irradiate all over the cortex and then concentrate back to their departure points (Pavlov, 1927). On the basis of these notions, Pavlov attempted to explain all the manifold properties of both positive and negative conditional reflexes and their complex interrelations.

The critical evaluation of the Pavlovian theory of cortical processes advanced by him on the basis of his experimental data, and the proposal of a new theory of conditioning based on the same data but with reference to the general principles of nervous activity developed by Sherrington, were presented in my monograph *Conditioned Reflexes and Neuron Organization* (Konorski, 1948, 1968). The title of this monograph was meaningful. In fact, whereas the Pavlovian theory of cortical activity, based on the irradiation of excitatory and inhibitory processes over the cortex and their concentration at their points of origin, could not be reconciled with the neuronal organization of the brain as it was conceived by Ramon y Cajal, the theory which I proposed was explicitly based on this conception.

It is understandable that achievement of the goal of explaining the properties of conditional reflexes by means of neural processes analogous to those, firmly demonstrated in lower parts of the nervous system, greatly strengthened by conviction the soundness of the general Pavlovian idea that conditional reflexes *could* be explained in neurophysiological terms. For, the only obstacle hindering this explanation so far, prevalent at that time among physiologists, was that the Pavlovian theory was quasiphysiological and quite alien to the real functioning of the nervous system. I was almost certain that, if Pavlov had from the very beginning tried to interpret his data on the basis of synaptic concepts and to indicate the affinity of his work to that of Sherrington, his ideas would have been understandable to neurophysiologists and fully acceptable. Therefore, I considered that it was a tragedy for the development of the Pavlovian work that at some definite turning point in the early twenties, he came to his unfortunate concepts of irradiation, concentration and induction of cortical processes, and thus his further theorizing went astray.

MY ATTITUDE TOWARDS BEHAVIORISM

It must be clear to the reader that I was in strong opposition to the behaviorism which accepted in full scope Pavlovian empirical terms (such as conditioned reflex, generalization, extinction, etc.). Praising Pavlov as the greatest *Psychologist* of our time opposed any idea of explaining animal behavior in physiological terms. In order to present my issue, let me take the view of two of the most influential scientists of my time, Skinner and Hull.

B. F. Skinner's Views

As is well known, Skinner decided in the early thirties to establish a purely empirical scientific discipline which would deal exclusively with description and systematization of animal and human learned behavior (Skinner, 1938) without a tendency to explain it by reference to any basic processes. In his most representative article pointing out his viewpoint (Skinner, 1950), he discards any theories explaining learning either on the basis of mental events, or physiological processes occurring, or assumed to occur in the brain. Here are the main points of his argumentation:

> A science of behavior must eventually deal with behavior in its relation to certain manipulable variables. Theories, whether neural, mental or conceptual, talk about intervening steps in these relationships. But instead of prompting us to search for and explore relevant variables, they frequently have quite the opposite effect. When we attribute behavior to a neural or mental event, real or conceptual, we are likely to forget that we still have the task of accounting for the neural or mental effect.

And again:

> Research designed with respect to theory is also likely to be wasteful. That a theory generates research does not prove its value unless the research is valuable. Much useless experimentation results from theories, and much energy and skill are absorbed by them. Most theories are eventually overthrown, and the greater part of the associated research is discarded.

I think that Skinner's discarding of the physiological approach in the analysis of animal behavior is groundless. As a matter of fact, almost all natural sciences aim to explain the hidden mechanisms of empirical data by proposing hypotheses, tested by new empirical data, which either confirm or reject them. I do not see any reason why the sciences of behavior should stand aside from this general rule of scientific development.

Skinner's main argument against the explanation of animal behavior with reference to central nervous processes occurring in the brain was that nobody could see these processes. This was why he considered that the term CNS (central nervous system), which the behavioral scientists deal with, was in fact the "conceptual nervous system," since its functions were concluded on the basis of stimulus-response relations (Skinner, 1938). But this contemptuous denotation is unjust and incorrect. Skinner is certainly fully aware that the behavior of animals does depend on the function of the central nervous system, in particular, of the brain. He also knows that the general principles of the functioning of this system are basically understood. Therefore, the goal of scientific research consists in determining the arrangement of nervous connections which can account for particular types of stimulus-response relations. Skinner also knows that Sherrington's fundamental work on the central mechanisms of spinal reflexes was based precisely on stimulus-response technique, since direct recording of the activity of spinal neurons was in his time impossible. Nevertheless, the "conceptual spinal cord" proved to be a reality and the principles of its activity were on the whole confirmed later by electrophysiological studies directly observing the activity of spinal neurons.

The Skinnerian approach to behavioral data seems to me the same as if a chemist were to describe the empirical properties of chemical compounds and their reactions, completely neglecting the molecular theory of the matter which explains the occurrence of these reactions. The similarity between such an imaginary approach of a chemist and Skinner's approach to the behavior of animals is even closer, if we consider that the molecular theory arose much earlier than scientists dreamed of "seeing" molecules and atoms. It, too, was purely conceptual.

What has been offered by the above approach to our knowledge? Since its principal task is the empirical study of behavioral response, it is reduced to a mere collection of facts, irrespective of their significance for understanding the central mechanisms by which they are controlled. It happens that some of these facts may be of prime importance from this point of view, but their proper evaluation must be done only by those people who are concerned with the elucidation of central mechanisms controlling animal behavior.

The above discussion on the validity of Skinner's general approach to the study of behavior should not in the least detract from his important methodological contributions in this field. Indeed, Skinner's methods are used in almost every behavioral laboratory and they play a significant role in the hands of those who aim at understanding animal behavior by physiological mechanisms.

C. L. Hull's Views

A quite different point of view was represented by another prominent American psychologist, C. L. Hull (1943). For Hull animal behavior was also the principal aim of his research work, but he attempted to systematize it by means of a number of concepts called "constructs," which intervene between the stimulus and the response and are chosen in such a way as to account for empirical data obtained in behavioral experiments. Here belong such notions as habit strength, reaction potential, inhibitory potential, and others. But Hull makes it clear that these constructs have no physiological meaning and are proposed because, according to his view, "the major neurological laws" were (in his time) not ripe "to constitute the foundation principles of a science of behavior." It is well known how popular Hull's system was among behaviorists and how much it has promoted the experimental work on animal behavior.

From my point of view the system proposed by Hull cannot by definition be quite satisfactory just because of its abstract character. After all, in the time when Hull undertook his life's work, the "major neurological laws" were fairly well understood. At least they were sufficiently developed to establish a theory of behavior which, although imperfect, could certainly fulfill the same role as was played by his abstract constructs. Therefore these constructs, based *only* on the empirical material from the field of conditional reflexes, might become misleading at the time when they should be translated into neurophysiological concepts.

Moreover, for me the Hullian system played a negative role in the development of our science. When reading Hull's principal treatise, one notices that his knowledge of neurophysiology was extensive and that he did emphasize that his system was transient and should be substituted in the proper time by a neurophysiological system. Unfortunately, this admonition was not obeyed by his followers. Therefore, when neurophysiology in the next years grew immensely and its discoveries *could* throw much light on the mechanisms of behavioral responses, psychologists continued to stick loyally to Hull's constructs, changing and improving them, but drawing no profit from neurophysiology.

Thus, willy-nilly there occurred in the science of behavior a most disappointing situation. Instead of coming closer and closer to neurophysiology, experimental psychology became, on the contrary, even more remote from it than in the time of Thorndike and Hull. The science of behavior proclaimed itself to be a self-contained scientific discipline, fully independent of brain physiology, and even reluctant to have any bonds with it. This unhealthy situation still exists, its clearest manifestation being the current use of the term "behavioral science," and the refusal of its adherents to study behavior within the scope of brain physiology. Since these adherents are also strongly opposed to introspective notions largely used by classical psychologists, the discipline exists in a vacuum. It is isolated from both physiology and psychology.

MY ATTITUDE TOWARDS TRUE PSYCHOLOGY

As it was argued in the preceding section of this article, the line of research conducted on the basis of either the Skinnerian or Hullian approach is directed toward an extension of our knowledge of behavior as such, without any attempts at understanding the cerebral processes on which this behavior is based. Therefore, this line of research has been denoted as the science of behavior. However, the investigators studying animal behavior along this line also use another term, no less popular than the previous one. They call this field "objective psychology." It is easy to see that this term is illogical, since psychology is by definition a field of science concerned with mental events or those events which we are aware of from our subjective experience or introspection. In opposition to this, the science of behavior is purely objective and rejects any references to psychic events. Thus, the term objective psychology should be avoided, since it includes a typical *contradictio in adjecto*.

True, psychology as a science of describing and analyzing mental events on the basis of self-observation, is an old discipline which does not need any defense. Usually two arguments are used against its validity. One is that very often the reports obtained from introspective observation by one person are unreliable, and other people cannot confirm them. But this is often true of objective observations as well. For example, when people look at the same object they do not necessarily agree about its visual properties. After all, this is why behavioral studies are often performed, by resorting to independent observations by two or more persons in order to obtain more reliable results. In fact, we do know how unreliable and misleading human perceptions can be and how cautious we must be to evaluate them properly. The other argument against introspection as a scientific method is that, while objective observations are, at least theoretically, "public," that is a number of people may observe the same object, the events "perceived" by subjective observations are by definition "private." Of course this is true, but it should not belittle their value. After all, an investigator who would like to test the generality of a particular subjective experience can present the stimulus by which it is elicited. He can show a picture evoking particular emotions to a number of persons of a given group and record what they are feeling while looking at it.

Finally, it should be noted that subjective observation is used in a very important field of science called psychophysics, which has allowed us to discover important properties of human perceptions. If we trust the observer's report of what he has perceived, why not trust him when he reports what he has imagined?

All of these seem so commonplace to everybody possessing common sense that I feel even embarrassed to mention them. Yet, I do know many "psychologists" who strongly oppose the scientific value of introspection, and if pressed about this issue, use a hypocritical maneuver. They claim that they base their statements not on subjective observations of other people, but on their objective verbal reports. By the way, this hypocrisy is quite naive, because if one is, for instance, interested in the classification of human emotions, he could hardly say that his interest lies in the classification of a definite class of verbal reports.

Another important question concerning descriptions of mental events is whether it is legitimate to attribute these events to higher animals. Certainly the naive misuse of such descriptions by laymen and even some scientists, who attributed a number of human experiences to animals on the basis of superficial and uncritical observations, led to denying any kind of subjective experiences to animals. This approach is again unscientific. If a species of organisms called *homo sapiens*, which possesses a highly developed brain for some mysterious reasons, is endowed with subjective experiences, then it must be admitted that higher animals, whose brains are very similar to those in humans, should also possess this peculiarity. Moreover, if behavioral and autonomic manifestations of various drives, such as hunger, fear, rage, etc., are in higher animals analogous to those in man, then there is no reason to negate analogous emotional experiences in these animals. If anybody would oppose this opinion on the grounds that subjective experiences in animals cannot be directly proved, we could show him that the same is true of all human beings, except himself. Yet I do not think that it would be reasonable for scientists to hold such solipsistic views.

To sum up, it is now fashionable among some groups of psychologists to discredit introspective methods of observations, considering them unscientific. Some of these psychologists, especially those engaged in experiments on animals, are consistent in that they are interested *only* in animal behavior, based on pure objective observations, and develop the theoretical systems in which subjective experiences do not intervene. Some of them, for instance, Tolman (1932), use terms denoting such experiences like expectancy; they regard them, however, as intervening variables. Others, especially those concerned with human psychology adopt a hypocritical attitude, pretending they do not care about mental events, but are interested only in external responses, among them verbal reports.

Despite the value that "objective psychology" may have had in bringing scientific rigor to the study of behavior earlier in this century, it seems to me that this attitude is in the present period of development of brain physiology particularly harmful. For all naturalistically-minded scientists, whether they are by profession physiologists or psychologists, are aware of the fact that mental events do depend directly on the cerebral processes and that no such events can exist without the functioning of these processes. In fact, both the methods of destruction of various parts of the brain and of recording evoked potentials in wakeful animals make the correlations between mental events and cerebral processes increasingly better understood. Although some decades ago psychologists *could* claim that the skull was a black box and that we could not even imagine what is going on inside, this black box is now illuminated by the penetrating light provided by the surgical knife, drugs, or implanted electrodes. Therefore, our long lasting dream of fixing correspondence between mental processes and cerebral processes does not seem unrealistic and is even not very far from realization. But this can be done only when psychologists stop being ashamed of their own scientific domain, return to studying mental events and help to bridge the gap between these events and neural processes. The sooner they do so, the better it will be for the development of our knowledge on the correlations between mind and brain.

SYNTHESIS

The above considerations, originating of course from my scientific development, lead me to specify the following possible domains of investigations which are directly or indirectly connected with brain functions.

1. The domain dealing mainly with subjective experiences. The method of investigation is here introspection, that is, observation of events occurring in our minds. This area was ex-

tensively studied in the nineteenth and early twentieth century. The monumental treatise by William James (1950) is a classic specimen of this discipline.

2. The domain dealing with subjective experiences plus their external effects. This is the typical human psychology of today if it is not biased by aversion to introspection. The works on emotions or motivations are good examples of such studies, since these are the phenomena in which subjective experiences are virtually inseparable from their autonomic and behavioral effects.

3. The domain dealing exclusively with behavior. While Skinner (1938) arbitrarily chose motor responses of animals for his investigation; Hull (1943), being closer to the physiological approach in the study of behavior, included also autonomic responses occurring in classical conditioning.

4. "Pure" brain physiology dealing with cerebral processes in anesthetized or immobilized animals, studied by electrophysiological methods. Of course, this domain has no direct relation to behavioral sciences. I have called it analytical neurophysiology.

5. The domain dealing with animal behavior (including autonomic responses) studies from the *physiological* point of view, that is with reference to the cerebral processes controlling this behavior. This domain is now developing with tremendous speed and efficiency, judging from the abundant increase in the number of journals each year, that it is hardly possible to follow it. It is called physiological psychology (the old term proposed by Wundt in 1910), neuropsychology, or the study of brain and behavior. All these names are synonyms.

6. The domain which includes the interdisciplinary study of brain functions, utilizing facts obtained from various sources. On the one hand, it makes use of the data collected by analytical neurophysiology which teach us about the functional properties of nerve cells, the interconnections between various parts of the brain, and the connections between the brain and peripheral organs. On the other hand, it deals with all relevant evidence both from the field of animal behavior and introspection, those phenomena which are *controlled* by cerebral processes. I have called this aspect of brain functions the integrative activity of the brain (Konorski, 1970), because the discipline dealing with

this activity is the true physiology of the brain which Pavlov attempted to establish.

Of course, the last domain specified here is closest to that called brain and behavior study, because the only differences between the two is that it does not neglect introspective observations in both normal and brain damaged human subjects. In my last book (Konorski, 1970) I emphasized how valuable may be the reports of some intelligent patients suffering from visual agnosia. They are able to describe their mental deficiences, which otherwise might completely escape our observation.

Now, having all these domains in mind, we may easily see that the domain concerned with the pure study of behavior is at least superfluous, if at all justifiable. In fact, as far as *human* behavior is concerned, according to our introspection it is inseparable from mental events. Accordingly, then it is a part of human psychology. As a consequence of the growing possibility of explaining these events by nervous processes occurring in the brain, human behavior will be more and more intelligible from the physiological point of view.

Even simpler is the situation with regard to *animal* behavior. This behavior is studied in special experiments which allow us not only to observe motor and autonomic conditioned reflexes elicited by particular conditional stimuli, but also to directly intrude into the brain in order to elucidate which parts of this organ, and in which way, they are involved in the formation and occurrence of these reflexes. Accordingly, the study of animal behavior has already become part of brain physiology, and its separation from that discipline is completely artificial.

I do realize that those scientists who were brought up on different scientific ideas from those advocated in this article, namely in the belief that the study of behavior should constitute a separate field of science, independent of kindred fields, will not be convinced by my argumentation. I think that this is because people engaged in the pure study of behavior are *ipso facto* not physiologists, but "behaviorists." They do not realize the explanatory power of brain physiology with regard to animal behavior. So I appeal in this legacy to those students who are not yet biased by their previous behavioristic training, and consequently have their minds open to other ideas, provided that these ideas are reasonable.

REFERENCES

Hilgard, E. R., Marquis, D. G.: *Conditioning and Learning*. New York, Appleton-Century-Crofts, 1940.

Hull, C. L.: *Principles of Behavior*: An Introduction to Behavior Theory. Appleton-Century-Crofts, 1943.

James, W.: *Principles of Psychology*. Vol. 1-2 New York, Holt, 1890. New ed. New York, Dover, 1950.

Konorski, J.: *Conditioned Reflexes and Neuron Organization*. Cambridge, Cambridge University Press, 1948. Reprinted with additional chapter, New York-London, Hafner Pub. Co., 1968.

Konorski, J.: *Integrative Activity of the Brain*. Chicago, Univ. of Chicago Press, 1970.

Konorski, J.: *Autobiography*. New York, Appleton-Century-Crofts, 1973.

Konorski, J., Miller, S.: Podstawy fizjologicznej teorii ruchow nabytych: Ruchowe odruchy warunkowe. Les principles fondamentaux de la theorie physiologoique des mouvements acquis: Les reflexes conditionnels moteurs. *Warszawa-Lwów, Ksianznica Atlas TNSW*. French Summ., 1933.

Konorski, J., Miller, S.: Conditioned reflexes of the motor analyzer. *Trudy Fiziol. Lab. I. P. Pavlova, 6* (1):119-278, 1936.

Miller, S., Konorski, J.: Sur une forme particuliere des réflexes conditionnels. *C R Soc Biol*, 99:1155-1158, 1928.

Miller, S., Konorski, J.: On a particular form of conditioned reflex. *J Exp Anal Behav, 12*:187-189, 1969.

Pavlov, I. P.: *Les Reflexes Conditionnels. Etude Objective de l'Activité Nerveuse Supérieur*. Paris, Alcan, 1927.

Pavlov, I. P.: *Conditioned Reflexes. An investigation of the physiological activity of the cerebral cortex*. New York, Oxford, Univ. Press, 1927.

Ramón y Cajal, S.: *Histologie du systéme Nerveux de l'Homme et des Vertébrés*. trans. by Dr. L. Azoulay. Paris, vol. 1-2, 1909-1911.

Sherrington, C. S.: *The Integrative Action of the Nervous System*. New York, Charles Scribner's Sons, 1906.

Skinner, B. F.: *The Behavior of Organisms*. New York, Appleton-Century-Crofts, 1938.

Skinner, B. F.: Are theories of learning necessary? *Psychol Rev*, 57:193-216, 1950.

Tolman, E. C.: *Purposive Behavior in Animals and Men*. New York, Appleton-Century-Crofts, 1932.

Wundt, W.: *Grundzuge der physiologischen Psychologie*. Leipzig, W., Englemann, 1874.

Chapter VI

EXPLORING WITH DRUGS*
The Way of a Neuropharmacologist

*I take this opportunity to express my appreciation to all my collaborators and in particular to Chuong C. Huang, Mohammad S. K. Ghouri, Brian F. Carr, John H. Daugherty and Peter B. Keen, who are currently sharing with me the continuing adventures of this search.

AMEDEO S. MARRAZZI

Dr. Marrazzi was born and brought up in New York City, where he attended and later taught at the College of the City of New York. After obtaining an M.D. and also marrying a classmate at New York University College of Medicine, he interned at Bellevue Hospital and then practiced medicine in New York City. He interrupted this to become a Christian A. Herter Fellow in Pharmacology at New York University and a member of the Pharmacology Department. He left his Assistant Professorship to head a new department as Professor of Pharmacology at Loyola University School of Medicine in Chicago, having been in the interim Visiting Investigator in Physiology at the Rockefeller Institute and Dazian Foundation Neurophysiology Research Fellow at the University of Chicago.

The following quote (Marrazzi, 1971) serves to summarize his subsequent career:

The study of the operation of the nervous system in health and in disease has led the author and his collaborators through a series of adventures in research that have developed into an increasing involvement with the mind and its disturbances. The evolution of this commitment to Experimental Psychiatry, the approaches that have been required and the insights that the data obtained have afforded constitute this progress report and expression of conviction in the need for interdisciplinary investigation.

An initial exposure to the practice of medicine strengthened the belief that, at its best, it constitutes a daily clinical experiment with each patient in which drugs provide the tools for dissecting and modifying the normal and disease processes. The focus on control systems with the greatest versatility in adapting to internal and external environments and with the greatest vulnerability to drugs, resulted in a convergence on the nervous system and its response to drug manipulation. Thus a neuropharmacologist came into being. In the process of developing suitable techniques and laboratories, the neuropharmacologist organized and headed two Departments of Pharmacology (Loyola Univ. and Wayne Univ.). Army Chemical Corps next provided the opportunity for exploration of the nervous system with more powerful substances both in the laboratories and in the field, and for the realization of a strong desire to reversibly reproduce and control derangements at the highest integrative levels including the mind. The neuropharmacologist thus became a neuropsychopharmacologist who subsequently, as Chief of the Clinical Research Division, put his experiments into the context of mental disease as Experimental Psychiatry.

The need for an expansion of the interdisciplinary approach and the greater availability of clinical rather than solely man-made disease made it natural to accept the VA's invitation to set up the first National Laboratories for Research in Neuropsychiatry. [Concurrently he was Professor of Physiology and Pharmacology at the University of Pittsburgh.] As the life of this successful pioneering operation approached a decade, the lure of a similar but completely on-campus operation culminated in the Hill Foundation Research Professorship of Neuropharmacology at the University of Minnesota. After thriving for five years, the project was again lured by the fuller recognition and potentialities afforded by the new laboratories and research ward of the new Neuropharmacology Division of the University of Missouri's Institute of Psychiatry in St. Louis, where the author is presently Professor of Psychiatry and Neuropharmacology and Chief of Neuropharmacology.

Among his firsts are: First paper on electrical recording of synaptic transmission to appear in the Journal of Pharmacology and Experimental Therapeutics (1939); Organized the first militarily sponsored Neuropharmacology Laboratory (Army Chemical Center, 1948); Organized the first completely interdisciplinary and integrated laboratory of Experimental Psychiatry (VA, 1956); First Hill Research Professor of Neuropharmacology (University of Minnesota, 1964).

E XPERIMENTATION MAY VERY PROFITABLY go beyond the observation of changes occurring without intervention, to the study of experimentally induced changes. The experimenter learns a great deal by entering the environment as an operator and so tailoring the situation to better provide answers to his questions. His skill in this determines whether the interpretive hazards of his participant role are outweighed by the more informative analysis made possible by manipulating and weighting factors at will.

The strategy of exploring reaction to environmental variations—constituting behavior—requires the capability of exercising control. The nervous system is such a controlling system whose end product is, indeed, behavior. Thus, it is a real advantage in the study of behavior to start with understanding the means of modulating the central nervous system.

A powerful and biological method of inducing reversible changes is that of altering the internal environment of the nervous system, i.e. the interneuronal chemical environment. The vulnerability of synapses to chemicals and drugs has long been recognized. The reaction to drugs, then, becomes the neuropharmacologist's touchstone. The nature and potentialities of the synaptic chemical or neurohumoral control can be explored with drugs characterizing, in particular, the nature of the response to those capable of producing dramatic behavioral changes.

It will become apparent that drug effects are achieved by biasing of synaptic equilibria which in turn control equilibria between regions of the brain, and that this synaptic and cerebral homeostasis is paralleled by behavioral homeostasis. The analysis of experimentally induced changes can often capitalize on the availability of clinical equivalents resulting from, so to speak, the experiments of nature and those of the therapist, who tries to cope with such disturbances in an effort to restore more adequate homeostasis or health.

How does the neuropharmacologist, now seen as the explorer of the nervous system with drugs, go about what may seem to be a bewildering complex task? He does so by keeping clearly in sight: (1) general biological principles that characterize the unit of structure and of function, *viz.* the cell, and (2) the essence of the intercellular communication and integrative, action or command system, that is the nervous system.

Dissection and analysis can achieve optimum results when the tools are sharp, the capabilities known and the nature of the material appreciated. The individual consists of a population of cells and so, in the first instance, he can only manifest properties that are contained in those common to all protoplasm interfaced with its environment by the cell membrane. These properties, in fact, are the same for all cells but aggregates of cells constituting tissues and organs specialize in some of these while retaining all the others. Neural tissue, for example, emphasizes excitability and conductivity. Appreciation of these fundamental biological facts determines the comprehension and most effective utilization of drug studies. Since the actions we are most concerned with are the reversible ones, it becomes evident that all that drugs can do is to increase or decrease the functions with which a cell is endowed. Accordingly, no matter how intricate the end result, we are simply dealing with only two kinds of actions, namely excitation and inhibition and their modification by blocking and enhancing agents, while the circuitry into which these actions are plugged determines the wide variety of manifestations that may result. A graded continuity of action that might otherwise appear to be merely a wide variety of effects is emphasized in the chart presented as Figure VI-1.

The essence of the nervous system is to be found in its

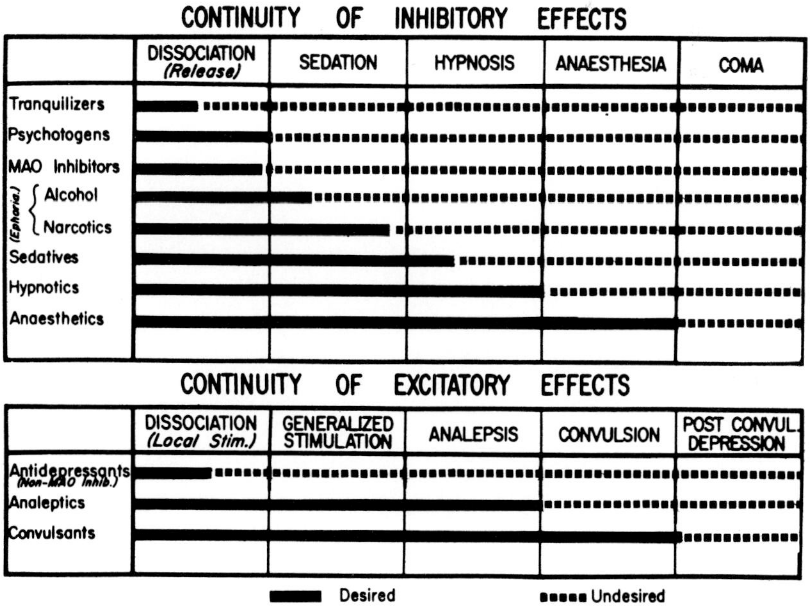

CONTINUITY OF INHIBITORY EFFECTS

	DISSOCIATION (Release)	SEDATION	HYPNOSIS	ANAESTHESIA	COMA
Tranquilizers					
Psychotogens					
MAO Inhibitors					
(Epheria.) { Alcohol					
(Epheria.) { Narcotics					
Sedatives					
Hypnotics					
Anaesthetics					

CONTINUITY OF EXCITATORY EFFECTS

	DISSOCIATION (Local Stim.)	GENERALIZED STIMULATION	ANALEPSIS	CONVULSION	POST CONVUL. DEPRESSION
Antidepressants (Non-MAO Inhib.)					
Analeptics					
Convulsants					

▬▬▬ Desired   ■■■■■ Undesired

Figure VI-1. Continuity of Inhibitory and Excitatory Effects

generation of input and output patterns, as a function of intercellular communication accomplished by changes in the critical
chemical environment at the synapses. The chemical nature of
the synaptic neurohumoral environment makes it susceptible to
modification by other chemicals or drugs and accounts for the
vulnerability of synapses to chemical and pharmacological influences. The factors involved, all potentially manipulatable, are
diagrammed in Figure VI-2.

We come then to the realization that these drug influences,
again, can only increase or decrease the processes involved in
neuroneuronal transmission, and, thereby, bias the push-pull
synaptic equilibrium between excitatory and inhibitory trans-
mitters, i.e. the synaptic homeostasis (Marrazzi, 1957, 1962a,
1966). Monitoring the response of transmission to candidate
chemicals (messengers) natural to the mammalian brain and to
their modifiers by recording the postsynaptic potentials evoked by
presynaptic stimuli, has enabled us to establish that cholinergic

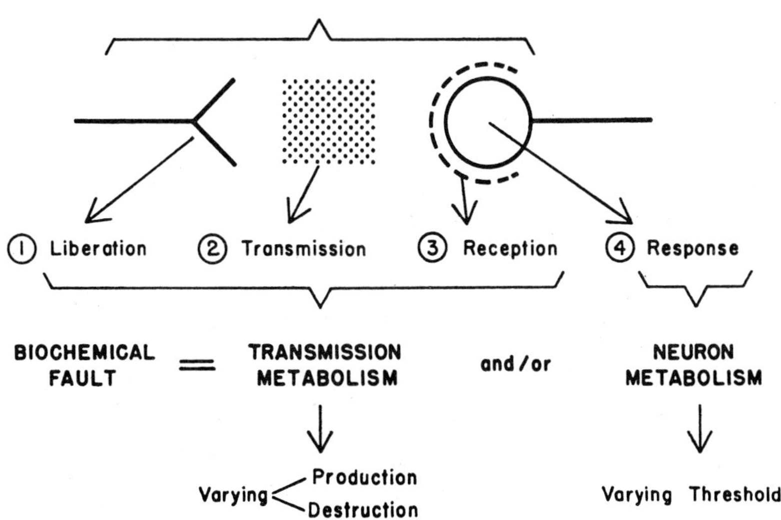

Figure VI-2. Potential Factors in Disturbed Synaptic Equilibrium

(Chakrin et al., 1968; Marrazzi, 1953) excitatory, and adrenergic (Marrazzi, 1957, 1958) and tryptaminergic (Marrazzi, 1957; Marrazzi and Hart, 1955) inhibitory, neurohumoral transmission systems operate in synaptic homeostasis. This is true of representative sites, Figure VI-3, we have sampled throughout the cerebrum, brain stem and cerebellum (Faingold and Marrazzi, 1972, 1973; Marrazzi, 1964). As dictated by the architecture that would make such synaptic homeostasis possible, our results from a large variety of synapses indicate that all neurons, indeed, have both excitatory and inhibitory presynaptic endings terminating upon them, with the varying richness and porportions of the respective endings contributing to the typical threshold differences characterizing specific areas. Figure VI-4 tabulates the data of our experiments on drug modulation of cerebral synapses and shows that our extensive testing gave results consistent with this interpretation. An example of simultaneously recorded cortical field and unit evoked potentials from the same site is presented in Figure VI-5, which shows the inhibitory action of close-arterially injected serotonin (5HT) with units recorded in various parts of the field potential cycle. Such modulation of homeostasis in the signaling and the controlling system is mirrored in the effector systems and the behavior thereby controlled, and in the accompanying affect and state of mind. The kinds of manipulations possible can now evidently be studied and accomplished through an experimental strategy that simply directs itself to modifying the excitatory and inhibitory processes—monitoring directly the actions achieved on synaptic inputs and outputs (Marrazzi, 1958, 1960), the effects produced behaviorally in the laboratory and in the clinic (Marrazzi, 1964b), along with the underlying neurochemical machinery supplying the necessary energy and producing the requisite synaptic and systemic messengers, including a potential second messenger, cyclic AMP. The latter could combine both roles.

The ordering of ideas, or classification is the first step in clarifying relations and interactions. In so doing, one deals with units and individuals, with populations and societies. Such studies can be conducted arm in arm by the pharmacologist and the behaviorist with mutual benefit.

Our own group has produced much evidence indicating that synapses and their drug sensitive mechanisms are *qualitatively* alike throughout the brain (Marrazzi, 1965), so that the differing patterns are a function of the varying thresholds of the responding postsynaptic cells. This important generalization (based on the sampling sites and methods in Figure VI-3 provides the kind of parsimony implied in the adaptive evolution that comparative anatomy and physiology suggest. The concept furthermore, on the one hand, denies unique sites of action of drugs on the brain and, on the other, recognizes central side or toxic effects as merely the undesired consequences of the inclusion of more and higher threshold synapses as the dose is elevated, cf. Figure VI-1.

The simplifying concepts proposed can help provide better analysis without necessarily dictating simple consequences and effects, for the factors in the equilibrium system as diagrammed in Figure VI-2 operate into and through circuitry of varying complexity determining the form of the overt manifestations.

FIGURE VI-3
GENERALITY OF CEREBRAL SYNAPTIC DRUG RESPONSE

Region	Sites Examined Recorded From	Evoked Thru
	1° Sensory Optic Auditory	Optic Radiations Auditory N. (Clicks)
Cortical	Association Lat. Gyrus Suprasylvian G.	Commissural Fibers A) Transcallosal or B) Transgyral
Subcortical	Lat. Geniculate	Optic Tract
Brain Stem Reticulum	Messencephalic Pontine	Pontine Retic. A) Sciatic Nerve B) Mesenceph. Retic.
Medulla	Phrenic Nerve	Spont. Resp.
Cerebellum	Vermis	Olive

		ACCUMULATORS (Preserve, Release, Inhib. Reuptake)	BLOCKERS
EXCITORS Cholinergic (Natural)	Acetylcholine	Antiche.	Atropine Curare TEA
Others (Unnatural)	Glutamate		
	Pilocarpine Nicotine		Atropine
INHIBITORS (Natural) Adrenergic	Adrenochrome Dopamine Norepin. Epin. Normetaneph. Metaneph. DMPEA	MAOI Amphet. Ephed.	CPZ Strych.
Tryptaminergic	Serotonin	MAOI	
Other Amines	GABA	Dilantin	Bicuculine Strych.
	Glycine		
	Histamine		Tripelennamine
"Peptides"	Bradykinin		
	Taraxein-like		CPZ
(Unnatural) Amines Catechol	Mescaline		Phenothiazines Reserpine (BOL vs. LSD) (LSD vs. Serotonin)
Indole	Bufotenine Harmine Psilocybin LSD BOL		

Figure VI-4. Drugs Modulating Cerebral Synapses

Furthermore the latter are also subject to secondary influences. The important possibility that local vascular effects of the drugs rather than direct neuronal actions are responsible for the observed phenomena—and it is certainly true that large doses have important local vascular contributing actions—is ruled out for smaller effective doses by demonstrating that the oxygen tension (pO_2) in the tissues underlying the recording electrode does not

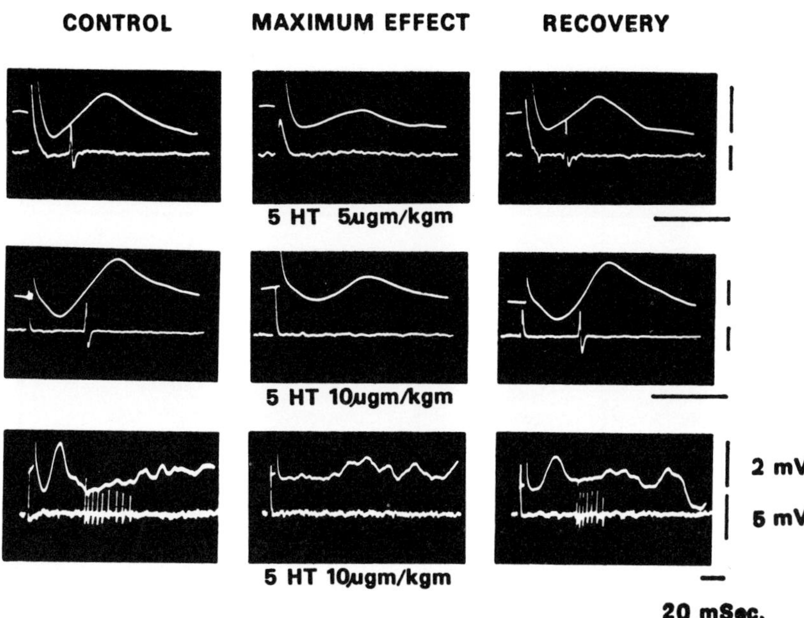

Figure VI-5.
SEROTONIN INHIBITION OF CORTICAL FIELD AND UNITARY
POTENTIALS IN SUPRASYLVIAN GYPRUS
Transcallosal stimulation 1 per 2 sec. Flexedilized Cat. Injection—iplilateral
common carotid artery

change or even changes in the wrong direction (Huang et al.,
1971; Huang et al., 1970). These data are tabulated in Figure
VI-6.

A different type of secondary effect that plays an important
role in the observed electrically recorded and, as we shall see
correspondingly in behavioral changes, is illustrated in Figures
VI-7 and VI-8 recording spontaneously firing cerebral cortical
units. In both the effects of acetylcholine (ACh) and serotonin
(DHT) the marked primary increased firing or excitation and
decreased firing or inhibition respectively do not return to their
control levels until they have passed through an intervening
secondary phase of postexcitatory depression, in the case of ACh,
and postinhibitory rebound in the case of 5HT. Failure to monitor
the effects continuously might easily lead to confusion of primary

EFFECT OF TRANSIENT ΔpO_2 ON CORTICAL EVOKED POTENTIAL			
pO_2	$\Delta\mu l.$	Procedure	E. P.
↓	4.0	CAROTID OCCLUSION	↓
	15.3	RESP. ARREST	↑↓
0	0	5 HT	↓
	0	HISTAMINE	↓
↑	0.1	MESCALINE	↓
	0.15	ACH	↑
	1.0	LSD	↓
	1.7	RESP.	0
	2.7	NE	↓
	5.0	E	↓

Figure VI-6. Oxygen Tension

and secondary effects. Since low threshold units would have a telescoped time course, sampling at any one point might seem to show differing effects for neighboring low and high threshold units. In fact, our analysis that distinguishes primary from secondary effects in 219 cortical units shows consistent primary excitation for acetylcholine and inhibition for serotonin, Figure VI-9.

The thresholds in question are confined to limited trigger areas on the cell surface, the receptors. The occupation and, in fact, competition for such receptors between active and less active substances, both with substantial affinities, results in the weaker substance blocking the action of the stronger. Thus, block by competitive inhibition is actually produced by a substance having a similar action to the one which it blocks (Ghouri, et al., 1973; Halasz, et al., 1969). Chlorpromazine (CPZ) block of 5HT and LSD is shown in the extracellular unit recordings, Figure VI-10.

Blockers may be general or quite specific, in which case they become very convenient pharmacological tools for discriminating actions and differentially modifying them for diagnostic and therapeutic purposes, Figure VI-11. The membrane nature and site of the specificity involved can be most elegantly demon-

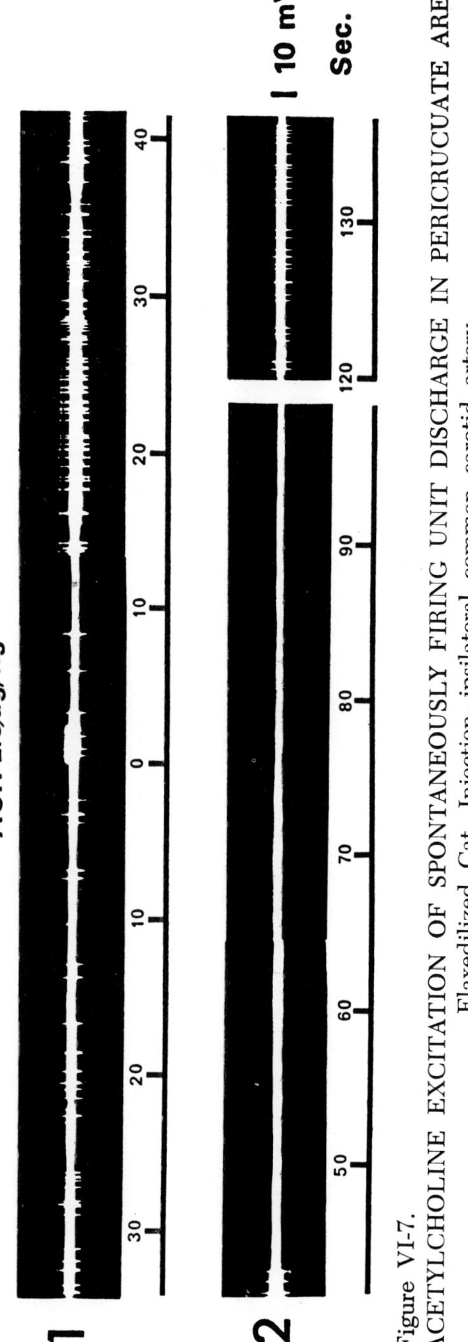

Figure VI-7.
ACETYLCHOLINE EXCITATION OF SPONTANEOUSLY FIRING UNIT DISCHARGE IN PERICRUCIATE AREA
Flaxedilized Cat. Injection—ipsilateral common carotid artery.

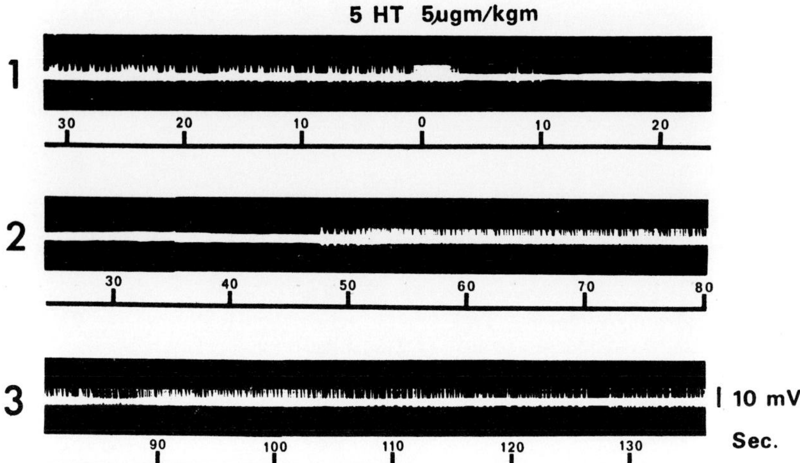

Figure VI-8.
SEROTONIN INHIBITION OF SPONTANEOUS UNIT DISCHARGE
IN PERICRUCIATE AREA
Flaxedilized Cat. Injection—ipsilateral common carotid artery

strated, as we (Huang and Marrazzi, 1973) have done for
serotonin, LSD and chlorpromazine, by intracellular recording,
which shows identical kinds of special changes for serotonin,
a natural cerebral synaptic inhibitor, LSD, a psychotogen acting
at the same site in the same way, Figure VI-12 (Upper AC
and Lower DC traces) and chlorpromazine, the prototype tranquilizer, again acting at the same site as a competitive inhibitor.
(The local anesthetic effects of chlorpromazine were excluded
as the responsible mechanism by showing lack of fundamental
similarity to the actions of a powerful local anesthetic, xylocaine.)
The data are tabulated in Figure VI-13.

A similar set of circumstances, probably operating through a
different set of receptors, is presented by the actions of the
cerebral inhibitors which are immune to the block by CPZ. We
have found this to be true for GABA and glycine, which, however, are specifically blocked by bicuculline, Figure VI-14
(Ghouri and Marrazzi, 1972; Huang and Marrazzi, in press). The
membrane parameters for these inhibitors again fulfill all the
criteria of inhibition but the transmembrane conductance changes

FIGURE VI-9
UNIT RESPONSES TO SEROTONIN AND ACETYLCHOLINE
(218 Units in 46 Cats)

Serotonin	*Inhibition*	*Excitation*
Suprasylvian Gyrus		
Transcallosal Evoked Units	24	0
Units Evoked by Local Cortical Stimulation	2	0
Spontaneous Units	13	0
Pericruciate Gyrus		
Units Evoked by Antidromic Stimulation of		
Medullary Pyramid Tract	6	0
Units Evoked by Stimulation of Thalamic		
V.L. Nucleus	8	0
Units Evoked by Local Cortical Stimulation	4	0
Spontaneous Units	63	0
Total	120	0
Acetylcholine		
Suprasylvian Gyrus		
Transcallosal Evoked Units	0	7
Silent Units	0	7
Spontaneous Units	0	16
Pericruciate Gyrus		
Units Evoked by Stimulation of Thalamic		
V.L. Nucleus	0	5
Silent Units	0	18
Spontaneous Units	0	38
Total	0	91

in the opposite direction, i.e. it increases indicating a different ionic channel and corresponding iontophore and triggering receptor.

A therapeutically less useful but analytically equally interesting group of substances is represented by strychnine, which turns out to be a nonspecific blocker of inhibitory receptors (Ghouri and Marrazzi, 1972; Huang and Marrazzi, in press). This raises the further possibilities that the block can be achieved either by interacting with some fraction that is common to various different types of specific inhibitory receptors—thereby contributing a nonspecific action—or by exerting its action beyond, i.e. "downstream" of receptors and therefore not being endowed by the specificity that is an attribute of receptors. Better comprehension of these

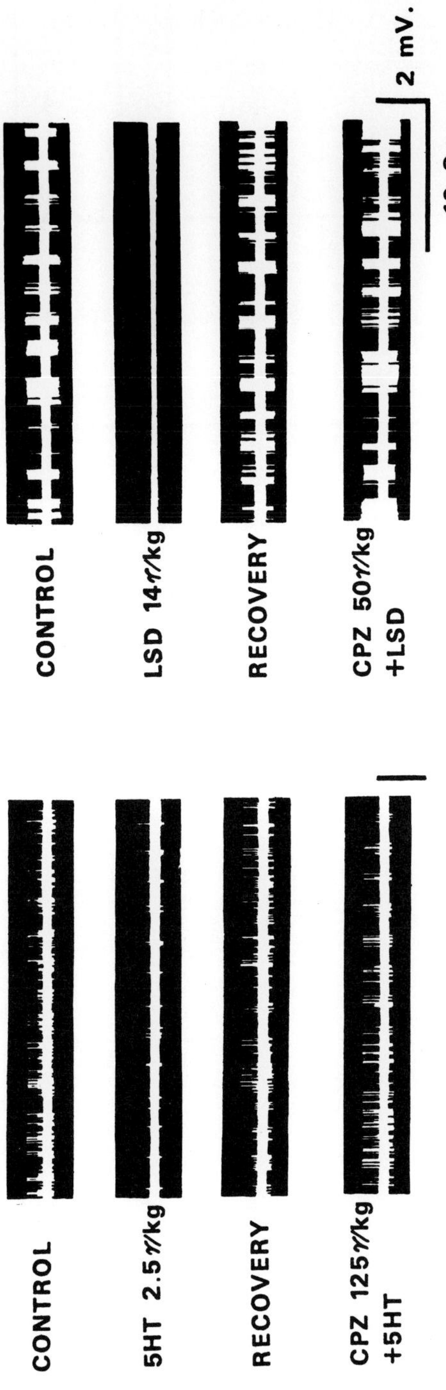

Figure VI-10. CHLORPROMAZINE BLOCK OF SEROTONIN AND LSD EXTRACELLULAR UNIT DISCHARGE IN PERICRUCIATE AREA

Flaxedilized Cat. Injection—ipsilateral common carotid artery

DRUGS	BLOCKERS				
	CHLORPROMAZINE	TRIPELENNAMINE	BICUCULLINE	STRYCHNINE	ATROPINE
INHIBITORS					
5-HYDROXYTRYPTAMINE	+	−	−	+	−
NOREPINEPHRINE	+	−	−		
HISTAMINE	−	+	−		
γ-AMINOBUTYRIC ACID	−	−	+	+	−
GLYCINE	−	−	+	+	−
GLUTAMINE	−	−	−		
EXCITORS					
ACETYLCHOLINE	−	−	−	−	+
GLUTAMIC ACID	−	−	−	−	−

Figure VI-11. Differential Block of Cerebral Synaptic Inhibitors and Excitors

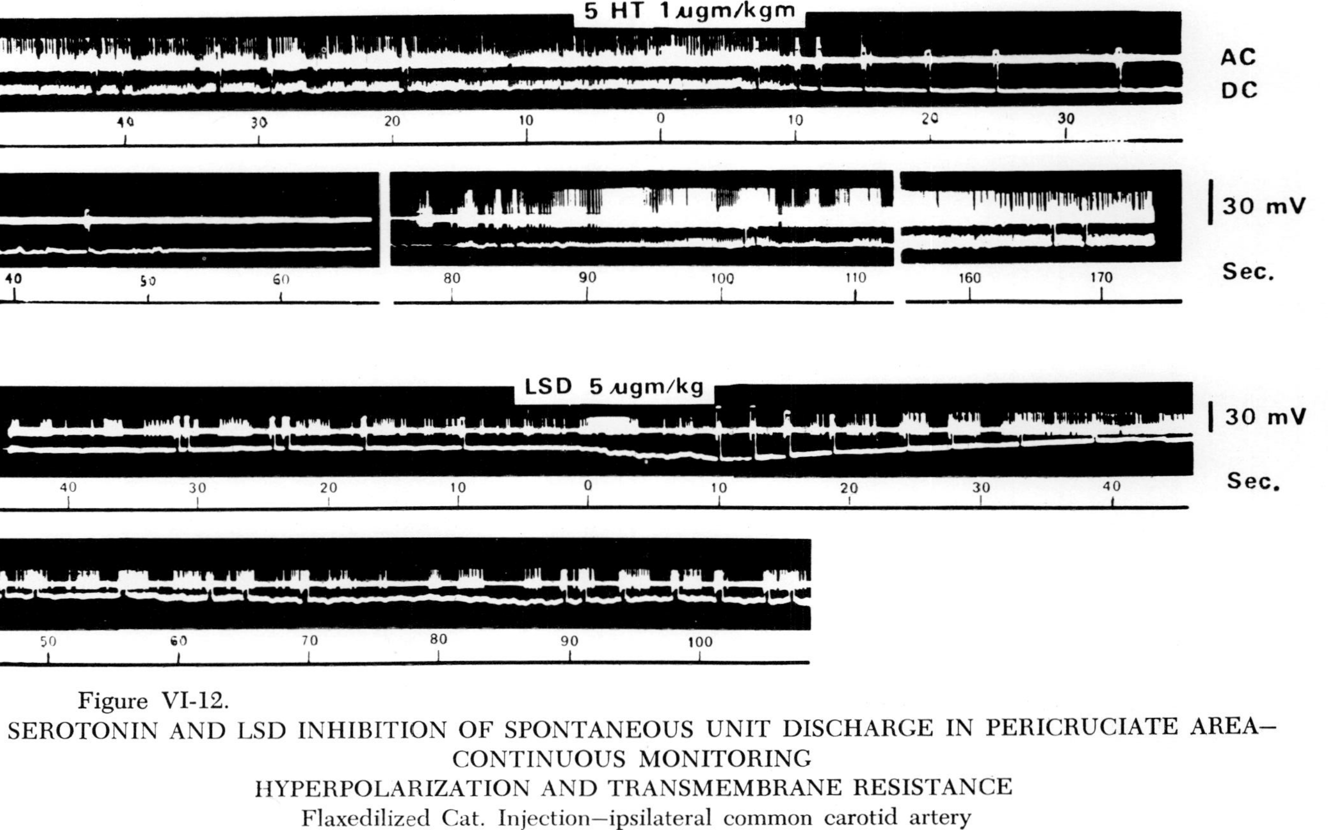

Figure VI-12.
SEROTONIN AND LSD INHIBITION OF SPONTANEOUS UNIT DISCHARGE IN PERICRUCIATE AREA—
CONTINUOUS MONITORING
HYPERPOLARIZATION AND TRANSMEMBRANE RESISTANCE
Flaxedilized Cat. Injection—ipsilateral common carotid artery

MEMBRANE CHANGES IN POSTSYNAPTIC INHIBITION BY DRUGS AND ITS BLOCKER					
Drugs		↓ Spike #s	↑ Polariz.	↑ Resist.	↑ IPSPs
Agonists	5HT	+	+	+	+
	LSD	+	+	+	+
Antagonist	CPZ	+	+	+	+
Anaesth.	XYL	+	−	−	−

Pericruciate Pyramidal Cell – Intracell. Rec.   Flaxedilized Cat

Figure VI-13. Membrane Changes

processes would contribute another key strategy in unraveling the critical role of the cell membrane in regulating exchanges at the interphase between the cell and its universe.

Accordingly, based on the neuropharmacological data we have outlined, we (Marrazzi, 1965, 1971) arrive at rational expectations for the output of the nervous system or behavior, if our insight into what we no longer regard merely as a "black box" is adequate. Discrepancies then become starting points for new and fuller insights. In this closely interrelated fashion we can, so to speak, bootstrap our understanding from available to more complete and testable information on the operation of the nervous system in health and disease, i.e. to the neurophysiology, neuropharmacology and neuropsychology, which, in our view, together describe a synthesis of behavior. This, then, can properly be regarded as the all-inclusive discipline—sometimes suggested by the cumbersome title of neuropsychopharmacology—with a clinical counterpart in psychiatry.

The finding in the blood of some schizophrenics of a fraction (50M in Figure VI-15) which we have been able to show is adsorbed to blood proteins and has a potent LSD-like cerebral synaptic inhibitory action blockable by chlorpromazine (Marrazzi, et al., 1959; Redick, et al., 1964) and our demonstration that

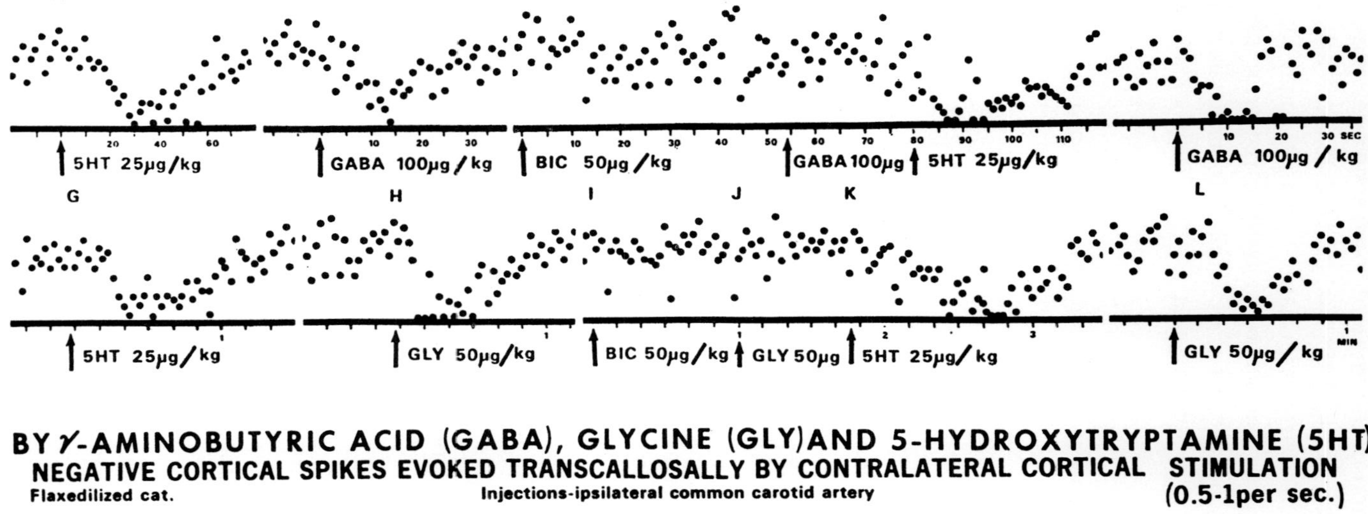

**BY γ-AMINOBUTYRIC ACID (GABA), GLYCINE (GLY) AND 5-HYDROXYTRYPTAMINE (5HT)
NEGATIVE CORTICAL SPIKES EVOKED TRANSCALLOSALLY BY CONTRALATERAL CORTICAL STIMULATION**

Flaxedilized cat. Injections-ipsilateral common carotid artery (0.5-1per sec.)

Figure VI-14. Bicuculline (BIC) Differentiation of Cerebral Synaptic Inhibition

DMPEA, found in the urine of some schizophrenics, has a similar action (Vacca, et al., 1968) suggests that there are, indeed, substances occurring in the disease state that could distort synaptic equilibrium to produce recognizable patterns of mental disturbance. Such agreement of laboratory and clinical data offers promise that this kind of analysis of disturbed behavior can be profitable.

By any other name—more or less elegant—behavior is still the all-important variable, the tangible and measurable output of the nervous system as it creates the overt manifestations of life. Such measurements range from the fractionated animal and human behavior ordinarily indicated by lever pressing or equivalents, closely controlled by the experimenter in signal bound responding or only shaped by him in operant conditioning, to the more complex patterns of behavior feasible to study in man, e.g. perception. Such patterns include the spontaneous experiments of nature available in the wards and clinics for the mentally disturbed.

The signal bound paradigm is valuable in analyzing the consequences, while from the operant conditioning paradigm one can hope to deduce the "signal" processes or contingencies that result in the "lawful" consequences. One can indeed, then, hope to use the two approaches in a complementary fashion rather than to denote allegiance to one or the other school of thought. The experimenter does intervene in both cases by using drugs to influence neural activity—to challenge and to restrain.

Restraint, in fact, would appear to be a powerful determinant in converting random activity into adaptive patterns suitably responsive to environmental happenings (Marrazzi, 1961). For this reason synaptic inhibition and its behavioral consequences become of prime interest, as well as because the catecholamine and indole psychotogens turn out to be potent cerebral synaptic inhibitors (Marrazzi, 1926b).

Since behavioral patterns beyond the simplest reflexes are bound to originate in circuits that are richly synaptic, it is not readily feasible to localize the actions responsible for the observed behavior to small numbers of synapses. It is evident, however, that increased latency in conditioned approach (Halasz,

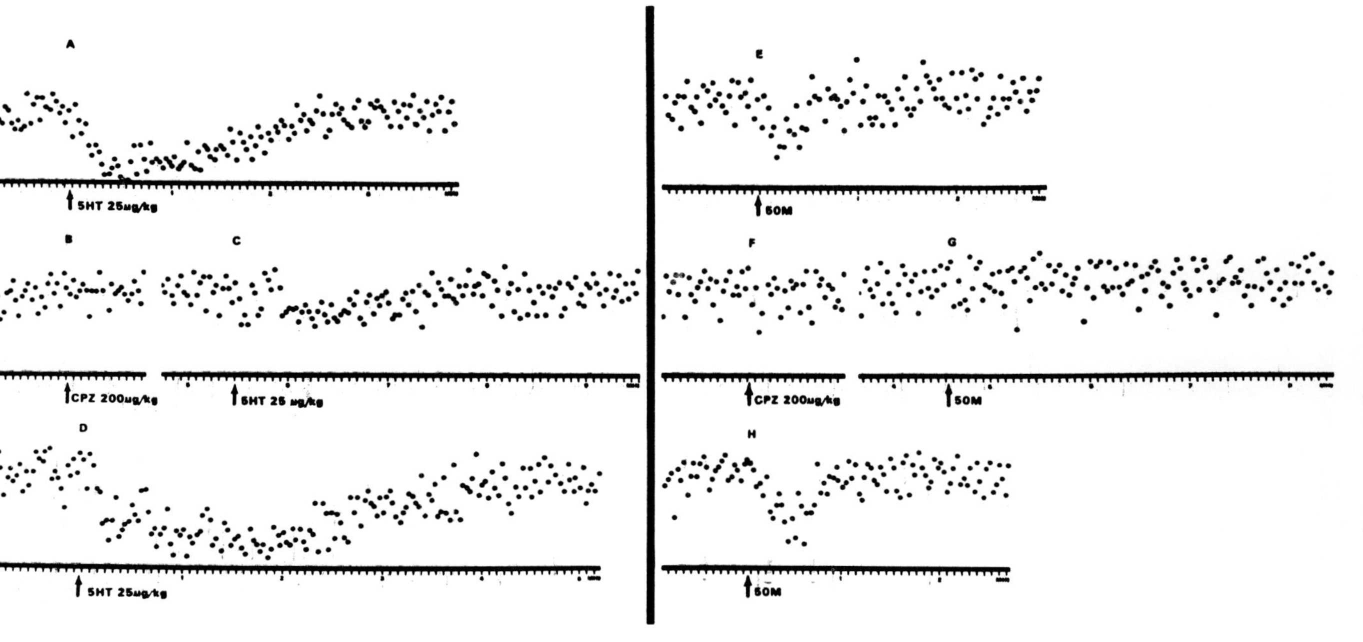

Figure VI-15. Cerebral Bioassay of 50M Serum Fraction

Formanek, and Marrazzi, 1969; Halasz and Marrazzi, 1964, 1966; Marrazzi, 1962b) (Figure 16, upper) and conditioned avoidance (lower) are signs of the inhibition (Marrazzi, 1962b) that more direct synaptic monitoring tells us to expect generally (Figure VI-3).

The intersignal and overresponding accompanying the loss of discrimination of the tones and of time (Davis et al., 1968; Halasz and Marrazzi, 1965; Marrazzi et al., 1973) and of economical correctness of choice as in the self-selection experiments (Marrazzi, 1962b) occurring, as they do, during the periods of smaller doses which obtain as the drug is entering and as it is leaving, that is, shortly after the onset and shortly before the offset, correspond to the release phenomena or disinhibition as in the example described above in the postinhibitory rebound seen in the records of postsynaptic potentials; while the delayed, reduced and incorrect responding during the intervening period of higher effective dose constitutes the major inhibition corresponding to the major synaptic change.

The cross-species validity of these findings (Figure VI-17) attests to their general significance. Furthermore, the predictability, even on the basis of limited synaptic sampling, of the behavior here observed attests to the generality of cerebral synaptic characterization by drugs, making allowance for diverse thresholds and richness of distribution (cf. also Figure VI-4).

On the basis, then, of the direct electrical recordings[1] as well as of clinical observation, one expects and, indeed, finds that chlorpromazine, as well as other phenothiazines, meprobamate and reserpine, offsets the behavior resulting from the exposure to synaptic inhibitors, including the catecholamine and indole psychotogens, in the manner of a competitive inhibitor. This is, small doses offset or compete, larger doses become additive and quite large doses, given by themselves, produce inhibition (Ghouri, et al., 1973; Halasz, et al., 1969), which although weak can sum to the point of eliciting the clinical picture of so-called toxic psychosis.

The conferring of a degree of selectivity results from the

[1](where, e.g. 5HT, CPZ and 5HT plus CPZ dose-response curves are parallel)

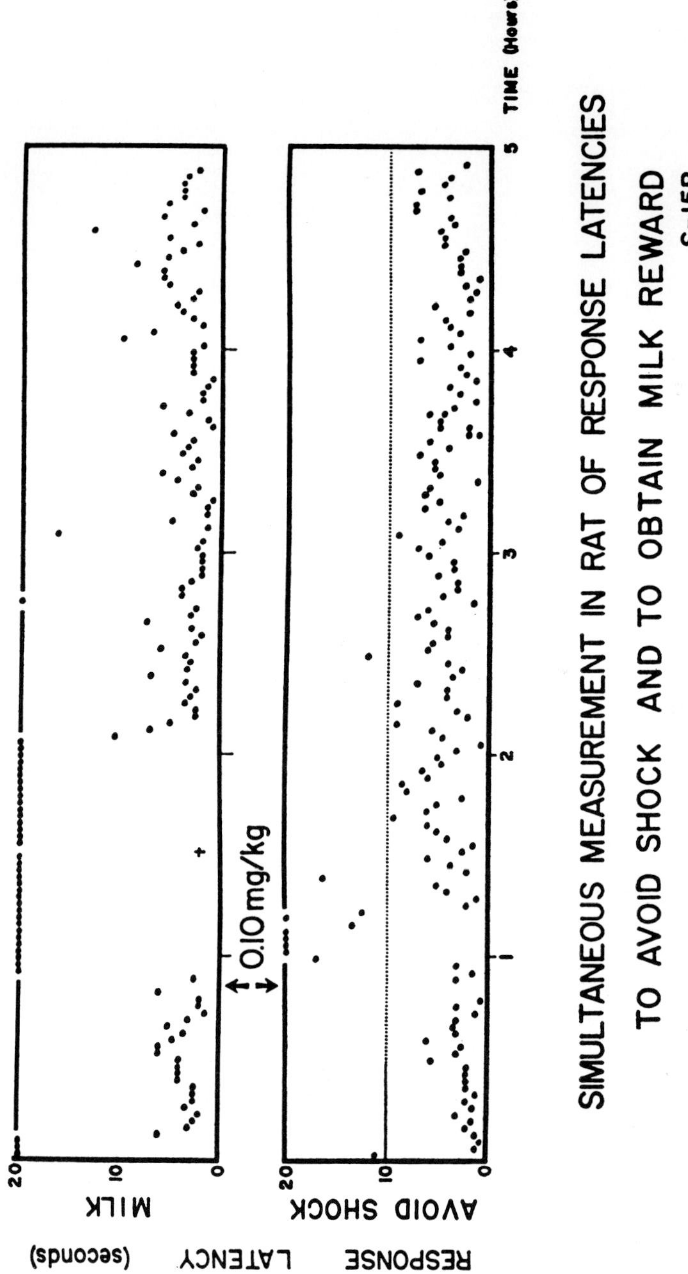

Figure VI-16. Effect of d-Lysergic Acid Diethylamide (LSD-25) on Approach and Avoidance Behavior

FIGURE VI-17
COMPARATIVE NEUROPHARMACOLOGY

Species	*Mode*	*Serotonin*	*LSD 25*	*CPZ Protection Vs*
Rat	Synaptic*	Inhibition		
	Behavioral		C.Ap.L. ↑ C.Av.L. ↑ Diff. ↓ Intersignal response number ↑	LSD 25 C.Ap.
Cat	Synaptic	Inhibition	Inhibition Intersignal response number ↑	Serot. ( ) ; LSD 25
Dog	Synaptic	Inhibition	Inhibition	
Monkey	Synaptic Behavioral	Inhibition	Inhibition C.Ap.L. ↑ Diff. ↓ Intersignal response number ↑	Serot.; LSD 25 LSD 25 on C.Ap.
Man	Synaptic Behavioral		Inhibition Hallucination Perceptual assoc. ↓ Timing Behavior # Discrimination ↓ Premature Responses ↑	LSD hallucination

↑ = increased; ↓ = decreased; C.Ap.L. = conditioned approach latency; C.Av.L. = conditioned avoidance latency; Diff. = differentiation (tone or time)
 *Synaptic in this table refers to transcallosally (except #) activated cortical synapses. However, as indicated in the table of "Generality of Cerebral Synaptic Drug Response," Fig. 3, synaptic inhibition by serotonin and LSD 25 is obtained at synapses throughout the brain.

differing distribution of thresholds, as may be reasonably inferred from the differential effects of psychotogens and tranquilizers on the major behavioral thresholds, i.e. of approach and avoidance, executed in the same subjects in the same sessions. Thus, as seen in part in Figure VI-16 and diagrammed in Figure VI-18, inhibition by psychotogens is exercised preponderantly on approach, that of tranquilizers on avoidance, while a simple sedative, like a barbiturate exercises its action about equally on both (Marrazzi, 1962b).

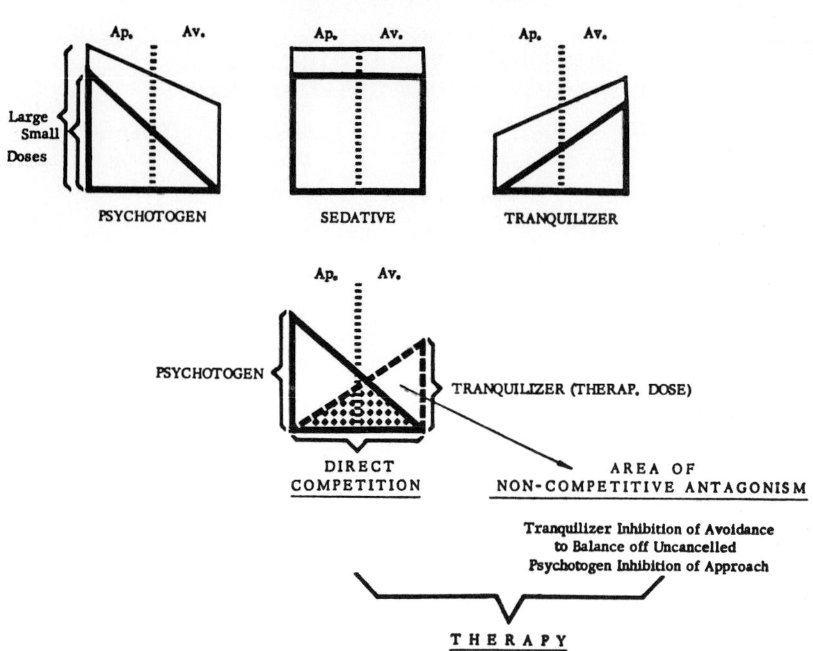

Figure VI-18.
NATURE OF PSYCHOTOGEN, SEDATIVE AND TRANQUILIZER
EFFECTS ON CONDITIONED APPROACH AND AVOIDANCE

Such data suggest that disruption of synaptic homeostasis is mirrored in the distortion of equilibrium between the major behavioral patterns of approach and avoidance. The data also make a definite distinction between the indiscriminate action of barbiturates and the more specific action of tranquilizers. In fact, the latter can be expressed numerically by observing the ratios of protective to depressive (larger) doses, which is one or less for simple sedatives and more than one for tranquilizers, cf. Table 2 (Morrazzi, 1962b) (Figure VI-19).

Inclusion of inescapable pain in the paradigm introduces an overriding requirement that can be met by simple sedatives and less specific depressants like barbiturates and meprobamate, which can control conflict behavior with pain as an inescapable consequence (Ray and Marrazzi, 1962), and reserpine, which more successfully reduces conditioned suppression (CER).

FIGURE VI-19
COMPARISON OF TRANQUILIZERS
SYNAPTIC PROTECTIVE AND DEPRESSIVE ACTIONS

Drug	Protective Dose vs. Mescaline mg./Kg.	Depressant Dose mg./Kg.	Safety Margin Depressant Protective
Chlorpromazine	0.050**	1.00	20
Promazine	0.075**	0.75	10
Reserpine	0.100	0.20	2
Phenobarbital	1.0*	0.75	0.75

*vs. Serotonin
**same vs. Serotonin

The human equivalents of the foregoing behavioral paradigms are at once more difficult, in that the problem for the subject to solve needs to be more complex, and potentially easier, in that verbal communication is possible.

Some particularly interesting and suggestive data are presented in Figure VI-20 where the judgment for timing behavior is tested in a DRL paradigm set at an optimum of ten seconds interresponse interval; so that premature responding fails to achieve reward (counts exchangeable for cigarettes) and over-responding, because of the time out feature at the end of each trial, is uneconomical. Even in these few subjects the variety of effects from LSD inhibition, i.e. loss of discrimination evidenced both as premature responding and as loss of optimum frequency pattern, are illustrated along with the worsening of the effects on time judgments of the ongoing psychiatric process, which we feel is also tapped in the LSD effect, and the improvement from chlorpromazine both when pitted against the natural process alone and against the same process aggravated by LSD. Again paralleling the animal experiments, chlorpromazine can not only ameliorate the performance but also, in larger doses, worsen it.

Perhaps the strongest support for our interpretations comes from their important use in aiding diagnosis and assessing the efficacy of therapy. This tests and carries on the thesis that interference with normal information processing, this is, interpreting

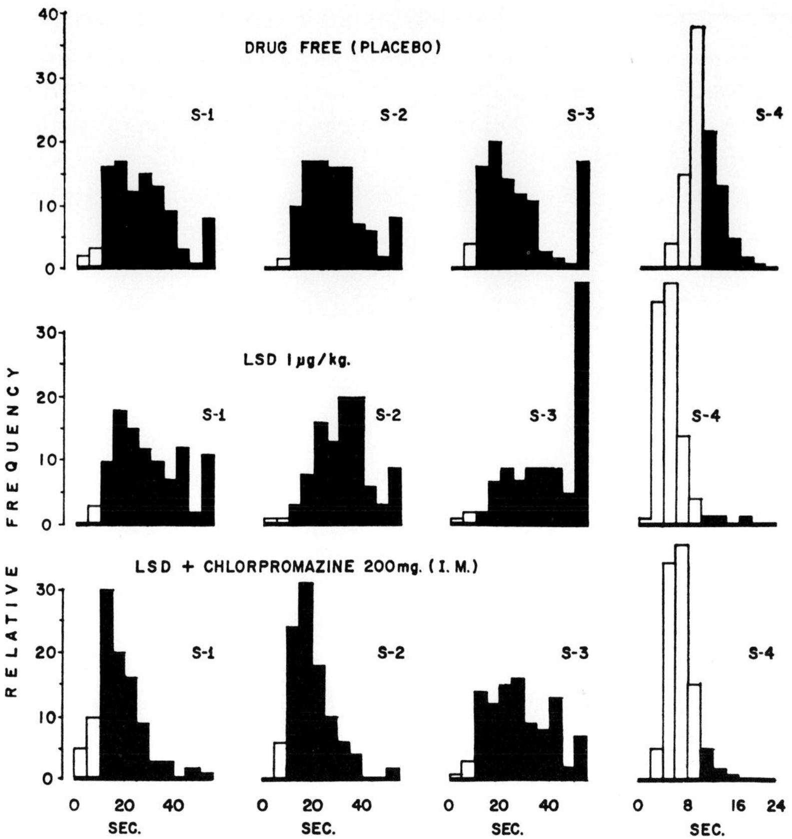

Figure VI-20. IRT Distributions DRL 10 Sec. Schedule

the news, in the light of the previously experienced and stored, by matching or by closeness of analogy, comes about by information under- or overloading resulting from distorted synaptic equilibrium. We have dealt with mostly the impaired and therefore inadequate communication between primary receiving and corresponding reference areas, the information underloading produced by cerebral synaptic inhibition as by LSD. Reasoning that existing impairment could be aggravated and thereby made manifest by a smaller dose of LSD than would be required in the normal, we have arrived at a challenging dose that is subclinical in the sense of not producing any or only rarely some mild overt symptoms—this is, euphoria—and to which the normals can adapt sufficiently to show no change in already perceived distortion, i.e. resolution of the experimental perceptual conflict monitored instrumentally, while the mentally disturbed perceive a much enhanced distortion paralleling the increasing absorption of the LSD (Marrazzi, 1966).

Since we believe that hallucination is an aberrant perception (Marrazzi, 1962d) we have set up a laboratory analog and equivalent, i.e. a perceptual conflict in either the visual (Marrazzi, 1970) or auditory (Marrazzi, et al., 1972) modalities and tested its resolution in a prechallenge self-control period and in the period subsequent to the LSD challenge.

The visual conflict is obtained by use of aniseikonic lenses to create disparate images in the two eyes while viewing a room, where binocular (depth) cues have been minimized by covering the five surfaces (room is open at one end where the subject sits) with leaves. The resulting distortion in this Ames room is tracked by the subject remotely operating a bar, pivoted in the center of the back wall of the room, so as to match or parallel the perceived slope, in a side wall or the floor, which develops as the conflict between the lens modified and the usual (remembered) image is resolved by a compromise. The auditory conflict is set up by use of the well-known delayed auditory feedback, which we quantitate by measuring the maximum tolerated delay without speech distortion or, more accurately, to the onset of minimal speech difficulty. Again self-control readings are compared to the effects of LSD challenge. In both situations the data are obtained completely instrumentally. The monitoring bar movements operate a servomotor to record the visual data, while the displacement of the playback head to obtain maximum tolerated delay of the auditory feedback is read from a scale.

For both modalities our (Marrazzi, 1970; Marrazzi, et al., 1972) results so far indicate the feasibility of (a) separating normals from mentally disturbed exhibiting a dissociative process and, in fact, of detecting marginal impairment, (b) thereby providing the means of making early diagnoses, (c) accordingly instituting prophylactic therapy and monitoring its effectiveness, (d) monitoring intensity of illness, which fluctuates cyclically in schizophrenia, and (e) monitoring the effectiveness of therapy whether somatic or nonsomatic.

Figure VI-21 provides an illustration of the use of a visual perceptual conflict in testing dissociation, in this case in a subject suffering from an early schizophrenic break. Figure VI-22 presents the charted data of repeated trials with an auditory perceptual conflict accomplished by delayed auditory feedback. The data consists of maximum delay times tolerated before earliest sign of impairment of speech, while Figure VI-23 graphs the increments, or deltas, between self-control (1 hr. average) and results of the immediately following LSD challenge (1 hr. average at maximum). The testing was repeated at intervals of ten[2] or more days without intervening therapy (entered above the base line) and at the end of two weeks of chlorpromazine therapy (entered below the base line). The percent differences of the means over this thirty- to thirty-five-week period between challenge with ("downrights") and without ("uprights") therapy gives a numerical expression of its effectiveness. It is to be noted in the series of seven patients said to be chronic therapy-resistant schizophrenics that four of them show an improvement ranging from about thirty to sixty percent, as shown on the left, while those on the right show sporadic isolated instances of improvement but no overall improvement as measured by the difference of the means.

The conceptualization, illustrated by the use of drug modulation of cerebral synaptic transmission, has evidently led to consistent findings at the animal and human levels at the signal monitoring and at the behavioral levels.

REFLECTIONS

Unlike the journal reports meant primarily to communicate data with the inferences and conclusions only as a result, we have attempted, we believe in the true spirit of this book, to give more emphasis to the thinking that generated the experiments and the extent to which the data supported it or led to new and more appropriate thinking. In this light, the experimenter emerges as

[2]Interval long enough to avoid acute tolerance.

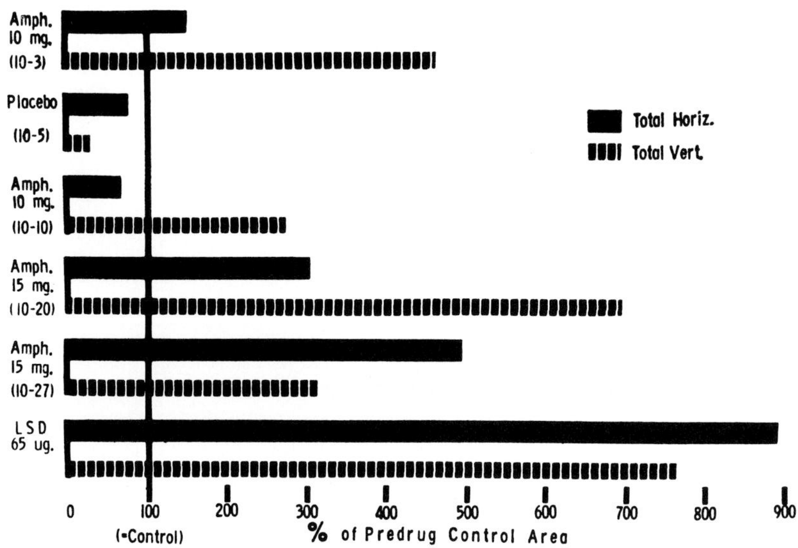

Figure VI-21. Visual Perceptual Conflict

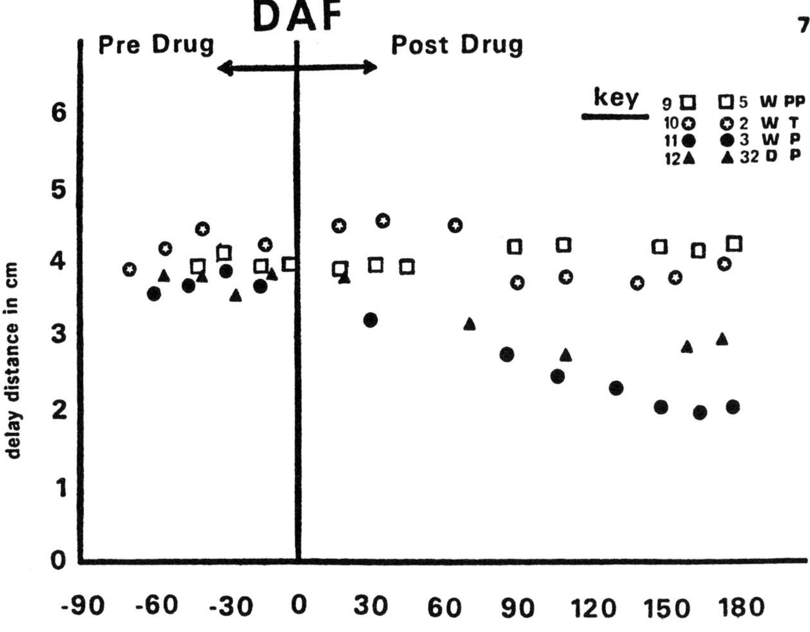

Figure VI-22. Auditory Perceptual Conflict

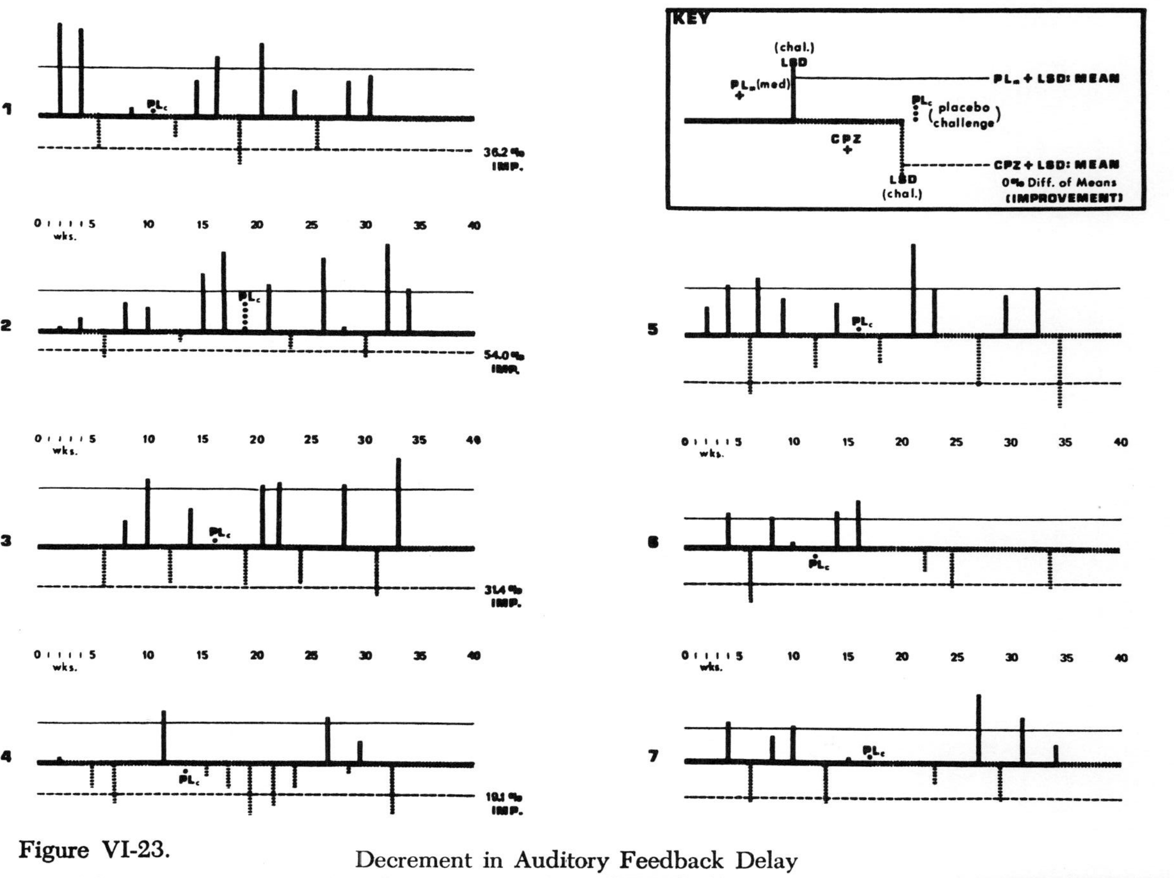

Figure VI-23. Decrement in Auditory Feedback Delay

LSD DISSOCIATION AND CPZ PROTECTION OF AUDITORY PERCEPTION IN SCHIZOPHRENICS
Reduction in Maximum Tolerated Delay

more than the coldly calculating logician ordering his results, but, indeed, as the adventurer logically exploring the pathways of thought by utilizing available and uncovering required new data by directed as well as serendipitous research.

He begins to achieve insight into the behavioral disturbances resulting from imbalances in individuals that occur in sufficient intensity and numbers to seriously unbalance the community, posing perhaps one of the greatest and most costly of our civic problems.

He finds drugs highly potent analytical as well as therapeutic tools to help him equally in laboratory research and in clinical practice which, at its best, is actually experimentation with very high stakes.

The suggestion of persistence of influence long after drugs have been metabolized, excreted and otherwise dissipated raises the question of state-dependent learning with a wider scope than its present exclusive application to the influence of drugs.

It, in fact, raises the most important question in understanding the operation of homeostasis, i.e. its temporary breakdown with restoration in normals subjected to great stress, e.g. the similar situation in the premorbid past history of mental patients, and the reason and nature of its failure without restoration when mental illness finally becomes overt and persistent.

We have put together many of our findings in arriving at a comprehensible and useful view of deviant behavior in man as exhibited in the mentally disturbed (Marrazzi, 1970, 1971, 1972; and Marrazzi et al., 1972).

The observed low threshold of drug induced inhibition, as by LSD, of negative feedback pathways,[3] coupled with the low inhibition threshold of association areas accounts well for the confusion state. This arises, then, both on the basis of input overload consequent to release from normal restraint (loss of negative feedback) and decreased ability to interpret due to impaired

---

[3]It is yet to be determined whether these include "presynaptic inhibition" which does operate by miniature negative feedback or recurrent pathways whose synapses could be expected to share generally similar properties, at least in part, to those effecting "postsynaptic inhibition."

access to past experience, from association output underload resulting from reduced communication.

A concept of hallucination as aberrant perception—of recognized or unrecognized stimuli—emerges, and this has been successfully tested as already noted.

Furthermore, the reasonable extension of this interpretation of the mechanics of disturbed behavior in terms of disruption of homeostasis leads to the view that this dissociative process is the fundamental underlying dysfunction in the types of mental illness characterized, as in the schizophrenias, by reduced coordination between primary and reference areas and, therefore, exhibiting various disruptions of information processing as manifested by hallucination, illogical thinking, learning disabilities and excessive or deficient and otherwise inappropriate affect.

Realization that malfunction of an adaptive system, Figure VI-24, will produce other inappropriate phenomena as evidences of over- and undercompensation, provides the key to the resulting overlay of secondary symptoms that these constitute. The latter, when entrenched or "learned," require separate therapy. Thus the strategy of both diagnosis and therapy is to detect and correct both the generating process and the persisting secondary phenomena, which need to be eradicated by some form of extinction therapy.

Drug intervention thus provides an experimental analog that warrants a literal interpretation of schizophrenia precisely as it is named—as the manifestations of a divided or functionally fragmented brain leading to "difficulty in reality checking." The "schizophrenic process" thereby becomes an underlying cerebral dysfunction, whose exact overt symptoms are determined by the individual's genetic and experiential background modulated by precipitating circumstances. The conceptual emphasis now focuses on identifying a process rather than engaging in a detailed matching or reproduction of an empirically selected clinical syndrome. The process turns out not to be specific or unique to the disease. On the other hand, it becomes possible to identify the process and its role in schizophrenia on the basis of the fact that the characteristic effects of the most potent mammalian cerebral

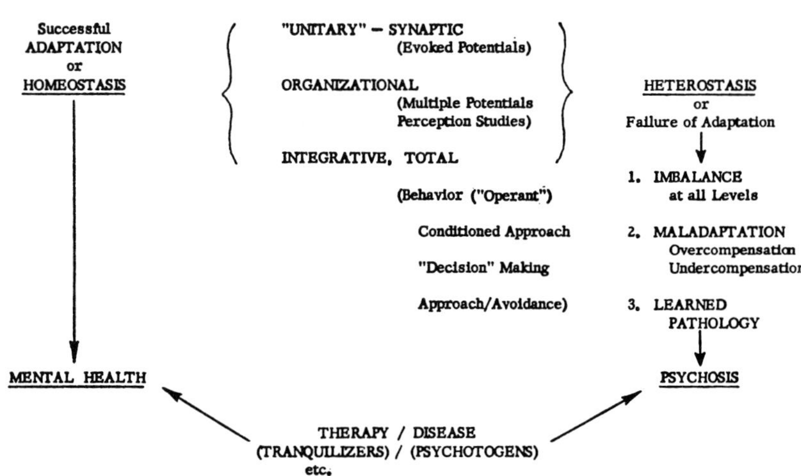

Figure VI-24. Cerebral Adaptive Systems

neurohumoral inhibitor, serotonin, of the powerful hallucinogen, LSD, and of the classical tranquilizer chlorpromazine, operate at the same membrane site in a *qualitatively* identical fashion but with great *quantitative* differences. The demonstration of the relation between inhibitory neurohumors, hallucinogens and tranquilizers, indicates that the "schizophrenic process"—which is aggravated by LSD and ameliorated by chlorpromazine—resides at the synapses controlling the normal processing of information (Marrazzi, 1972; Marrazzi, et al., 1973).

One can add to the implications for diagnosis and therapy already mentioned the possibility for training in adaptation by graded exposure during the periods of improved adaptation (and presumably improved learning ability) or remission that are so typical of schizophrenias. In this way LSD could be an aid to behavioral therapy much beyond the advantages of simply promoting ventilation and readier exposure of the patient's deranged thought processes.

In this connection the use of drugs as tools leads to the further testable suggestion that learning could be effected by an increase, with repeated use, of low threshold receptors in the pathway of an appropriate and therefore positively rewarding response or of an inappropriate and therefore negatively rewarding one.

The experimental credo represents faith in causality and in the worthwhileness of its testing by the experiments of the laboratory and of life. The applicability of basic research in furthering the solution of biomedical problems, as in the development of our "clinical yardstick" for mental disturbance, is a natural and expected outcome of the cooperation, maximal stimulation and the eventual dovetailing—even though often seriously displaced in time—rather than the irrational competition that fails to recognize the wisdom of exercising due patience in harvesting the fullest return from the research dollar invested in fundamental research.

The advantages of an integrated approach in the study of an integrating system become quite evident. The problems are certainly intriguing and demanding and the solutions, though incomplete, have, indeed, served to better define the persisting questions which continue to engage our attention and fascination.

Recognizing the learning process as education in the exercise of inhibition so as to narrow random responses in order to effect the purposeful manipulation of our environment for better fulfillment and the achievement of a happy life, puts it in better perspective to cope with the mounting problems created by implementing fully man's endless ingenuity.

REFERENCES

Chakrin, L. W.; Shideman, F. E., and Marrazzi, A. S.: The *in vivo* synthesis and release of tritium labeled acetylcholine by cat cerebral cortex. *Int J Neuropharmacol*, 7:351, 1968.

Davis, S. H.; Han, M. H., and Marrazzi, A. S.: Behavioral DMPEA-mescaline ratio—Elimination of differential relative to cerebral transmission. *Fed Proc*, 27:278, 1968.

Faingold, C. L., and Marrazzi, A. S.: Pharmacological identity of some cerebellar synapses. *Proc 5th Int Cong Pharmacol*, San Francisco, July, 1972, p. 66.

Faingold, C. L., and Marrazzi, A. S.: 5-Hydroxytryptamine and histamine effects on reticulo-cerebellar evoked potentials. *Fed Proc*, 32:221, 1973.

Ghouri, M. S. K.; Daugherty, J. H., and Marrazzi, A. S.: Differential blockers characterizing cerebral biogenic amine sites. *Proc West Pharmacol Soc,* Vol. 16, Squaw Valley, California, February, 1973.

Ghouri, M. S. K., and Marrazzi, A. S.: Cerebral synaptic modulation by agonists and antagonists. *Proc 5th Int Cong Pharmacol,* San Francisco, California, July, 1972, p. 81.

Halasz, M. F.; Formanek, J., and Marrazzi, A. S.: Hallucinogen-tranquilizer interaction: Its nature. *Science, 164:*569, 1969.

Halasz, M. F., and Marrazzi, A. S.: Psychotogen vs. tranquilizer on monkey conditioned approach. *Fed Proc, 23:*103, 1964.

Halasz, M. F., and Marrazzi, A. S.: Disinhibition of conditioned behavior by cerebral synaptic inhibitors. *Pharmacologist, 7:*173, 1965.

Halasz, M. F., and Marrazzi, A. S.: Releasing effects of LSD 25 on differential conditioning in cats. *Fed Proc, 25:*261, 1966.

Huang, C. C.; Faingold, C. L., and Marrazzi, A. S.: Noncorrelation of chemical cortical evoked potential effects with altered pO_2 and other nonspecific factors. *Fed Proc, 30:*434, 1971.

Huang, C. C.; Ghouri, M. S. K., and Marrazzi, A. S.: The differentiation of direct synaptic from cerebral vascular drug effects. *Pharmacologist, 12:*253, 1970.

Huang, C. C., and Marrazzi, A. S.: Analysis of drug block of LSD/5HT/ GABA by monitoring neuronal membrane changes. *Fed Proc, 32:*303, 1973.

Huang, C. C., and Marrazzi, A. S.: Studies of bicuculline block of GABA cerebral synaptic inhibition by monitoring neuronal membrane changes. *The Physiologist,* Vol. 16, in press.

Marrazzi, A. S.: Some indications of cerebral humoral mechanisms. *Science, 118:*367, 1953.

Marrazzi, A. S.: Messengers of the nervous system. *Sci Amer, 196:*86, 1957.

Marrazzi, A. S.: The effects of certain drugs on cerebral synapses. The Pharmacology of Psychotomimetic and Psychotherapeutic Drugs. *Ann N Y Acad Sci, 66:*496, 1957.

Marrazzi, A. S.: Study of adrenergic cerebral neurohumors in relation to synaptic transmission mechanisms. *Exp Cell Res Supp,* 5:370, Academic Press, New York, 1958.

Marrazzi, A. S.: Methodological problems in neuropharmacological research. Roundtable methodological problems in neuropharmacological research. In Wortis, J. (Ed.): *Recent Advances of Biological Psychiatry.* New York, Grune & Stratton, 1960, p. 379.

Marrazzi A. S.: Inhibition as a determinant of synaptic and behavioral patterns. Pavlovian conference on higher nervous activity. *Ann NY Acad Sci, 92:*998, 1961.

Marrazzi, A. S.: The influence of the experimental laboratory on psychiatry towards the turn of the century. In Hoch, P. H., and Zubin, J. (Eds.):

Symp. on the Future of Psychiatry. American Psychopathological Assoc. New York, Grune & Stratton, 1962a, p. 19.

Marrazzi, A. S.: Synaptic and behavioral correlates of psychotherapeutic and related drug actions. Some biological aspects of schizophrenic behavior. *Ann NY Acad Sci, 96*:211, 1962b.

Marrazzi, A. S.: Pharmacodynamics of sympathomimetic and marginal sympathomimetic drugs. In Nodine, J. (Ed.): First Hahnemann Symp on *Psychosomatic Medicine.* Philadelphia, Lea & Febiger, 1962c.

Marrazzi, A. S.: Pharmacodynamics of hallucination. In West, L. J. (Ed.): *Hallucinations.* New York, Grune & Stratton, 1962d.

Marrazzi, A. S.: The generality of cerebral synaptic drug response and its relation to psychosis. In Wortis, J. (Ed.): *Recent Advances in Biological Psychiatry.* New York, Grune & Stratton, 1964a.

Marrazzi, A. S.: Animal techniques for evaluating antipsychotic drugs. In Nodine, J. H., and Seigler, P. E. (Eds.): *Animal and Clinical Pharmacologic Techniques in Drug Evaluation.* Chicago, Year Book Publishers, 1964b.

Marrazzi, A. S.: An experimentalist looks at psychiatry. In Wortis, J. (Ed.): *Recent Advances in Biological Psychiatry.* New York, Plenum Press, 1965.

Marrazzi, A. S.: Restoration of cerebral homeostasis. Basis of biological treatment. In Rinkel, M. (Ed.): *Biological Treatment of Mental Illness.* New York, L. C. Page & Co., 1966, p. 222.

Marrazzi, A. S.: A neuropharmacologically based concept of hallucination and its clinical application. In *Origin and Mechanisms of Hallucination.* New York, Plenum Press, 1970, p. 211.

Marrazzi, A. S.: Neuropharmacology and experimental psychiatry, the evolution of a project—A progress report. *Schizophrenia, 3*:47, 1971.

Marrazzi, A. E.: A neuropharmacologically generated concept of psychotic process and its clinical application. *Psychopharmacol Bull, 8*:60, 1972.

Marrazzi, A. S., and Hart, E. R.: The relationship of hallucinogens to adrenergic cerebral neurohumors. *Science, 121*:365, 1955.

Marrazzi, A. S.; Huang, C. C.; Ghouri, M. S. K., and Carr, B. F.: Extra- and intracellular analysis of the "schizophrenic process" during diagnostic and therapeutic drug intervention. Paper presented at Soc Biol Psychiat meeting on "The Biology of Schizophrenia," Montreal, Canada, June, 1973.

Marrazzi, A. S.; Renfrew, A. G.; Hart, E. R., and Wilson, J. E.: The effect of blood protein fractions on cerebral synaptic transmission. *Fed Proc, 18*:419, 1959.

Marrazzi, A. S.; Woodruff, S., and Kennedy, D.: Perceptual challenge to measure illness and therapy. *Am J Psychiat, 128*:886, 1972.

Ray, O. S., and Marrazzi, A. S.: Pharmacological and behavioral analysis of conflict behavior in rat. *Fed Proc, 21*:415, 1962.

Redick, T. F.; Renfrew, A. G.; Pieri, L., and Marrazzi, A. S.: A cerebrally active small moiety from "taraxein-like" blood fractions. *Science, 141*: 646, 1964.

Vacca, L.; Fujimori, M.; Davis, S. H., and Marrazzi, A. S.: Cerebral synaptic transmission and behavioral effects of dimethoxyphenylethylamine: A potential psychotogen. *Science, 160*:95, 1968.

Chapter VII

MEDICAL RESEARCH IN A FEDERAL AGENCY

William S. Middleton

A native of Pennsylvania, William Shainline Middleton was born in Norristown on January 7, 1890. His medical degree was granted by the University of Pennsylvania School of Medicine (1911). After an internship at the Philadelphia General Hospital (1911-12) he entered upon a career in academic medicine at the University of Wisconsin Medical School. Here he served in the advancing ranks of Clinical Instructor of Medicine to Professor of Medicine until 1955. From 1935 to 1955 he was Dean of the Medical School while he maintained his clinical and teaching responsibilities. Emeritus status was bestowed upon him by the Regents of the University in 1960.

His academic continuity was interrupted by both World Wars and he was personal adviser to Surgeon General Raymond Bliss, United States Army, in the Korean Affair. In World War I he served both in the British Expeditionary Forces and the American Expeditionary Forces in France (1917-19). In World War II as Chief Consultant in Medicine to the European Theater of Operations he saw service in Great Britain and Europe (1942-45). Withdrawing from the academic scene in 1955, for eight years he was Chief Medical Director of the Veterans Administration.

Upon his completion of this term of service, he became Visiting Professor of Medicine at the University of Oklahoma (1963-64). Upon the conclusion of this appointment he returned to Madison as Consultant in Research and Education at the Veterans Administration Hospital. In 1970 he was named Distinguished Physician by the Veterans Administration. He continues his bedside study and teaching.

Over the years his 300 publications have indicated his interests. The fields of cardiovascular, respiratory and hematopoietic disorders have received especial attention. His studies in medical history have been assiduously pursued. A master (1952), he served as president of the American College of Physicians (1950). A founding member, he was president of the Central Society for Clinical Research (1933). His further society affiliations include the Association of American Physicians, Association of Physicians of Great Britain and Ireland (honorary foreign member), American Society for Clinical Investigation, American Clinical and Climatological Association, American Association of the History of Medicine (president, 1934), College of Physicians of Philadelphia (nonresident fellow), Royal College of Physicians of London (fellow) and Royal Society of Medicine (honorary fellow).

Academic honors have come to him as follows:
Doctor of Science, Pennsylvania 1946; Cambridge 1950; Wisconsin 1971.
Doctor of Laws, Temple 1956.
Doctor of Humanities, Franklin and Marshall 1957.
Doctor of Letters, Marquette 1958.
The University of Pennsylvania Alumni Award of Merit was granted him (1943) and the Centennial Award of Northwestern University is also his (1951). He was the Alfred Stengel Memorial medalist of the American College of Physicians in 1962. He was decorated by the United States, Great Britain and France for military service in World War II. In 1958 he received the Exceptional Service Award of the Veterans Administration.

THE VETERANS ADMINISTRATION DEPARTMENT of Medicine and Surgery operates the largest hospital system in the United States. With such vast resources and responsibilities from a clinical standpoint comes not only the opportunity, but the moral obligation, to advance the sum of human knowledge and welfare by research. The veteran population, while predominantly adult male in its constituency, actually covers every segment of our citizenry from the sociologic, economic, cultural and ethnic standpoints. By reason of the intimate relationship of the agency with the veterans, long-term contacts and sustained follow-ups are assured. Indeed, in our modern society there exists no parallel situation for the detailed study of the life history of specific diseases and of the aging process.

In a profound sense, Public Law 293 (January 3, 1946) was the Magna Charta of the medical profession in the Veterans Administration. By its provisions, the formulation of professional policies and the implementation of the medical functions of the agency were assigned to the Chief Medical Director, a physician, who in turn was answerable directly to the Administrator of Veterans Affairs. Its terms released physicians, dentists and nurses from the regulations of Civil Service and afforded the prerogatives of professional leadership and advancement that had previously been denied them. Concomitantly the evolution of the Deans Committee concept was reaping rich harvests. In essence, this plan, whose details were embodied in Policy Memorandum No. 2 (January 30, 1946), was a gentleman's agreement to effect an affiliation between Veterans Administration hospitals and medical schools in the areas of mutual interest, i.e. service, teaching and research. Appointments to the medical staff of an affiliated hospital are made upon the recommendations of the respective departmental chairmen of the medical school. The manager (director) of the Veterans Administration Hospital retains the veto power but rarely exercises it, since differences are quite regularly reconciled before the nomination is officially made. Such appointees have faculty status and discharge academic functions in the medical schools. The house staff members, as a rule, are recruited by the medical school and rotated through the Veterans Administration Hospital services.

The Deans Committee plan has brought splendid dividends to both affected parties. Without financial outlay the medical schools have gained great clinical facilities that with the *increasing demands for health personnel have proven providential* in education and training. In fact, there is growing pressure to locate new or replacement Veterans Administration hospitals adjacent to medical schools. The advantages to the American veteran from this arrangement cannot be overstated. The association has vastly improved the recruiting potential of the agency's institutions. The infusion of new life and blood into the system together with the teaching attendant thereon has greatly advanced the quality of medical care. With the resurgence of clinical activity came the clamant demand for research facilities. In *Technical Bulletin,* August 5, 1948, there were cited provisions "for the establishment of a general research laboratory in every teaching VA hospital and in some of the nonaffiliated hospitals."

Radioisotope facilities received separate consideration. The regulations for the authorization and operation of these units were herein outlined. Obviously the recruitment inducement of research opportunities could not be overlooked; but it was subsidiary to the patent challenge of the medical problems to be solved.

In 1946 at the suggestion of Michael E. DeBakey, follow-up studies of certain medical problems arising in World War II were undertaken by the National Academy of Sciences-National Research Council under the subsidy of the Veterans Administration. Gilbert W. Beebe directed these surveys, whose subjects were:

> 1955 — "A Follow-up Study of World War II Prisoners of War."
> 1956 — "A Follow-up Study of War Neuroses."
> 1957 — "Peripheral Nerve Regeneration: A Follow-up Study of 3,656 World War II Injuries."
> 1961 — "A Follow-up Study of Head Wounds in World War II."

Occasional further research projects were funded by the Veterans Administration in medical schools and other institutions. However, these advances were desultory and their pattern was not cohesively organized. To remedy this obvious defect the advice of the National Research Council was sought. Already this body had rendered constructive counsel in the Follow-up Studies and in the Committee on Prosthetic Devices. In response they appointed the Committee on Veterans Medical Problems that proved extremely effective in the formative period.

Singularly, although with the passage of time and the growing strength of the medical staffs of the Veterans Administration hospitals intramural research was steadily replacing studies by extramural and contractual grants, no specific appropriation for general medical research was voted by Congress until FY 1955. At that session $4,800,000 were appropriated for this purpose. As a corollary to the improved staffing and service under the Deans Committee system, the burgeoning demand for an increase in research emerged.

Renewed professional interest and vigor, observed in every hospital staff favored by an active program of research so generated, reflects itself in greatly improved veteran care. The dividends from this sound program of medical research, so invigorating to the Veterans Administration, do not stop with the system but permeate medical thought and practice throughout the civilized world.

The first direct general medical research monies from Congress, $4,800,000 (FY 1955) were followed by an appropriation for medical research of $5,379,200 in FY 1956. Meanwhile upon the advice of the Research Committee, a careful survey with a projection for a ten-year period had been prepared by the Department of Medicine and Surgery. This projection was to prove most opportune by the crowding events of the forthcoming year (FY 1957). The Department requested a research allotment of $10,000,000. In the hearing before the Subcommittee on Appropriations of the House, the Chairman, Representative Albert Thomas, took vigorous exception to this item. He stoutly maintained that research was not a function of the Veterans Administration. In spite of all representations to the contrary he held his ground. Nor was he dissuaded by the evidence of its immediate and removed advantage to the American veteran and to the public at large.

Our appearance before the Committee on Appropriations of the Senate evoked an entirely different reaction. Senator Walter G. Magnuson chaired the meeting in place of Senator Carl Hayden. The increase to $10,000,000 (FY 1957) was in our judgment a sound level for growth. Senator Magnuson took me quite by surprise when he said, "Doctor, with your background I am amazed that you bring in such a meager exposition of the needs and opportunities of veteran medicine. I have been advised that industry and business assign ten percent of their operation to research. At that rate, you should be asking for $60,000,000 instead of $10,000,000!" As the Senator was speaking, I realized that his information came from a lobbyist for a prominent philanthropist greatly interested in health affairs. I indicated the impossibility of an intelligent use of public monies for research on a widely fluctuating annual scale. Our plan of carefully graduated increases assured effective utilization of the appropriated sums for staffing and equipment, for which I would give a clear accounting. With an increase from $5,000,000 to $60,000,000 such a reconcilitation would be impossible. The ultimate appropriation (FY 1957) was for $10,000,000.

However, the official record (84th Congress 2nd Session, Report No. 2041) on this issue reads:

> The committee finds that the Veterans Administration which spends approximately $607 million for hospital care of its patients in 118,608 beds, is spending only $5,679,200 for medical research. The committee feels that this is not adequate in proportion to the size of the problem, and believes that further funds should be applied to the clinical evaluation and laboratory research on new treatments for arteriosclerosis of the heart and brain, including long-term use of anticoagulants, special diets, use of nonfeminizing estrogen as a means for the prevention or reversal of arteriosclerosis in the vessels of both the heart and brain.

Further directions of study were suggested. Continuing,

> The committee requests that a plan be submitted by the Veterans Administration to the Appropriations Committee for next year outlining an accelerated program against these major causes of death and disability among our veterans in order that hospital costs might be cut and that the veterans might be returned to normal living, able to work and be self-supporting.

The Congressional Record-Senate for June 6, 1956, afforded Senators Magnuson and Morse a forum for their views that ignored the strictures placed upon the Department of Medicine and Surgery by the Bureau of the Budget and the Congress. The other side of the picture is interesting. No sooner had the appropriation bill been signed that I had a call from Representative Thomas, "Doctor, what are you going to do with all the money we gave you? Now you won't squander this money by spreading it around a lot of hospitals, I hope. I'd like to see you just put it on three or four. Just put a lot of money down in Houston and build something that's worthwhile!" Indicating my dependence upon the advice of expert counselors, I thanked him for his interest and support.

To meet the sustained technical but effective opposition of certain members of the House of Representatives to medical research in the Veterans Administration, recourse was had to the traditional legislative device of redefining the stated mission of our agency. In this instance the expedient consisted of the insertion of the phrase, "including medical research" to the existing mandate of Congress to the Veterans Administration for "a complete medical and hospital service." (85th Congress, Public Law 85-857, Section 4101, September 2, 1958). The provisions of this Act were to become operative January 1, 1959, whereupon legal obstacles to medical research in the Department of Medicine and Surgery no longer existed.

The projection of Congressional support of medical research in the Veterans Administration is reflected by these figures:

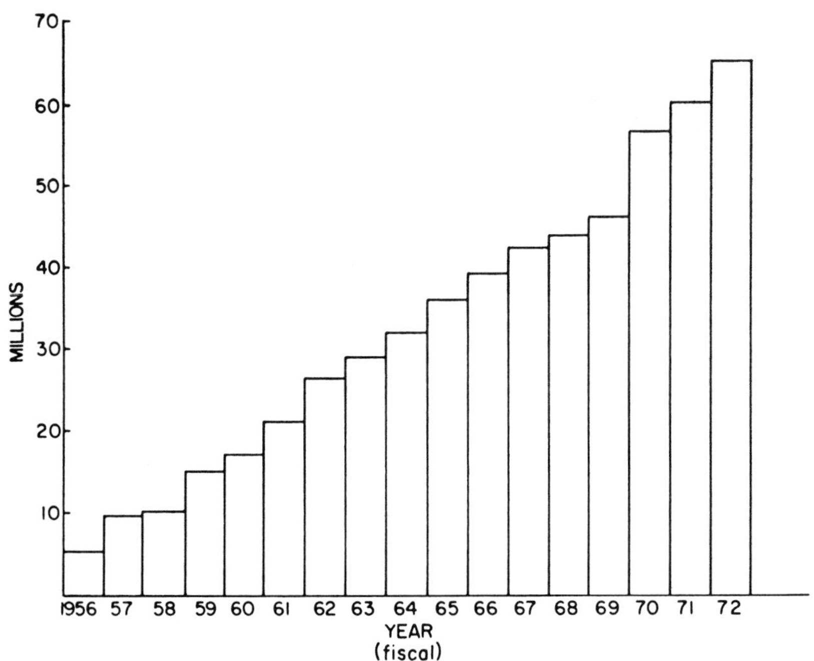

Figure VII-1. Congressional Appropriations for Medical Research

1956 —	$ 5,379,250	1965 —	$36,508,000
1957 —	10,000,000	1966 —	39,983,000
1958 —	10,344,000	1967 —	42,911,000
1959 —	15,344,000	1968 —	44,472,000
1960 —	17,344,000	1969 —	46,616,000
1961 —	21,500,000	1970 —	57,134,435
1962 —	27,000,000	1971 —	60,686,000
1963 —	29,500,000	1972 —	66,703,000
1964 —	32,572,000		

Particular attention is directed to the planned accessions in the appropriated sums. Isolated from the inordinate pressures of well motivated sources external to the agency, the Veterans Administration has pursued a conservative pattern of fiscal responsibility that has protected both the research worker and the mission of the Department of Medicine and Surgery. Private foundations and Federal agencies contribute materially to the support of research in the Veterans Administration. These sources are especially screened.

Since research was not accepted as an element of the medical mission of the Veterans Administration until after World War II, the planning of hospitals with the vast expansion at this period omitted this important detail of space requirement. Improvisation was the natural order of the day. Kitchens, store rooms, closets and any space that could be transformed to research laboratories was fair game for the avid workers seeking breathing room for their studies. In 1950 in forty hospitals with active research programs, the *total* research space was only 75,000 square feet!

The scanty provisions for research facilities in post-World War II construction had by strenuous representations been extended to an average of 11,700 square feet for the 500-bed general hospital (1962). At that time the national minimal standards called for 20,000 square feet. By FY 1963 a total of 1,211,470 net square feet for research was recorded. However, the Veterans Administration has fought a rear guard action and down to the present time has not been able to meet the physical requirements for adequate research space. The plans for the most recently constructed 500-bed general hospitals in the system assign from 20,000 up to approximately 40,000 square feet to this vital function. In FY 1971 the total research space was 1,694,137 square feet.

As a result of the deliberations of an *ad hoc* commission of representatives of Federal agencies called by Paul A. Hawley, Chief Medical Director, Veterans Administration, the responsibility for an active program, ostensibly directed toward the care of casualties from atomic sources and to defense procedures against the same, was placed clearly upon the Veterans Administration. Implied in the terms of reference moreover was the exploitation of this modality on the broadest medical front. Of particular significance was the inclusion of George Lyon in this preliminary planning group, for upon him was to devolve the evolution of the remarkable programs of radioisotope study in the vast hospital system of the Veterans Administration and the training of teams ("Radef") in Civil Defense. His active leadership in the Radioisotope Safety Training in the Navy and his participation in the atomic exercises ("Reflux Test" and "Cross Road") qualified him admirably for his appointment as Special Assistant to the Chief Medical Director-Atomic Medicine (April 20, 1948). In this capacity he answered directly to Chief Medical Director Hawley on all matters pertaining to atomic medicine. The Veterans Administration established a pattern of research and service in this area that set the pace for civilian medicine.

Our interest is general scientific advancement not individual credit. So vast have been the contributions of the Veterans Administration to atomic medicine that Procrustean privilege must be involved to afford even a glimpse of this situation. In 1949 Benedict Cassen and his associates constructed the first radioisotope scanner in the University of California-Los Angeles. However, its clinical application in thyroid scanning was made upon patients in Veterans Administration Hospitals (Wadsworth and Long Beach, California) by Herbert Allen, Jr., Raymond Libby and M. E. Morton. With greatly improved techniques and equipment all scanning methods to outline internal organs took their roots from the humble beginning of the wide calcium tungstate scintillation counter. In effect this technique brought nuclear medicine to the clinic.

Turning to a distinctly independent Veterans Administration

contribution, the original work of Solomon A. Berson and Rosalyn S. Yalow (Bronx) on radioimmunoassay is conspicuous. From the first announcement of their basic concepts (1957) this team with their associates has pursued broad biologic and physiologic studies of the polypeptide hormones with a precise definition that has shed light not only upon the basic problems but on vast areas of clinical endocrinology. From the primary interest in the study of insulin their investigations have extended to include growth hormone, parathyroid hormone, adrenocortical hormone, gastrin and other polypeptides. The fundamental observation, derived from the studies of insulin, showed that by labelling the same with I^{131} a distinction could be made between this compound in the subject under insulin therapy and the untreated control. In the treated group antibodies to insulin developed, and by chromatographic and electrophoretic techniques the free and the bound insulin could be separated. The controls had no insulin-binding antibodies. In essence, these principles apply to all peptide hormones tested. Actually this technique has proved applicable in other fields of study, *viz.*, Australian antigen. In a letter written shortly before his death, Berson referred enthusiastically to the inviting new vistas of "Big Gastrin," "Big ACTH," and "Big, Big Insulin." In his opinion the heterogeneity of peptide hormones offers unusual promise for productive investigation.

With the vast resources of the Veterans Administration and the encouragement of study in the esoteric field of nuclear medicine, it is not surprising that the radioisotope units in the many hospitals should pioneer in a number of areas. At Los Angeles William H. Oldendorf made original observations of cerebral blood flow. The transit time of an intravenously injected radionuclide through the brain was established for the normal subject. With this background the effects of physiologic and pathologic alterations were measured. The clearance of various drugs from the blood affords an interesting correlation with their immediate action and a possible explanation for addiction to the same. Heroin, for example, is cleared on a single passage through the brain, whereas morphine is removed at one percent the rate of heroin.

Oldendorf and his associates approached the problem of the mental deficiency of phenylketonuric subjects in a unique manner. Selenomethionine Se 75 was used as a tracer to establish the penetration of the blood-brain barrier of the rat. Preloading with intravenous nonradioactive L-methionine or L-phenylalanine effected a reduction in the uptake of selenomethionine Se 75 by the brain. In the rat, the inhibition of the uptake was greater with phenylalanine than with methionine. Furthermore, this effect appeared at lower plasma concentrations of the aminoacid than is encountered in clinical phenylketonuria. The natural transfer of these observations was its application to the clinical problem. Among nine phenylketonuric patients statistically significant reductions of the selenomethionine Se 75 uptake were established as compared with twelve matched controls who were mentally retarded. The conclusion of the saturation of the blood-brain barrier for selenomethionine Se 75 by the native high blood phenylalanine in phenylketonuric patients would appear justified.

The evolution of an appropriate agent for renography was directed toward the elimination of the adverse reactions to earlier chemicals (or drugs) designed to study the form and the function of this organ. Manuel Tubis (Los Angeles) developed sodium orthoiodohippurate labelled with I^{131} (1960). Termed Hippuran, this agent became universally employed to visualize the kidney and to approximate its excretory function. Certain recent changes in the product (I^{123} for I^{131}) afford some advantages.

Conspicuous among the recent contributions of Veterans Administration medical research has been the work of Marcus A. Rothschild (Bronx) on albumin synthesis in the body. He proved that thyroid and cortisone greatly enhanced this synthesis. By sophisticated methods he established a colloidal osmotic mechanism for the regulation of albumin synthesis. At least in part this effect is mediated by the interstitial colloid content of the liver. By emphasis on the known extravascular pool of serum albumin in the skin, Rothschild focused attention on its importance in burns. Most revealing were his observations relative to the effect of alcohol on albumin synthesis. Contrary to the accepted clinical viewpoint, a majority of the alcoholic cirrhotic patients on an adequate diet demonstrate a normal capacity to synthesize serum albumin within a few days after the withdrawal of alcohol. Furthermore, the addition of small quantities of tryptophan will prevent or promptly reverse the toxic effect of alcohol in this important function of the liver.

One of the most brilliant cooperative studies in medical history has been the Cooperative Chemotherapy of Tuberculosis. Before the advent of streptomycin, the curves of morbidity and mortality from tuberculosis had shown a definite decline in this country. The eradication of bovine tuberculosis had practically eliminated scrofula, bone and joint tuberculosis. Education of the laity as well as the medical profession speeded the earlier recognition of all forms of tuberculosis and thereby favored the control of its dissemination. Collapse and excision of the affected areas of the lung served their limited role in the advance. Nor can the conservative regimen of the sanatorium care be overlooked. Its hygienic measures of rest, diet, fresh air and sunlight supported the patient while Nature was resolving the pathologic process.

The incidence of tuberculosis among American veterans reached its crest of 15,940 in 1954. John B. Barnwell had been recruited to direct the attack on this major problem. In 1939 Selman A. Waksman and his associates had announced the discovery of streptomycin which in their studies disclosed a bactericidal action on cultures of the mycobacterium tuberculosis (1944). William F. Feldman and H. Corwin Hinshaw of the Mayo Clinic established the remarkable capacity of streptomycin to stay the course of otherwise fatal tuberculosis in guinea pigs. Promptly this experimental experience was transferred to tuberculous patients in Minnesota (1945).

Barnwell enlisted the services of Arthur M. Walker, an associate at the University of Pennsylvania (under Professor A. N. Richards) and at the University of Michigan, who proposed an expansive study of the chemotherapy of tuberculosis. To speed the accurate evaluation of streptomycin this team (Barnwell and Walker) included in the proposed study hospitals of the Army and Navy as well as the Veterans Administration. To assure adequate control in the administration of streptomycin and in the assessment of its effects, stringent rules were imposed. Random sampling of the eligible tuberculous subjects divided them into a group who would receive the drug to be tested and a similar number who would take only a placebo. Both groups received the conventional hygienic care of patients with pulmonary tuberculosis. A further precaution was imposed in the double blind procedure. Neither the patient nor any member of the attending medical team was apprized of his therapeutic status.

Fitzsimons Army Hospital, Sampson Naval Hospital and five Veterans Administration Hospitals (Sunmount, New York; Brockville, Ohio; Hines, Illinois; Livermore, California and Rutland Heights, Massachusetts) were designated for this momentous study at the outset. Furthermore, the effects of the therapy were susceptible of objective demonstration in the physical status of the treated as compared with those who did not receive streptomycin. The ultimate criteria came in the roentgenologic changes in the pulmonary lesions and the disappearance of the mycobacterium tuberculosis from the sputum. Since the information relative to the treatment was centralized in an office removed from any hospital engaged in the study, the results were read impartially and without bias. The caution of the leaders was further voiced,

> The Veterans Administration is not, and should not be, in a position to make the first clinical trial of the new drug . . . . Once a new drug has been tried, however, and has been shown to have some promise of effectiveness without undue toxicity, the VA is peculiarly, and perhaps uniquely, fitted to conduct a large-scale investigation of its effectiveness and the best regimen for its administration.

The initial group of participating hospitals (7) was steadily advanced to twenty-two (20 VA). "A Preliminary Statement Concerning The Effects of Streptomycin Upon Tuberculosis in Man" that was to revolutionize the treatment of this disease, appeared as *Veterans Administration Technical Bulletin,* August 4, 1947. As a measure of the thoroughness of the inquiry a panel of recognized phthisiologists (8-12) reviewed the X-rays of the tuberculous patients before and after treatment with streptomycin. Their conclusion of its efficacy, especially in the improvement or resolution of exudative lesions, was a milestone in the acceptance of this drug. The Statement dealt in some detail with the results of streptomycin therapy in other forms of tuberculosis.

Measured conservatism characterized the reports of the results of the Cooperative Chemotherapeutic Study. Still the enthusiasm of the teams could scarcely be submerged, as witness such passages as the following (*Veterans Administration Technical Bulletin* 10-34, August 5, 1947):

> In tuberculous lesions of the lung the panel's verdict read:
>
> It will be recalled that, by terms of the protocol, all lesions were progressive or stationary at the time streptomycin treatment was initiated. According to the jury, little or no effect was demonstrable on the old fibrous or caseating type of lesions. In the case of exudative lesions, on the other hand, 81 percent of the votes noted improvement, i.e., the lesions either "disappeared" or became "smaller" or "harder." Fifty percent of the votes indicated that in the light of the jurors' past experience these changes would "never," "rarely" or only "occasionally" have occurred on bed rest alone within a comparative period of time. The results observed in the Army and Navy series were superior to those.

Even more emphatic was the position taken in regard to the efficacy of streptomycin in the treatment of miliary tuberculosis and tuberculous meningitis.

> The immediate dramatic clinical response of patients with meningitis, the unprecedented resolution of pulmonary miliary lesions, and the startling diminution of all signs of acute infection in desperately ill individuals of both groups make the treatment of these two types of disseminated tuberculosis by streptomycin mandatory and provide incontrovertible evidence of the chemotherapeutic activity of streptomycin against the tubercle bacillus. It is believed that the mortality rate of acute miliary tuberculosis will be definitely lowered. It is doubted that the eventual mortality rate of meningitis will be appreciably reduced.

Particular attention was drawn to the tendency for resistant strains of the mycobacterium tuberculosis to emerge under continued streptomycin therapy. Its toxic reactions were carefully documented and among them the singular propensity for eight cranial nerve injury was emphasized.

Other drugs have joined in the incomplete conquest of tuberculosis; but the study of streptomycin established the beachhead. Furthermore, the pattern of the attack layed out by Barnwell and Walker is accepted as the prototype for subsequent controlled therapeutic studies. The aggregate gain in personal health and survival from this study is inestimable. Monetary savings, vast as they are, shrink into insignificance in comparison with the restoration of countless tuberculous patients to healthy, normal lives through the beneficence of streptomycin and its companion antituberculosis drugs. Certain figures, involving the responsibility of the Veterans Administration in this respect, bear witness to the magnitude of this contribution:

Hospitals (for tuberculosis) — *Patients*

1954	21	15,940 (In all V.A. Hospitals)
1964	4	6,000 (In all V.A. Hospitals)
1969	0	2,400 (In all V.A. Hospitals)

An important supporting element in the sustained contributions of the Veterans Administration to the control and the treatment of tuberculosis is the laboratory for the study of resistant strains of the mycobacterium tuberculosis (and related organisms) under Gladys C. Hobby and her associates (East Orange). The precision and definition of their results have afforded clinicians an assurance and a security that have greatly extended the acceptance of the therapeutic effectiveness of a sequence of new drugs.

As indicated, the brilliant success and the wide applicability of the Cooperative Study of the Chemotherapy of Tuberculosis attracted the attention of the entire medical world. By the same token, the Department of Medicine and Surgery recognized even more forcibly its unsurpassed opportunity to exploit this avenue of approach in the investigation of a vast number of clinical problems. The Research and Education Division in the Central Office gave direction and organization to a number of other cooperative studies; but the incentive to sustained cooperative effort stemmed from the workers in the field. At a given time (FY 1970) some thirty odd cooperative projects were active in the system.

The objectives covered a wide range of medical, neurologic, psychiatric and surgical problems. Every effort is made to bring all forces together for the study of a common problem. In the interest of coordination of research, for example, the approach to the study of coccidioidomycosis included representation from five (5) Veterans Administration Hospitals in the Southwest, an Army, a Navy and an Air Force Hospital, one civilian hospital, two universities, one State College, the Communicable Disease Center (Atlanta), the Naval Biological Laboratory (Berkeley) and the National Institute of Allergy and Infectious Diseases (Bethesda). With the participation of the National Cancer Institute the Cooperative Studies in Cancer are constructively organized from functional and geographic standpoints to insure coverage and communication. In the Veterans Administration Hospital, Washington, D.C., a section of thirty beds is assigned for cooperative studies in the chemotherapy of cancer with the National Cancer Institute.

In selecting the Cooperative Study of Antihypertensive Agents for special discussion, the pattern of approach rather than its substance is emphasized. Yet, there emerges a fundamental conclusion that would be difficult, if not impossible, to evolve from independent research.

Arterial hypertension is one of the most serious problems confronting medicine today. When all accepted causes for this objective sign with its concomitant organic changes have been excluded, there remain a vast number of patients with hypertension whose etiology cannot be assigned. Because of the growing importance of this group, a double blind control study was undertaken on a cooperative basis under the chairmanship of Edward D. Freis (Washington). Eight Veterans Administration hospitals participated. Strict criteria were applied in the selection of candidates for this study. For the uniformity of returns, the Committee agreed upon a classification that incorporated the cogent factors of the systemic criteria along with the levels of diastolic pressure. In scoring the findings in each group double weight was accorded the fundal changes and the diastolic pressure.

The responses to the several antihypertensive drugs were susceptible of careful evaluation. Combinations of reserpine and hydralazine proved more effective than either alone or a placebo in mild and moderately severe hypertensive patients. In the latter group the cited combination proved as effective as reserpine plus ganglionic blockers. Independently there was no distinction among the ganglionic blockers. Generally, the response was more prompt and greater in magnitude in the severe than in the mild hypertensive patients. The supplementation of chlorothiazide with hydralazine and reserpine was attended by better results than with chlorothiazide alone.

Perhaps the most significant results of this surpassing co-operative study emerged from the marked divergence in the morbidity and the mortality figures for the treated as compared with the control (placebo) group. Both in the 115 through the 129 mm Hg (diastolic) group and in the 90 through 114 mm Hg (diastolic) group the incidence of serious complications or terminal morbid events was much higher in the control (placebo) than in those treated with antihypertensive drugs. Indeed this circumstance became so apparent in the mild (90 through 114 mm Hg) hypertensive patients that the study was concluded (April 1964-May 1967) rather than deprive this group of the protection of antihypertensive agents.

Incidentally, Leonard J. Skeggs (Cleveland) was the first to isolate hypertensin I and hypertensin II from the blood.

Despite extended studies of the effectiveness of anticoagulants on the morbidity and mortality of myocardial infarction, no agreement had been reached after a long period. The Veterans Administration undertook a cooperative study of the matter. (Richard V. Ebert, University of Minnesota, Chairman) Fifteen hospitals participated in the effort. Beginning in 1957 and utilizing random selection of comparable patients, in so far as feasible, and the double blind technique of treatment a total of 747 patients suffering myocardial infarction was divided into two groups. One group received placebos and the other bishydroxycoumarin. In the division no differences in the occurrence of prior arrhythmia, shock and cardiac decompensation appeared between the two groups. All patients were followed for two years or to death. More than one half survived for five years. Most significant, however, were two circumstances. The death rate of the anti-coagulant treated patients for the first three years was lower than the controls. After three years the survival curves of the two groups converged and by the fifth year there was no statistical difference. Under anticoagulants the incidence of recurrent infarction and congestive failure was distinctly lower than in the controls.

The application of medical electronic data processing to the mass interpretation of electrocardiograms has been the chief target of Hubert V. Pipberger (Washington). At the outset the electrocardiographic signals in analog form were transferred to the magnetic tape. These signals were then converted to the digital form for automatic analysis by the electronic computer. A high degree of accuracy of interpretation was achieved. Long distance operation of this procedure (Veterans Administration Hospital, Martinsburg, West Virginia to Veterans Administration Hospital, Washington, D.C.) was a first demonstration of this prospect. Refinements in technique have improved the diagnostic range of this approach and have added new potentials for the automatic analysis of certain high frequency notches. With a conservative attitude Pipberger looks upon such analyses not as diagnostic criteria but as distinctive marks between the normal and abnormal.

Automation found an unusual but logical application in cardiac pacers. The pathophysiologic consequences of certain cardiac arrhythmias, as atrioventricular heart block with Adams-Stokes syndrome, offered a natural target in the replacement of the disturbed natural conduction system by an artificial pacemaker. With the cooperation of associates in electrical engineering, William Chardock (Buffalo) constructed one of the first of the effective devices for this purpose. The implanted pacer was activated by a transistor and has found a wide range of usefulness in cardiac patients. Atomic energy has more recently been employed by this group as the power source.

With the increasing demand for more involved and more

complicated laboratory tests, any device for their simplification and expedition is welcomed with avidity. Leonard J. Skeggs (Cleveland) first devised an automatic method for colorimetric analysis. Much of the automation of laboratory procedures, presently utilized, stems from his personal contributions and derivatives therefrom.

The aging male population of American veterans affords an unprecedented opportunity for the study of carcinoma of the prostate. Sixteen hospitals participate as the Cooperative Urological Research Group (Clyde E. Blackhard, Minneapolis and George T. Mellinger, Kansas City, Chairmen). Following the conventional stages of prostatic carcinomata, various therapeutic attacks were pursued after an accepted protocol. In 1971 adhering to the random sampling of patients and the double blind method of applying therapy, statisticians evaluated the results. In 288 patients with stage I or stage II carcinoma, radical prostatectomy was uniformly performed. One half of this group in addition received supplemental estrogens; the other half, placebos. A significant increase in fatal cardiovascular complications attended the use of the supplemented estrogens. In stage III or stage IV carcinoma 1,764 patients received one of several therapies, i.e. placebo, estrogen, orchiectomy plus placebo, or orchiectomy plus estrogen. The survivals of the patients with stage III receiving placebo, estrogen or orchiectomy plus a placebo were quite comparable, while the surviving rate of those treated by orchiectomy plus estrogen was better. In patients with stage IV carcinoma, there was no statistical difference among the patients receiving the several (4) methods of treatment.

An arresting note was struck by the high incidence of cardiovascular complications in those patients receiving estrogen therapy. In the light of this circumstance the trial of reduced doses of diethylstilbestrol (5.0 mg to 1.0 mg) was undertaken. The Group recommended the latter dose of estrogen in stage IV patients, but its deferment in inoperable stage III and stage IV patients until they become symptomatic. Further studies of therapeutic agents are being pursued by the Cooperative Urological Research Group.

For many years Ludwik Gross (Bronx) has pursued the study of oncogenic viruses. Not only have his investigations been directional and productive, but in certain respects he has blazed new trails and opened wide horizons in neoplastic research. The experimental transmission of a series of tumors by the injection of cell free filtrates of the abnormal tissues, viz., rabbit myxomatosis (Sanarelli), chicken erthromyeloblastic leukemia (von Ellermann and Bang), chicken sarcoma (Rous), rabbit fibroma and papilloma (Shope) and mouse mammary carcinoma through nursing milk (Bittner) among others, gave the basic thesis for Gross' approach to the problem of mouse leukemia.

His primary success resulted in the transmission of Ak-leukemic extracts of Ak embryos to neonatal C3H mice (1951). The choice of the strains of mice was determined by the high natural incidence of leukemia in Ak lines (females, 71 to 85 percent; male, 52 to 77 percent) while C3H mice have a low spontaneous occurrence of this disease. The frequency and the onset of the leukemic condition bore an inverse relation to the age of the mice at the time of the subcutaneous or intraperitoneal inoculations. The younger the mice the earlier and more regular was the production of the leukemia.

Gross' investigations took him deeply into the genetic and other factors in the pathogenesis of experimental leukemia. His sound efforts have established beyond a peradventure the viral etiology of mouse leukemia. He has also isolated a virus from the leukemic tissue that has induced carcinoma of the parotid gland upon inoculation in other mice. A variety of other "solid" tumors, *viz.*, mammary carcinoma, fibromyxomata and medullary adrenal tumors, has been similarly produced. Gross has been nationally and internationally recognized for his outstanding contribution. Most recently Gross has immunized guinea pigs against leukemia.

Oscar Auerbach (East Orange) and his associates have made a notable contribution to the knowledge of the pathogenesis of bronchogenic carcinoma. Although the accusing finger of several observers had earlier incriminated cigarette smoking in its etiology, it remained for Auerbach and his team to fix this point by meticulous studies of the entire tracheobronchial tree of smokers and nonsmokers and other approaches (1957, 1961). As histological criteria the following changes in the bronchial mucosa were noted:

    a. Basal cell hyperplasia
    b. Stratification
    c. Squamous metaplasia
    d. Carcinoma *in situ*

They adduced incontrovertible evidence of an ascending scale of histologic changes in the bronchial mucosa with increasing cigarette smoking (0 in nonsmokers; 11.4 percent of those smoking 2 or more packages a day).

To complete the circle of evidence Auerbach, Hammond, Kirman and Garfinkel (1970) have produced histologic changes in the bronchial mucosa of smoking dogs. Again there was a quantitative influence on the degree of change incident to the amount of smoking. Filters (cellulose-acetate) apparently lessened the cellular reactions. In eighty-six dogs submitted to smoking cigarettes in quantities comparable to man up to 875 days with and without filters, and eight nonsmoking controls, all groups had some bronchoalveolar tumors. However, the incidence was lowest (25 percent) in the nonsmoking dogs and highest (79.2 percent) in the non-filter smokers. Furthermore, pleural and transpleural invasion of this type of tumor and early invasion squamous cell carcinoma occurred only among smoking dogs.

With the wide range of clinical and pathological problems in veteran patients with neurological conditions, the magnitude and comprehensive order of research in this field may be anticipated. The subjects range from profound neurophysiological and neuropharmacological approaches to epidemiologic studies. In an especially esoteric field Robert Efron (Boston; Martinez) has made conspicuous contributions. In the Pavlovian tradition he controlled certain types of epilepsy by conditioned inhibition. When the aura was long and physical agents were the apparent inciting stimuli to such ictal episodes, this approach by inhibition appeared more effective.

Efron's further attention to the invariant time-dependent

properties of all perceptions promises to open new vistas for research in neurology. Essentially he has found that measured in milliseconds the perceptual onset latency was not related to the duration of the stimulus but the perceptual offset latency was longer for brief stimuli than for those above the critical level. By elegant technique he has established this common temporal characteristic for sight and hearing and has correlated the same with the electrophysiological activity of the associated neural tracts. The possible bearing of these observations on aphasia and agnosia offers a fresh approach to their understanding and management.

The high incidence of cerebral vascular lesions in the veteran population has stimulated many cooperative therapeutic approaches. Among these have been anticoagulants, estrogens, MER-24, and Astromid-5. No sustained advantage has been assigned to any of these agents after extended study. Particular interest attaches to the Veterans Administration experience in another neurologic disease. Fortuitously, a patient with pulmonary tuberculosis complicating multiple sclerosis experienced a remarkable remission in the neurologic manifestations while receiving isoniazid for the tuberculous condition. The repetition of this unanticipated result led to a carefully controlled study of the effect of isoniazid on multiple sclerosis. The knowledge of its unpredictable course with the frequent occurrence of remissions ranging from months to years in duration led to a conservative, if not skeptical, outlook on the part of the majority of the physicians concerned. However, lay science writers so raised the hopes of the afflicted and their families and friends, that a definite answer was imperative. The results were disappointing in that no benefit attended the administration of isoniazid to patients with multiple sclerosis under controlled conditions.

Among pioneers in the area Andrew V. Schally (New Orleans) has directed his studies to the amazingly productive field of the neurohormones elaborated by the hypothalamus. In turn, by precise techniques he has isolated and identified these hormones with the specific functions of the release of growth hormone, adrenocortical hormone, thyrotropin and luteinizing hormone from the anterior pituitary. The synthesis of these neurohormones opens a most inviting field for endocrinologic research. Their promise of eventual broad clinical application affords a prospect of surpassing importance. Of immediate interest is the synthetic production of TRH (thyrotropin releasing hormone) by the New Orleans group. They have indicated the possibility of an early diagnosis of mild thyrotoxicosis with this product. Theoretically TRH may ultimately find a place in the treatment of metastatic carcinoma from the thyroid by increasing the activity of such sites for attack by I^{131}.

The studies of Noble J. David and his associates (Durham; Miami) on fundus angiography are especially significant. The fluorescein technique of Dollery et al. was refined by special equipment and photography to afford accurate information relative to the integrity of the central retinal artery and its branches. The venous pattern of this area was likewise studied. They have emphasized the pathophysiology of changes in the blood flow in the retinal vessels with reference to the carotid arterial system and to variations in the intraocular and intracranial pressure. These studies have been extended to the experimental evidence of endothelial damage in the retinal arteries of monkeys from emboli of autologous fibrin clots. Actual leakage of fluorescein into the retina occurred subsequent to the lodgment of such emboli. Even with experimental air embolism this evidence of endothelial injury was adduced.

By serendipity David and his group made a major contribution to fundus angiography. The short wave lengths (470-500 nm) utilized in fluorescein angiography do not penetrate to the choroid coat, which is obscured by the interposed pigment. In seeking a technique to afford a photographic differential between the arterial and venous oxygen saturation of the pial vessels, indocyanine green was employed. This dye absorbs infrared wave lengths quite avidly. The success in this direction, while not quantitatively valuable in the original quest, offered the promise of the visualization of the choroidal vascular system, since the pigment epithelium permitted the penetration of red and infrared wave lengths (750-900 nm). Their observations relative to the rapid circulation of the dye in the retromacular choroid offers an area for detailed study that is being pursued with refined physiologic and ophthalmological techniques.

The transplantation of organs has captured the imagination of man for centuries. Blood transfusion constituted the first practical application of the principle. In this respect, years passed after Lower's experimental transfusion (1665) and Denis' transfusion from a lamb to man (1667) before the sustained advances of the 20th century. Especial security came with the grouping of blood for compatibility and with its preservation. The chimera of organ transplantation still fascinated the layman as well as scientist. The establishment of compatibility between the donor and the recipient has witnessed a substantial improvement through refined techniques in recent years. Renal transplantation has shown the greatest growth of late and a number of Veterans Administration teams have been productive in this field. Thomas E. Starzl and his associates (Denver) have been major contributors.

Successful as has been the Denver group in the technical performance of the renal transplantation, even greater significance attaches to their sustained efforts to interpret the mechanism and the control of rejection. By splenectomy and thymectomy prior to the surgical procedure, improvement of the results in experimental animals led to their adoption in the human subjects. These measures supplemented the conventional immune suppressive agents, i.e. general body X-ray radiation, azothioprine, prednisone and actinomycin, according to the indications. The challenge of orthotopic liver transplantation was met by carefully designed animal experiments before the approach to the patient. After an extended experience with this procedure (33) they concluded that hepatic tumors should be excluded from the indications. The longest survivors have had biliary atresia, the victims of which obviously afford a maximum of biologic and histologic reserve. Eight of the group (33) lived longer than one year. Emphasizing the serologic and anaphylactic reactions to their foreign (horse) source, the detailed observations on the preparation and use of heterologous antilymphocyte plasma, serum and blood promise a further protection against transplant rejection. In the work on antilymphocyte preparations there has been a close cooperation with investigators in the University of Edinburgh.

As indicated, the responsibility of the agency for research in prosthetic devices and sensory aids was early recognized by Congress (1948). In essence the entire program, although centrally organized and coordinated in the Prosthetic and Sensory Aids Service, involves a complex system of research and development in the diversified fields of prosthetic and sensory aids. To this end at the present time the Veterans Administration has eight centers and, through contractual relations supports in varying degrees, studies in twenty-five universities and laboratories with related missions. The technological range of these studies is beyond the purview of this review; but every device for the rehabilitation of veterans handicapped in locomotion or other skeletal orders immediately becomes available to all individuals so afflicted. For example, this program is now supporting in part the studies on externally powered arm prosthesis in several institutions. From a technical standpoint the evolution of the hydraulic and the pneumatic control mechanisms has afforded stability and adjustment to changes in stride and peace that prove most advantageous to the amputee. Infinite pains and skills have vastly improved braces and supports.

The activities of this Service are conspicuous in the development of sensory aids. Technological advances have improved the reading range and the mobility of the partially sighted and the blind. A laser typhlocane, developed under contract with academic and technical scientific organizations, utilizes certain highly sophisticated equipment to render the position of obstacles and the levels of approaches perceptible to the blind. Several devices have been developed to improve the learning-teaching prospect of these veterans. In fact this aspect of the rehabilitative program holds a high priority in the overall mission of the Service.

The Veterans Administration has a large stake in the other disabilities of veterans. In the field of deafness, with the Committees on Sensory Aids and Prostheses of the National Academy of Sciences-National Research Council, standards are set that are reflected in the production and utilization of hearing aids by the afflicted, both veteran and nonveteran. Every physical measurement available has been brought to the study of gaits in the physically handicapped and applied in the evolution of appropriate canes, braces and prostheses.

With the population situation in mind, the problems of aging have come to occupy an important place in planning health care. The veterans constitute an element of the citizenry that is best adapted to a controlled study of all factors entering into normative and pathologic aging. As earlier cited, the veterans comprise a large group, male adults in the main granted, who by special provisions of the law are in sustained contact with a governmental agency, the Veterans Administration. This relationship is extended by the provisions of the law for medical care in its hospitals and clinics. Obviously there could be no more perfect setting for the exploration of the many factors entering into the aging process.

The Boston Outpatient Clinic is engaged in a continuing Normative Aging Study. By periodic examination of older veterans in physical, laboratory and psychological parameters, a longitudinal inventory of the individual may be obtained. Hopefully a disclosure of his elements of strength leading to longevity may give leads to the recognition and correction of faults in their less sturdy fellows. With the cooperation of the University of Chicago and Brandeis University an interesting study of 1,600 Spanish American War Veterans of a total 18,600 survivors is directed toward their psychological reactions with reference to their socioeconomic adjustments. Scores of projects are being pursued toward the elucidation and amelioration of physical, physiologic, pathologic, metabolic and chemical changes incident to advancing years. The results of these investigations may have a distinct socioeconomic impact on the aging population at large.

Approximately one half of all hospitalized veterans suffer from emotional illnesses. The great gain of recent years has been the reversal of the curve of bed occupancy in the hospitals of the system from these ills. The advances in psychopharmacology have contributed, first, by their independent action and then significantly by the accessability of emotionally ill patients to adjunctive measures under the influence of tranquilizing and mood-elevating drugs. Cooperative studies are in active operation to evaluate the influence of chemotherapy on psychiatric conditions, as schizophrenia and on acute alcoholic withdrawal. The pressing problem of drug addiction is under study, *viz.*, marijuana by Leo E. Hollister and his associates (Palo Alto). Of especial significance has been the Veterans Administration-National Institute of Mental Hygiene Collaborative Study on Lithium Carbonate in Affective Disorders under Robert F. Prien, Coordinator (Perry Point). Eighteen hospitals treated 255 manic patients with a random choice of lithium carbonate or chloropromazine. Prior to therapy the patients had been classified as highly active or mildly active by the degree of psychomotor activity. Chloropromazine proved more effective in the highly active, whereas lithium carbonate was preferred in the mildly active patients. The side effects may weigh the balance in favor of their primary choice; but patients receiving lithium carbonate did not experience the fatigue and sluggishness of the chloropromazine treated patients.

With an extensive experience in an expanding field of medical research, the Veterans Administration came to an appreciation of specific needs in highly esoteric fields that could not be met by the many hospitals engaged in this activity. In the interest of the economy of highly skilled personnel and expensive sophisticated equipment, the pattern of Research Support Centers was evolved (1962). A geographic distribution was planned, as follows: Eastern — West Haven, Connecticut; Midwest — Hines, Illinois; Southern — Little Rock, Arkansas; Western — Sepulveda, California. Representatives manning these Centers afforded research workers in the hospitals of their geographic area counsel and direction in research design, statistical techniques, scientific data organization, data processing, computer programming, biomedical engineering and such other spheres of assistance as their expertise might offer. A further function was the registry of special equipment and resources that might be transferred to meet the urgent requirements of another research group, i.e. Instrumentation Loan Bank (Little Rock).

Theoretically the concept of the Research Support Center met rising demands for such services effectively. Obviously, not all skills could be afforded by even four such Centers; so that certain special requests were channeled to the point where the requested services were available. The early days of their operation were pronounced successful. Then with a growing strength in the Deans Committees' association, the reference of the problems of an earlier period to the qualified staffs of the affiliated universities gradually siphoned the requests from the Research Support Centers. This circumstance, with other administrative problems, has led to the decision to discontinue the Centers.

Constructive planning for medical research must perforce consider the encouragement and recruitment of potential strength in the rising generation. There are a number of variations on this theme which basically is designed to attract the desirable research staff. Obviously the intellectual climate, affiliations, equipment, personnel and the research outlet must afford the major attractions. In 1956 the clinical investigatorship was initiated. By its terms young physicians with a flair for study and demonstrated research potential are appointed for three years. During this period they will pursue independent investigation, or, if locally determined, they may work with senior members of the staff. During the individual's tenure a division of his time not to exceed twenty-five percent, will be spent in clinical work on the wards. In the main such appointees are being groomed for academic careers. A high percentage of the clinical investigators remain in staff positions in the Veterans Administration. Then, too, men of productive promise may merit continuance in a new category, i.e. medical investigator. The term of this appointment is four years and subject to review, it may be renewed.

The research (now research and education) associate program (1962) is admittedly a recruitment device. In areas where it is difficult to maintain a well-balanced staff, as psychiatry, psychology, pathology and radiology, such posts are available upon the completion of the respective residencies. In this relation the stipend is at a staff level and the opportunities for self-improvement in education and research rest largely upon the incumbent.

Traineeships are also offered in limited numbers. The senior medical investigator (1959) is at the opposite pole. Selected on the basis of established eminence in a given field of medical research, his status is permanent. The roll of its recipients is impressive:

> Samuel H. Bassett, Los Angeles (deceased)
> Edward D. Freis, Washington
> Oscar Auerbach, East Orange
> Ludwik Gross, Bronx
> Jay T. Shurley, Oklahoma City
> Norton Grossman, Los Angeles
> Solomon A. Berson, Bronx (deceased)
> Paul Heller, Chicago
> Rosalyn S. Yalow, Bronx

The William S. Middleton Award for outstanding medical research in the agency was established in 1960. The recipients and their recognized contributions read like an American registry of science:

1960:	Solomon A. Berson Rosalyn Yalow	— Radioimmunoassay of insulin.
1961:	Hubert A. Pipberger	— Automatic processing of cardiovascular data.
1962:	Leslie Zieve William C. Vogel	— Studies of phospholipids and phospholipidases.
1963:	Stanley Ulick	— Chemistry and metabolism of corticoid hormones.
1964:	Robert O. Becker	— Electrical control systems in living organisms.
1965:	Lucius B. Guze George M. Kalmanson	— Host-parasite relationship in chronic pyelonephritis.
1966:	Leo E. Hollister	— Psychopharmacology.
1967:	Leonard J. Skeggs	— Automation of laboratory procedures.

1968: Thomas E. Starzl — Organ transplantation-antilymphocyte serum and globulin.

1969: Roger H. Unger — Metabolism of fats and carbohydrates with relation to diabetic therapy.

1970: Andrew V. Schally — Physiology and biochemistry of hypothalamic neurohormones.

1971: Marcus A. Rothschild — Synthesis of serum albumin.

The Survey of Medical Research in the Veterans Administration was conducted by the Division of Medical Sciences, National Research Council, under a federal contract with The National Academy of Sciences. Chester S. Keefer chaired a distinguished committee and Robert I. McClaughry served as Director of Studies. Its report (July 5, 1960) covers in detail the origin, organization and operation of this vast program. In submitting the report of the Survey to Sumner G. Whittier, Administrator of Veterans Affairs, R. Keith Cannan wrote:

> Two considerations are emphasized. The first is that the fostering of research—the pursuit of new medical knowledge and understanding— is inextricably woven, historically and intellectually, into the administration of the best possible medical care. The second is the inescapable fact that research is a highly individual enterprise. The wind of ideas bloweth where it listeth. It can be encouraged, it can be coordinated. It cannot be directed by remote control.

The Survey report is a remarkable document. The recommendation "that the legislative and executive arms of the federal government explicitly accept the principle that the Veterans Administration is obligated not only to provide optimum medical care to the veteran, but also, to the extent of its professional and physical resources, to contribute to the advancement of medical knowledge through research and to the dissemination of medical knowledge through education for the benefit of the nation as a "whole," essentially states the position of the Department of Medicine and Surgery of the Veterans Administration. Obviously no pains were spared to obtain accurate, objective evidence. Inquiries at sources, within and without the agency, served to limit bias. The gross deficiencies in the physical and financial support were freely exposed. Its recommendations were both perceptive and constructive. The quality of the research product of the Veterans Administration had earned the respect of scientific peers. Avoiding invidious comparisons the scientific output of research workers in the Veterans Administration stood at least on a par with that of comparable Federal agencies. Any effort to compare their productivity with university researchers starts with a distinct difference in missions. The Department of Medicine and Surgery has the primary mission of patient care. Research and teaching, so essential to the maintenance of superior medicine in the care of patients, must perforce take a secondary position. By the same token, if merely by the enhancement of recruiting alert, active members to the Veterans Administration, the encouragement and the support of research have redounded to the advantage of the people of the civilized world as well as the American veteran. Building on the foundation of past organization and achievement, medical research in the Veterans Administration will go to even greater heights in the future.

Chapter VIII

HOW TO DO BASIC MEDICAL RESEARCH

IRVINE H. PAGE

Irvine Page was born in Indianapolis in 1901. He graduated from Cornell University in 1921 with the bachelor of arts degree in chemistry and later from the Cornell Medical College in 1926 with an M.D. After an internship at the Presbyterian and Bellevue Hospitals he became the Director of the Chemical Division of the Kaiser Wilhelm Institute in Munich from 1928 to 1931. In the years following he was named Director of the Lilly Laboratory for Clinical Research in Indianapolis (1937-1945) and then Director of the Research Division of the Cleveland Clinic Foundation (1945-1966).

Doctor Page in his most productive scientific career authored, co-authored and edited ten scientific books including Chemistry of the Brain, 1937; Experimental Renal Hypertension, 1948; Strokes, 1961; and Serotonin, 1968. He has also published scores of scientific papers and is presently Editor-in-Chief of the journal, Modern Medicine.

His notable research accomplishments are in his investigations on the mechanisms of arteriosclerosis, shock and hypertension. It is out of this work that he isolated from blood the vasopressor substance, serotonin, identified as 5-hydroxytryptamine. And his classic accomplishments in the understanding of angiotensin are well known.

For his contributions Dr. Page has accumulated no less than sixteen awards including the Albert Lasker Award (1958); the AMA's Sheen Award as "Outstanding Doctor of Medical Science in the United States" (1968); the "Heart of the Year" Award (American Heart Association, 1969); and the Stouffer Prize,

(1970). He has received in addition seven honorary doctoral degrees from universities world wide.

Dr. Page has been president of the American Society for the Study of Arteriosclerosis, the American Heart Association, the American College of Clinical Pharmacology and Chemotherapy and is a Founding Member of the Institute of Medicine in the National Academy of Sciences.

THERE IS NO SINGLE *best* way to do basic research, thank Heaven! But before I tell you how I did it, let me tell you briefly about my etiology, or as I wrote some years ago, "How I Got That Way."

Fifty years ago research was an odd-ball pursuit and there was little money for it. My father-in-law, semi-facetiously said to me, "When are you going to stop doing research and make an honest living practicing medicine?" It was an era in which research was mostly under strong, often brilliant, authoritarian leadership. Research was an elitist activity only because there were so few of us and under the circumstances why should there have been more of us? Mediocrity had a hard time. Technicians and apparatus were scarce, hence were shared. Only "the chief" had a secretary and mostly you paid your own way to meetings. The government neither supported research, meetings nor committees!

Yet in retrospect, the era was amazingly productive of great basic research. My experience has obviously shaped my present views which generally are considered too authoritarian and inconsistent with the "thrusts," "delivery" and "goals," words so dear to the hearts of laymen and government employees. According to current standards, the age was too critical, too financially prudent, too antidemocratic and too rigid. It insisted on everyone's participation in the *work* of research, instead of emphasis on the promotion of one's political future. It is easy to see why I am skeptical of the broad use of systems analysis in basic research, of planning by committees, of Conquest of Cancer Crusades, of vague endeavors at international cooperation in research and of the complete faith that money is the key to most great discoveries. Do you suppose that when Roentgen inadvertently saw the shadow of the bones of his hand, he thought he had a cure for cancer? In short, at heart I am a "butterfly net" type of researcher who only systematizes after a natural phenomenon has been surely identified, impelled by medical sympathies to bend my energies, and others that I can persuade, to bring research to the aid of patients. What I have to say reflects fully my own biases. But among great research workers curiosity is usually associated with a vivid imagination which precedes discovery. This is succeeded by intuitively and perceptively chosen experiments needed for proof.

THE FORMAT

My ideas about the type of organization in which research is done is not critical but that the environment it creates is. The only general cant is that all research be done the same way or with the same goals. Diversity of living is the essence of life and as well of research. Scientific opportunism of the "band wagon" type, led by the chemotactic action of money, power and committees, is anathema. Mobility, heterogeneity, freedom, intuition, animosity, individuality are all terms of high significance in research. We are slowly losing these qualities in the name of systematization, administrative order and concentration on goals. Bureaucratic government stands ready and eager to further homogeneity. Quantity can never substitute for quality. Sad to relate, there are but few with sufficient creative talent to exert any important effect on the development of science.

One other cant is the notion that *all* medical research be done in medical schools. Having worked in one of the great Kaiser Wilhelm Institutes in Germany for three years, the Rockefeller Institute for Medical Research for seven years, the Indianapolis City Hospital for seven years and the Cleveland Clinic for some twenty-seven years, I believe these alternatives are quite as acceptable as teaching institutions. Sir Hans Krebs recently noted that in Great Britain over the past twenty years the lead in scientific excellence has passed from the universities to research institutes where teaching and administration were light.

THE RESEARCH ENVIRONMENT

It seems to me that most of the great advances have been accomplished by individuals, or limited numbers of gifted scientists, male and female, working in wholly dedicated teams. Certain kinds of research require especially large groups but the smaller, usually the better. There is no such thing as the head of the research project being a head *in absentia*. If travel and committee meetings are more important than laboratory work, he should become a roving ambassador. This is why I have long believed that much of policy and committee work should be done by older men who have already had their big chance at research. But I do not believe that retirement from laboratory work should be mandatory; only from administration and active leadership. There are many examples of the most creative age as being a scientist's so-called "declining years." I like to think of "declining" as declining invitations.

In many commercial laboratories, "the director" may be the administrator and in no sense involved in the direction of the research. This is not good nomenclature and already has blemished the name; whatever the head of the team is called, he should make certain that everyone on the team receive full credit for his contribution despite the impatience of the scientific community as shown in many journals where everyone other than the first author is made to join that most prolific and anonymous author named et al. Research work is just as entitled to identification with its creator as an artist who paints a picture.

To be a true scientific *leader* is a great responsibility. He must be able to communicate a fire and enthusiasm for discovery, the technical understanding, the associative mind that puts new ideas in usable juxtaposition and who earns the respect and loyalty of those with whom he works.

I have spent nearly fifty years in active research under many important "chiefs." I have nothing but respect, gratitude and affection for all of them beginning with Dr. G. H. A. Clowes at the Marine Biological Laboratory in Woods Hole, to Geheimrat Richard Willstätter in Munich, Germany, to Dr. Donald Van

Slyke at the Rockefeller Institute in New York. They all participated in the work I did at the bench, they helped my position
by taking some of the responsibility for the published reports,
they provided richly rewarding discussion and never interfered
except to keep me on the track. This is quite different from the
type of research that now threatens to preempt public funds.
Special committees "identify" the "critical" problems, organize
and direct their execution, and pay for them. This is much like
the Russian system of "research for the people." Aside from the
productivity of the system itself for which I have grave misgivings, the cost in time and money is staggering.

The one goal of research should be *discovery* and its proper
documentation. Secondary are such things as gaining respect from
one's peers, maintenance of the integrity of the community of
scientists and the great body of knowledge entrusted to them to
add to and purify by telling the whole truth. If only because
research is a so very human endeavor, full credit must be given
to those to whom it is due. Abuses should be dealt with openly
and courageously lest they proliferate. Competition should be
kept vigorous, collaborative and friendly.

The freedom to choose one's own subject and how to study
it is a complex problem when a team is involved. Many university
departments allow complete freedom, often with less than the
highest standards of performance. Others are much less per-
missive. Where a team of scientists is concerned, then a broad
subject usually is selected and for its study the team built around
its needs. The more diverse the team the better!

I believe that even when a particular subject is chosen, that
very wide latitude especially in regard to the different skills involved should be given, so long as the *general* goal is the same.
In my own experience, cardiovascular research was the major
concern, but the team consisted of clinicians, pharmacologists,
physiologists, surgeons, bioengineers, physical and organic chemists and morphologists. Cooperation was no problem because it
was always in one's own interest to cooperate for everyone to
make progress.

As a generality, I believe every man should be given a period of about twenty years of almost untrammeled research before he is called upon to participate in administration and outside activities. If he has what it takes, he will be well launched on a scientific career of excellence and will need no further guidance. Others do better when they always stay well within the framework of an ongoing tightly knit team.

One of the most serious dangers to creative research is to work in a laboratory loaded with expensive, complicated equipment. The equipment too often dictates the approach to the problem. Government grants greatly augment this tendency along with the rigidity often imposed by overplanning. When discovery no longer has a thrill and if you only find out about it when told days or weeks later, either you are not doing your share or have become too old to care.

I am also much opposed to the overuse of technicians. I doubt that a beginner in research should have even one until he is thoroughly familiar with the methods to be employed. Only when work becomes routine is a technician desirable. Too much time is often taken up simply finding something for the technician to do.

The contemporary idea that the representatives of the public should participate in the policy decisions of research I accept with great reserve. There are many exceptionally able laymen who can effectively participate. But when *representatives* are chosen by groups such as labor, consumer, business, etc., with little regard for competence in either the problems themselves or their administration, then the system is likely to be disastrous. Good research depends far more on interpersonal valuation of other scientists who are themselves successful researchers.

While I believe basic research should be put to use whenever a use can be found, I have little sympathy for slogans such as "Science for the People," or the demand that science be "made relevant." I know of no science which ultimately will prove irrelevant. True, there are priorities that *seem* more relevant at the moment and the genial scientist often knows them. But there are other times when such guesses are wholly misleading. For example, it will not be easy for a supercommittee to decide for the researchers of the Cancer Crusade what avenues to explore to arrive at cures for cancers. The wrong selection of priorities could easily retard progress.

THE POWER OF THE PRESS AND GOVERNMENT

I include the problem of the power of the press and of government because in my lifetime they have grown so incredibly important.

The press no longer simply reports news but it makes it, along with the reputation of many scientists and physicians. From such reputations often comes the power to extract large amounts of taxpayers' money from the government which, in turn, may be reflected in the kind of research and environment which will be created.

I believe in cooperating with the press but not in seeking them out. But the cooperation must go both ways. The press should not be left in doubt about your true thoughts. I have little patience with the researcher who raises false hope and exaggerates, fails to mention others in the field and panders to the power elite. If that is the price of becoming "a celebrity," I prefer others to pay it.

The example provided by the first transplantation of a human heart should give us all pause for thought. Never before has the public been treated to such a Roman circus. Dr. Christiaan Barnard was hailed as having made the "breakthrough" of the century; performed a "surgical miracle." Surely no one would have quarreled with performing a few such operations to show their technical feasibility and highlight tissue rejection problems. A dignified, conservative and factual report could have been made to the medical community and a quiet announcement to the press. Certainly there would have been a period of excitement but it would have soon cooled had all involved not kept it at white heat. False hopes were raised, reputations were made and lost, the objectivity of research was seriously degraded, the human and monetary cost were prodigious. After four years tempers are beginning to cool and cardiac transplantation is coming into the perspective that it should have had at far less cost within about a year. Most of those involved have now become highly defensive, including the press. The critics who initially were so vigorously denounced for being conservative and skeptical have now been labeled obstructionists to scientific progress.

Government too has become an important factor in the conduct of research by its power to give money and by setting priorities. These are critical areas which need constant and courageous surveillance. Creeping federalization of science is becoming one of science's greatest threats. The most recent and blatant example is the Conquest to Cure Cancer, which promises a new era in science methodology but an era which is as likely to be bad as good.

It is often highly impolitic to criticize a colleague or powerful political or business figure in public. In its crudest form this is illustrated by the Lysenko affair and the more recent misuse of psychiatry as punishment for dissent. But even in the United States the beginnings of this ugly crime against Truth were shown by the black list discovered to exist in the Department of Health, Education & Welfare, or more subtly by the snubbing of dissidents by the power elite of Washington. But if this responsibility for open and honest discussion is not taken seriously by those who are in a position to make proper value judgments, then we should not be surprised if we do not command the respect we think is our due. In the past two decades too often the scientific community was publicly silent in the face of obvious dishonesty or grossly exaggerated claims. The resultant Roman circus and demeaning of research hurt us all. A laboratory, team, or department should stand for something its peers esteem.

The current trend of active government participation in the planning of basic research with high political visibility such as the attempt to develop an artificial heart which by 1970 would have been commonly implanted is likely to be disastrous if only because of its overpromise. The extension of the idea of government planning with its evident confusion of basic and technological research to other areas of biomedical research is frightening.

I hope those so deeply imbued with the need for *planned* basic research will examine closely the results of both planning of even applied research to large new cities as in Sweden and Brazil, or the effects of current economic planning. This does not say that planning has *no* place but rather that its place should be restricted and prevented from interfering with research in which far fewer variables are understood. It is interesting to note here that in the very critical pharmaceutical industry there is only one center in this country supported solely for *fundamental* research in biology—the Roche Institute of Molecular Biology. Even with a budget as large as $4.5 million, it sets its own course! With all the talk about support of basic research by industry, how little of it is not market-oriented. The Institute's long range objective is to yield benefits to humanity in terms of scientific progress. On such a horse I would put my money.

As Ronald Hare described the steps that led to the discovery of penicillin by Fleming, the one certain thing that would have prevented it would have been planning and "adequate" financing. Chance and the trained, genial observer are still paramount to great research.

Chapter IX

MAN'S NONPHYSICAL NATURE

J. B. Rhine

During the years of his youth, J. B. Rhine tacitly assumed a ministerial career to which he had made an early commitment. But as college drew near Rhine's interest in theology began to wane as he found himself drawn to the sciences. In the middle of his sophomore year at the College of Wooster he gave up his preministerial program of study and planned an escape into nature, a life in the woods, and finally decided to devote himself to forestry. Accordingly, in 1917 he left Wooster for duty in the Marine Corps and made plans to attend the Michigan School of Forestry upon his discharge from service.

In 1920 Dr. Rhine married Louisa Ella Weckesser and together they went to the University of Chicago to get the basic biology for a career in forestry. They were greatly stimulated by the challenging scientific debates which were prevalent at the time — issues such as Lamarkian inheritance and the mechanist theory of life.

While working for their degrees in plant physiology, the Rhines began exploring psychical research. They spent a year at the Boyce Thompson Institute at Yonkers doing botomical research and taught for two years at West Virginia University before making up their minds to try out psychical research as a possible field for science. After a year at Harvard in preparation and one at Duke with Professor William McDougall, they accepted invitations to stay on at the latter to work in psychical research.

The combination of McDougall, Duke, and the challenge of the new field were ideal. There, they found opportunity, tolerance and encouragement, sharing in the stimulating culture of a university community. There, they were generously sustained by the unique institution of American philanthropy which has created the university itself and which through the years, continues to support their research efforts.

THE AIM

THIS IS A CONDENSED account of a search for a better understanding of the nature of man, a quest that has held my interest for over a half century. The central problem that has served as a thread in the development of this scientific inquiry and that of my wife, Louisa E. Rhine, is concerned with the incomparable mystery of man's uniqueness. We have been asking what it is that truly distinguishes him from the other known orders of nature—first of all, the physical order.

This may appear a pretentious undertaking as we formulated it at the graduate student stage. But, even before the sobering experience of fifty years of effort, we had no anticipation of either an easy or an early conquest in the attempt. Our expectations were even modest enough to allow us now some feeling of advance as we look back at the beginning.

THE BEGINNING

As a starting point for this account, I chose the sending of two letters of inquiry that I wrote in 1922 from the Botanical Laboratory of the University of Chicago, where my wife and I were working for advanced degrees in plant physiology. The letters were addressed to two well-known psychologists, Dr. Joseph Jastrow at Wisconsin and Dr. William McDougall, F.R.S., at Harvard, and in both I inquired about the status of the claims and findings of psychical research. We knew that Jastrow had been critical of this subject, but that McDougall had been actively interested.

Both men replied promptly, each one in line with his already known attitude; that is, one was discouraging and the other encouraging. McDougall also answered a question about the Hodgson Fund for Psychical Research at Harvard, saying it was currently being used to aid Dr. Gardner Murphy in his studies on that subject. We decided to go on toward our degrees but to pursue our interest in the subject of psychical research by reading all that McDougall had written on the subject, while keeping an eye on Jastrow's criticism as well. Mc-

Dougall's *Body and Mind* proved to be a decisive influence in keeping us on the trail of psychical research. It was exhilarating to discover that this great man himself had long been making the kind of research that seemed to us most worthwhile.

Our restlessness had not been generated by lack of appreciation of plant physiology. The attempts in that branch of science, then relatively new, to bring the physical sciences to the study and understanding of life processes in plants was fascinating. There were many attractive mysteries emerging from these studies that promised to reveal glimpses of the nature of living functions. As chemistry students, too, we marveled at the "magic" of newly discovered enzymes with which our studies came partly to deal, and were fascinated at how much better chemists the humblest plants were than the best experts in the universities. But there were some strange problems hammering even more demandingly on the windows of our curiosity: the tantalizing unknowns of the human mind grouped under psychical research. They raised the question whether man might not have hidden aspects in his makeup that would, if known, profoundly alter the picture of him science had so far painted.

Why did we not then turn forthwith to psychology? We had been exposed to undergraduate psychology before we entered biology, but nothing of what interested us now in psychical research had ever been mentioned. This field of psychical research was indeed a weird and wild collection of claims, almost entirely incredible; we were doubtful about them and could easily understand Jastrow's attitude. Yet, we argued that, if McDougall's view was correct *to any degree*, we could not afford to miss it by dropping our interest at this point.

Moreover, there were names of other scientific men associated with these psychic claims. Surprisingly, many of them at that period were physicists: Sir Oliver Lodge, Sir William Crookes, Lord Rayleigh, Sir William Barrett, and Sir Joseph J. Thomson; only a few were in psychology (such as McDougall and William James), and there was but one eminent physiologist, whose name, Charles Richet, reassured us. Whatever their specialities, however, these distinguished "witnesses" helped us to decide to find out, without hastily burning our bridges, on what basis they had been led to look into the problems of psychical research.

THE CIRCUMSTANCES

The times, too, had much to do with our decision. The long, drawn-out warfare between religion and science was still at a high pitch in this country. Verbal battles between fundamentalist theologians and some of the more popular names in science of that day were getting public attention. Watsonian behaviorism, which had recently exploded in psychology, had a very considerable impact on religion. The "monkey trial" was going on in Tennessee, and even on the University of Chicago campus, the Baptist theologian Shailer Matthews had lined up a series of speakers on science and religion (in alternation) in an attempt to bridge the widening gap between these disciplines. My wife and I sat through them all, realizing increasingly that the sciences really had the heavy artillery on their side and that for the student mind, neither theology nor philosophy could save religion in that sort of contest.

On the other hand, it was plain enough too that not one of the sciences was really touching the central issue—whether, as Matthews put it, there was evidence of "personal forces in the universe." All that scientists had to offer on their part were physical forces. They knew no other principles. Psychology, such as it was then at the University of Chicago, was not even represented in the series. Rather, as seemed obvious to us, quite another branch of inquiry was called for if man's peculiar nature was to be understood scientifically. That branch was psychical research. If there was anything in the least scientifically sound about its claims, this type of study was needed; at the very minimum it offered a way to bring the materialistic theory of man to an objective test.

But science, too, like formal religion, had lost much of its authority for us, especially because we saw that our biology teachers were less than objective about challenges to mechanism and the psychologists too overreactive to anything suggesting dualism. But thanks to both professions, we had almost learned to rely on objective experimental methods for answers to such provocative questions. So the fact that both these (as all the other) professions wanted nothing to do with psychical research did not completely deter us; we think now we were fortunate in having acquired both a respect for scientific method and, as a consequence of our uprooted theology, an unsatisfied curiosity as to what man's nature really was.

Not that ours was an original thought; it was pretty much the burden of some of the works we had been reading, particularly those by Frederick W. H. Myers, Sir Oliver Lodge, and William James. The book by McDougall, already mentioned, most explicitly raised the question of man's nature with respect to the physical world and even pointed the way to a search for the answer.

Why it was that we two were so much interested in these psychical research claims as to take this step can be explained briefly. In both cases, there were personal circumstances that oriented us rather positively toward religion until the college years introduced us to the sciences. But from there on, we came to regard supernaturalism as logically unacceptable; and although I had enrolled as a preministerial student, I decided to drop out when I finally realized that psychology gave no support to the assumption of volitional freedom. It was, of course, supposed that morality depended on free will and it seemed to me that without it, the ministry would be futile.

Actually, neither of the two systems of authority, the religions or the sciences, promised an acceptable solution to the problem we faced in 1922. But even with all its dubious connections, psychical research seemed to offer at least a possible *direction* in inquiry. At our age and stage we were willing to take the risk of making at least an evaluative inquiry while still adhering faithfully to the standards of objective science to which our training and judgment had already committed us. We accepted, too, the rule that the more improbable an hypothesis, the stronger the evidence required to make it acceptable.

PSYCHICAL RESEARCH THEN

What was the state of psychical research in 1922? The Society of Psychical Research in England had, in its forty years of existence, assembled many volumes of scholarly studies, principally reports on studies of the communications of mediums. It had been the belief of the spiritualists that a medium (usually in a state of trance) was capable of communicating between an assumed spirit world and that of the living. Moreover, the evidence of such communication was in itself considered to be a kind of demonstration of the existence of discarnate spirits of the deceased, and consequently proof of postmortem survival. This effort at proof was a step that none of the major religions of mankind had ever taken; it was an aim at producing verifiable, repeatable demonstrations of one of religion's major doctrines.

For my wife and me, educated to some extent in the mechanistic psychology and biology of the day, this alleged evidence would at the same time offer a forthright disproof of the view of living man which currently prevailed in the sciences of life and mind. The materialistic theory would soon be dead if these supposed spirit communications could be proved to be what was claimed for them. While still strongly reserved about such a fantastic claim, we could at least appreciate the fact that people like McDougall had the forthrightness to be objective about it and the courage to help to bring it to scientific test.

Here, of course, is where the warnings against psychical research may have had a certain restraining value (although we were certainly not ignorant of the risks). Our growing skepticism about the authority of scientists had been reinforced considerably by the controversies of the times. McDougall and John B. Watson were drawing swords in open debate over behaviorism. We heard Ivan Pavlov, the Russian physiologist, famous for his conditional reflex research, lecture at Chicago on the inheritance of acquired characteristics as proved by his own experiments with mice, but soon thereafter, he discovered he had to withdraw his conclusions. Even in physical research, scientists were bitterly controverting each other over a Boston medium,

Margery, who was charged with fraud. At that stage, we were more strongly repelled by the cantradictory claims than attracted by the grain of truth that just might possibly be found.

In the meantime, we had obtained Ph.D. degrees at the University of Chicago, some experience in scientific research and teaching (in plant physiology at West Virginia University), and some years of study of the literature of psychical research, including a year shared between Harvard and Dr. W. F. Prince at the Boston Society for Psychic Research. Then, in 1927, an offer was received that allowed us to work for a short time with Professor McDougall, who in the autumn of that year went to Duke University to establish a department of psychology. We had arranged to study, under his supervision, a collection of stenographic records of messages obtained from a number of mediums. This material had been collected by a Detroit educator, John F. Thomas, under conditions of special precautions, based on the use of token objects sent with the stenographer instead of with the actual presence of the "sitter" (the person seeking communication).

Accordingly, we agreed to spend a semester at Duke to evaluate these records but also to appraise as far as possible, the scientific possibilities of the field of psychical research as a whole. The trial semester grew into a year and the year into a succession. I was given a staff position first in philosophy and psychology combined and later one with full time in psychology, with liberty to pursue psychical research.

BUT DO MEDIUMS REALLY MEDIATE?

The findings of our analyses indicated, we thought, that the information given by the mediums could hardly have been obtained sensorially. Something beyond their known abilities seemed definitely to have been indicated; however, there was no sufficient basis for attributing the source to the discarnate individuals. The medium could (with the special powers which her practice implied she possessed) have got all her information from the very same sources we tapped in checking for accuracy. We therefore decided, and McDougall concurred, that no conclusion of proof could be reached on this type of material because the alternative explanation could not be eliminated.

This judgment was later confirmed in the firsthand studies of a medium (Eileen J. Garrett) that were conducted in the Duke Psychology Department. In these laboratory experiments, the controls were adequate to avoid leakage of information from the sitter to the medium and to insure a highly objective estimation of success. Thus, the experiment served the first requirement, that of testing the medium's capacity for what was then called "supernormal knowledge" (and which came to be called extrasensory perception). But it still left us no way to answer the second question, that of whether the medium actually was in contact with the discarnate sources in question.

Here the story definitely turned a page as this finding regarding mediumship was fully appreciated, and the judgment was reached that the method of mediumship was logically not adequate to the problem of demonstrating communication with a possible spirit world. In the course of time, enough others besides Professor McDougall and ourselves reached a similar decision that there seems to have been no seriously large division over the question.

During those years, the emphasis on mediumship in the societies for psychical research gave way preponderantly to experiments on extrasensory perception (ESP) which we had already begun to investigate side by side with the mediumistic studies. When, in the early 1930's, parapsychology was, with Professor McDougall's sponsorship, introduced to the psychology laboratory, we were able to carry out experiments in telepathy and clairvoyance and to develop methods of improved control to make these tests as carefully controlled as the psychology laboratory at that stage could contrive.

Such spontaneous extrasensory experiences as telepathy and clairvoyance had been reported by many persons who were not mediums, and the collections of reports of such occurrences made up a substantial part of the literature of psychical research. There had even been some tests of these abilities conducted earlier. Professor Charles Richet, among others, had given card-guessing tests for clairvoyance to schoolchildren and hypnotized patients in the 1880's. G. H. Estabrooks had tested fellow students at Harvard in the 1920's for what was called telepathy. By following these earlier attempts, improving somewhat on the card-guessing methods already used, and devising a new set of test cards, my colleagues and I at Duke made some advances in the card-test procedure; these techniques were already in use especially in clairvoyance testing, when the opportunity came in 1934 to test Mrs. Garrett's mediumship.

Mrs. Garrett demonstrated significant ability in the standard tests for clairvoyance and what was called "telepathy" (better called general ESP or GESP). She also showed about the same order of success whether she was tested in the normal state or in trance. Precise comparisons cannot be made as to the amount of knowledge given by Mrs. Garrett in the card-guessing tests with that given in her "messages," although she succeeded in both.

FROM MEDIUMSHIP TO ESP

By this time, our thinking had advanced considerably with regard to the interpretation of the expanding ESP results. It was much easier to administer and control tests of clairvoyance than those for telepathy. For instance, only one test subject was needed, and the experimenter himself could administer the card-guessing test and do so under conditions that excluded all sensory contact with the cards. Thus, they could be concealed in various ways, with opaque envelopes or screens, or with the use of other rooms or buildings.

The monograph *Extrasensory Perception*, published in 1934, contained a series completed just before going to press, in which 300 trials in card-guessing (for clairvoyance) were carried out with the subject (HP) in one building and the experimenter (a graduate assistant, J. G. Pratt) with the cards at a distance of 100 yards, in another. The level of success obtained was highly significant, about 40 percent, while the chance average expected was only 20 percent. The conditions ruled out all conceivable sensory alternatives to the ESP hypothesis known at the time. Such precautions had not been taken earlier in either psychology or psychical research, and still further safeguards were planned as they became justifiable. At this stage, in the first report of six years of exploration, it seemed safe to conclude that the occurrence of clairvoyance had been demonstrated; and by the time the book was bound, the case was confirmed by HP several times over.

The experiments with telepathy, however, were a different story, and a much less conclusive one. This was because the problem is a much more complex one. Telepathy is the direct mind-to-mind transfer of thought without sensory mediation, but it was discovered that all the earlier telepathy testing had been conducted with a sending agent *looking at an object*, while the receiver attempted to identify the sender's thought of it. Since this condition did not exclude clairvoyance, the results could not be conclusive of telepathy.

When we conducted tests *without* the sender having an object on which to concentrate (e.g., using a pack of coded cards instead), the scoring rate obtained was approximately equal to that made by the same subject in clairvoyance tests. I then began to suspect that only one basic ability was involved and initiated use of the term "extrasensory perception" as an inclusive term. Even so, as will be explained later, the findings on the question of telepathy were not sufficiently conclusive for that specific type, but at least they were evidence of ESP of one type or another.

ESP AND SPACE-TIME

What principle of nature could account for this card-guessing exchange, even at short distances? Once we were fairly satisfied it was genuine ESP the next question was: If it is real, does it not have to be physical? What other type of causal principle does science have? And, if physical, will it not have to be affected by space and time? Yet, as we already knew, the results of the clairvoyance tests with a distance of 100 yards (and later at still greater distances) appeared to rule out the expected distance effect. Certainly, the inverse square law was never in any case applicable. As far as we could tell, the test results showed no true relation to the distances whatever, just as the distances involved in spontaneous ESP experiences had seemed to make no observable difference (e.g., in frequency of cases). This naturally made it even more exciting then to try the effect of time discrepancy on ESP; that is, to test subjects for precognition. If there is no effect of distance, why not expect a similar independence of time? We knew, of course, that many people had reported spontaneous ESP awareness of future events, experienced in dreams and intuitions.

Fortunately, it was comparatively easy to modify the clairvoyance method for use in precognition testing simply by having the subject try to predict what the order of the target cards *would be* after the pack was shuffled. This card-guessing test for precognition was first made in December 1933, and again with subject HP; again, too, the test gave significant results. The first method of shuffling was by hand, with a number of variations subsequently applied. All the various hand-shuffling methods gave similar success; this aspect made no difference. The aim was to see first whether the subject could do well enough to justify an advance in method. After that, a program was set up to determine whether the method was really adequate for the randomizing of the order of the cards. (This development is reviewed in great detail in my wife's book, *ESP in Life and Lab,* in 1969).

For a long time, however, this shuffling was not considered good enough for a firm conclusion on precognition. For that and other reasons, we decided to hold the precognition findings for later publication. These new results themselves raised fresh questions that could not be immediately answered; for example, the question of whether the hand shuffling of the cards (by the experimenter) provided adequate randomization. In fact, as the experiments continued, it was found that neither the hand shuffling nor even shuffling by machine was entirely adequate to the test. Approximately five years passed before the first report on precognition appeared, and even long after that, there were further advances in the method of target selection.

It was, however, a new finding (i.e., psychokinesis) from our own laboratory that most complicated the interpretation of the precognition data. As a result, we had to begin the precognition project over again several times. Yet, in spite of these frustrations, it was a rewarding experience to realize that we were engaged with so significant an issue as the mental transcendence of the physical order of time. Even in this retrospect of forty years, it is hard to pass over this point without a pause for reflection on its meaning.

The survival hypothesis had been important (at least for the two of us) primarily for its implication of the transcendent nature of the *living* man, important though other aspects were. But the method of mediumship turned out to be incomplete (because the very powers needed for contact with possible discarnate minds could reasonably be assumed to give access to all the sources required for the verification of the messages). At this same point, however, the evidence was coming in strongly to show that ESP was not limited by space-time; various kinds of barriers (like walls and mountains) seemed to make no difference; cards could be identified even when piled up in a box or when reshuffled at some future time. If no physical property limits this exchange, it has in principle the same transcendent quality as the survival hypothesis itself implies.

Thus, as one road (that of mediumship) was closed, at least for the present, another (the trail of the ESP research) was opened. The new evidence from the card tests suggested a non-physical capacity in man that seemed to indicate, in a less spectacular but more dependable way, a concept of man something like that which had been expected of the survival doctrine—namely, that living man had a way of communicating that was not only extrasensory, but extraphysical too. This discovery seemed a great challenge to further research and, of course, we already had the methods necessary for a start.

It was therefore decided as early as 1935 to turn major attention to the study of ESP and related abilities and their bearing on the nature of man. This meant discontinuing for the time being research on survival. We decided to shelve it until, if ever, a more clean-cut approach could be made. As it was, no decision either way seemed to us possible then, and none has occurred to us since.

A DECADE OF INTERRUPTIONS

This is not a history of parapsychology or else there would be space given here to two major interruptions that occurred to the ESP research at Duke during the period from 1935 to 1945. These disturbances were the controversy over ESP, and World War II; the one took most of our time, the other took most of our workers, and both seriously retarded our progress. But, since the research program did struggle along through the difficult decade and regained strength after the mid-forties, largely through the support of other psi workers elsewhere in this country and Western Europe, I will use the space those intrusions would take to give instead more of an account of the positive developments themselves. I think it fair to say that if the destructive criticism of this period had even been halfway justified, the psi research movement could not have survived; but, since it has, and in a moderate degree has even thrived in spite of disruptions, that phase can safely be ignored for the present.

Scientific readers will realize that new lines of discovery advance only as other research workers have succeeded in verifying the new findings. This happened to the ESP work at Duke with a few investigators almost from the first, and later with increased numbers; the continuance of the new field was thereby assured and by 1937, it became necessary to found the *Journal of Parapsychology*. Some reflections on this period, especially as they relate to general appraisals, will come at the end of the chapter. The main story picks up again here, right after the first encouraging results of the tests with precognition.

PSYCHOKINESIS

The precognition research was still in its infancy when it received a lively competitor. This was the initial demonstration of psychokinesis (PK), or mind over matter, that began in January of 1934 and only a month after the first precognition tests.

PK is a sort of complementary link with the ESP effect, the parapsychical pair being closely analogous to the sensorimotor combination; thus, the two "psychic powers" together became the entire *extra*sensorimotor interaction of the individual with his environment.

At that time, all this comparison was much more vague in our minds than it is today. Yet we knew from the background of psychical research that the range of spontaneous psychic happenings included not only the ESP type of experience, but also unexplained physical happenings—the clocks that unaccountably stopped at the time of a death, the pictures that fell when someone closely connected with them died; and many other such phenomena. The spiritualist seances, too, had produced physical happenings attributed to spirit agency, and the term "telekinesis" had been introduced to identify these.

Until 1934, nothing had occurred to us that would bring the claim of mind over matter to the type of laboratory test that the card-guessing methods had done for the three subtypes of ESP. In January of that year, however, an incident took place that provided me with an idea.

A young gambler visited me to discuss our ESP experiments, in which he had an interest. In the lively conversation that followed, he asserted his belief that a mind-over-matter principle was often involved in dice-throwing games; he was immediately invited to demonstrate his idea by throwing dice on the floor in a corner of my office. In a matter of minutes, the ESP subject HP was brought in to compete, and both men were successful enough in "beating chance" to help me to decide to follow up. During the years that followed, there was the necessary refinement of methods to exclude one by one all possible counterhypotheses to that of PK and, equally important, to develop a procedure that could, after publication, be taken over by other interested experimenters for possible confirmation.

The dice-throwing tests went steadily and rather successfully on from that date, but it was not until 1943, nearly ten years after the beginning of the PK tests, that the time seemed right for the first publication of the PK work in the *Journal of Parapsy-*

chology. This delay was in great part due to the ESP controversy, but it was also caused partly by the war and by the difficulty of surrounding the PK tests with as firm safeguards as had been used with clairvoyance and precognition. The dice tests could be controlled well enough with regard to possible imperfections in the dice or the use of skill in throwing them. A more sensitive point lay in the recording methods. Advances had been made with the use of double observation and eventually with photographic recordings, but the perfect control (as good as that in a well-designed precognition experiment) was not easy to achieve in PK.

Then, in 1943, came the analyses of the quarter-distribution (QD) of the scatter of hits on the record page in PK tests. These were found when we analyzed old records preserved over the period before publication began. They were reported in the *Journal of Parapsychology* in 1944 and 1945 (and reviewed in my wife's book, *Mind Over Matter,* in 1970). To put it briefly, the records of the entire twenty-four series of earlier PK experiments were examined and of these, eighteen were found to have record sheets on which the page could be divided into equal quarters by drawing median vertical and horizontal lines. Because ESP record sheets had often shown declines of scoring rate across the page to the right and down the page, examination of the PK records was begun for comparison. Most of the eighteen eligible experiments showed that the upper left (first) quarter had by far the most successes and the lower right (fourth) the fewest on the page. When the entire eighteen were compounded by suitable mathematical methods, this diagonal decline (from first to fourth quarter) of the number of hits showed a difference of "astronomical" significance. Not only that, but there were other equally striking evidences of the consistency of the decline when there were smaller sections of the page that could be systematically reexamined.

Quite evidently, something had gone on in these tests that neither the experimenter was looking for nor the subject aware of. It was obvious that none of the common experimental counter-hypotheses could be suspected to have had any bearing on these hitherto unnoticed declines. These had to be due to some consistent way in which the subjects had reacted to the place on the record page on which the data were being recorded as the testing went on. It was, in fact, a position effect on the process of PK itself, confirmed over and over again by different subjects in different experiments with a wide range of methods and test conditions. It was evidence of lawfulness of such a quality that an invitation was publicly extended for a reexamination by a qualified committee. It was not accepted, but the laboratory had an independent recheck made on the entire QD analysis and published the results.

DISTINCTION OF TYPES

The establishment of the occurrence of PK was, in my judgment, best accomplished by these diagonal declines in the quarter distribution of the page. But years before that occurred, PK got into the precognition testing as a counterhypothesis that required changes in procedure for such testing. One investigator had already reported an experiment in precognition with the use of dice, but abandoned the method when he learned through correspondence about the PK tests. In the Duke Laboratory, the precognition tests had already progressed to the use of mechanical shufflers when it was discovered that subjects could, to a better than chance degree, hand shufle the cards in one pack to match the order in another one; this technique was called the "psychic shufflle." Then, when the mechanical shufflers were introduced in precognition work, even with completely mechanized operation, it was found that test subjects could significantly influence the fall of the cards in the machine. In fact, it turned out to be surprisingly difficult to design precognition tests in which PK could confidently be ruled out; and an occasional individual can still be found today who will argue that the present elaborate techniques of randomization are not sufficiently conclusive.

But the tables were turned then and precognition became a counterhypothesis for the explanation of PK test results. Eventually, this forced some changes in the PK test designing too. It was argued that precognition might enable the PK test subject to foresee the way the dice would fall, and thus find out which face was most favored in a given series. If, then, the subject was allowed to select the target face for each run of trials, such precognition (if it occurred) could be a factor. This led to added safeguards and more regulation of the test procedures; the choice of target face by the subject was eliminated. But probably the QD evidence of PK just mentioned is the best bulwark against even this counterhypothesis of recognition in PK test results.

Similar debates went on during the mid-forties particularly with colleagues in England who were concerned over the question of whether the test design for clairvoyance properly excluded the occurrence of telepathy. It was argued that, because in the checkup the experimenter would see the symbols (which he could not see during the trials), the subject might well use precognitive telepathy (if there is such a capacity) in guessing ahead what the experimenter would see in the checkup. This called, then, for modification of the clairvoyance test procedure and some fresh experimentation in which there was no such regular order observed by anyone involved in the checkup.

Again the argument was reversed and turned against telepathy. The point was made that, even though in a pure telepathy test, the agent or sender used a code method and thus *did not have any objective record* of the real targets of which he was thinking at the time, nevertheless the decoded records of the later checkup would be available through *precognitive clairvoyance*. This led to extremely complicated pure telepathy tests, carried out first by Elizabeth McMahan at Duke and later by S. G. Soal in England, which were designed to get around this complication and rule out even precognitive clairvoyance, far-fetched as this may seem.

It seems best not to allow the rather momentous decision recording the establishment of telepathy to be conceded at this point. To prove the direct mind-to-mind exchange would require exclusion of the possibility of clairvoyance of any accompanying physical indices (e.g., vocal organ changes and brain activity) in the organism. This may at first look like a mere academic quibble; however, ESP test subjects have already been shown to be able to obtain information produced by a formula programmed into a computer and scored only in terms of total trials and hits; so we had better hold open the idea that the same ability might succeed in clairvoyantly "picking the brain" of the sender in the tests for telepathy. We may consider telepathy a likely but unproved possibility and keep the question open.

THE UNITY OF PSI

On the side of similarities between these types of parapsychical abilities the information was rather more impressive. The very grouping of them all under the heading of "psychical research" (or, as we began to call it in 1934, "parapsychology," after the German "parapsychologie") meant that they appeared to have something in common. But other common features emerged from the researches going on; first, there was the inability to explain psi phenomena in terms of the familiar natural processes of sensorimotor exchange on which all the other sciences depend. For both ESP and PK, there was no such basis of mediation, no evidence of organs of reception or response.

Then, too, the same difficulty of reproducing and controlling the effects applied to both types. This made experimentation difficult and even made spontaneous experiences rare. Again, if a person had one type of psychic ability and was adequately tested, it was usually found that he had them both. The test conditions affecting one type (e.g., producing declines) would apply to the other. Still other common features will be discussed in the sections that follow.

This brief summary of the common characteristics of the types will indicate why we came in the course of time to think of one general capacity as underlying all the types of psi abilities, much as the popular term "psychic ability" implied. Eventually, it appeared that one unitary parapsychical function underlies this group of phenomena, giving it at least the impression of functional unity. Robert H. Thouless and B. P. Wiesner suggested the use of the Greek letter "psi" to designate this concept of unity and this has become general usage.

The term psi is more than a mere conveniece of exchange;

even as the concept of unity took shape in our minds, we recognized the fact that precognition seemed to be just clairvoyance of future events and PK seemed to suggest a principle of reaction in its inverse relation to clairvoyance. Psi thus becomes a hypothetically reversible subject-object interaction (and if telepathy occurs it would be also a subject-subject interaction). More important perhaps, PK cannot be imagined as operating effectively without ESP; so it is much easier to think of the two types as functioning in some way as a unitary process.

NO PHYSICAL LIMITATIONS

But, in this search for clues to man's nature among the hidden channels of the personality, one primary query has been waiting at every turn: What really goes on here? One wants to know first if this psi effect is real; if so, then how is it going to fit into the world of the known natural sciences? But this calls for a still more precise question to start with: Is the psi process itself physical or nonphysical? More specifically yet, have any measured relations been found between the psi effect and physical conditions; for example, when two distances are compared? And what about the precognition tests in which the time barrier is introduced? In PK research, too, the same type of question arises: Do physical aspects of the targets make a difference—for example, their densities, sizes, shapes, numbers, and other material characteristics of the dice (or other target object used)?

Naturally, some psi workers have been strongly motivated to find any possible physical characteristic of psi imaginable. In fact, if any least relationship could be reliably demonstrated between psi and physics, it would have solved most of the practical problems of parapsychology, making it a "hard" science almost overnight. Funds would have been available, recognition would have come easily, and all the university doors would have opened wide long ago.

As it is, only a few psi workers have reported that they obtained even slight effects to suggest a physical relationship, and these seem not to have appreciated the difficulty of designing a test that controls against psychological biases associated with the problem; the subject's belief or preference has to be taken into account as well as the actual condition. To most psi workers, it is rather evident that psi does not behave like a physical process, as the terms are used today, and that it shows a consistent independence of physical conditions in its operation.

The establishment of the nonphysicality of psi, little as we know what it is if not physical, opens up a new world. So basic a finding will profoundly affect the major sciences as the fact becomes fully realized. For the present, however, conservative scientists are not yet ready to consider the immensity of the consequences. The habit is strong of thinking of mental processes as not requiring a distinct classification with regard to physics.

But now the psi evidence forces the issue. It is no longer a speculative question. In an experimental science, the answers from well designed experiments become definitive. A great many people in psychology and philosophy have long been fancying the mind as a sort of epiphenomenon, an ineffectual reflection of what goes on in the "real" world of brain physics. But, as McDougall suggested in *Body and Mind,* and as John Beloff, with more evidence to go on a half century later, concludes in his *The Existence of Mind,* parapsychology furnishes evidence of the existence of mind. The latter rightly added that it is the only experimental proof of such existence.

CAUSALITY AND ENERGETICS IN PSI

It would be wrong to say that psi has *nothing* to do with physics. In fact, it may be only through changes registered in the physical world of the subject that we can learn about the occurrence of psi. When one is dealing with psi test results, he does obtain physical changes that are directly or indirectly measurable, like anything else in science. It does not matter that most of these are statistically evaluated; a great deal in the other sciences is in the same category. The dice (and whatever other physical targets are used) are influenced as they roll; we must assume that they have to be affected physically in order to register a PK effect. An alteration of a physical system is of course no mere imaginary matter. Such effects, as the word implies, assume the transfer of some *causal* influence needed to induce the change. Even the admission that we do not yet know the determining principle does not prevent us from inferring that an unknown energy must be involved. Then, after this first logical step is taken, we proceed to study the hypothetical energy, with a view eventually to giving it a description and a name—in this case it is likely to be a psi, psychic, or parapsychical energy, or perhaps just "mental."

Even on the ESP side, communication between a subject in Paris, Zagreb, or South Africa, and target cards in Durham, represents a communication which can be as well called an energetic exchange as any of the other several types of exchange that are possible at such distances. In all tests of psi with distance, the results registered are in the end physical effects; they may have to be if they are to leave any record; but most of the time they are indirectly registered (e.g., embodied in a dream report or transcribed on a record sheet). But then the message in any typical physical communication at a distance must also be "translated" into another physical form for the end product to be comprehensible.

Since we now have a case, I think, for the inference of some sort of psi energy, we can go on to assume the causal efficacy of psi as long and as far as causality is a usefully descriptive word in scientific discourse. I do not know about the future usefulness of the concept either in physics or parapsychology; it is hard to see how causality could function in precognition, although it seems to do so. However, with so little known about how precognition operates, what psi energy is like, and the nature of mind in general, it seems best just to keep the challenge of this great problem in focus and watch for an opening to penetrate further into it. As Arthur Koestler has suggested in the *Roots of Coincidence,* these mysteries of the two fields have something in common if only in their similar challenge to the conventional sciences.

At the stage of psi research in 1950, the stock taking was generally encouraging. It looked as though the types of psi were experimentally distinguishable as surface phenomena, but united through a common underlying process. That is, psi was considered as a unitary but reversible function, easy to regard as being the same sort of two-way exchange as sensorimotor (SM) communication—it was extrasensorimotor of ESM action. Whether anything took the place of the senses and muscles, there was as yet no sign or even suggestion.

Because the complex stimulus-response mechanism used in the normal SM exchange was lacking, ESM, or psi communication, appeared even more strangely distinct, but the consistent absence of any discoverable physical intermediation offered the first big step of explanation. Psi, being nonphysical, would seem to need no ports of entry and exit—no senses, no muscles, no glands. It does indicate a profoundly distinct, undiscovered mode of interaction; yet, it has to interact physically or it would not be experienced. This psi interaction with the environment registers and generally makes measurable changes; psi therefore must be in some broad expanded concept of the word, an *energetic* determinant.

In such a mid-century summing up as this, there was, from the viewpoint of the research, an impression of substantial gain in knowledge, but, as always, further questions. For example, what was the distribution of psi? Was this ability an individual gift, a species endowment, or was it a normal inheritance of all behaving organisms? The nonphysical character of psi seemed, even by itself, to be a firm beginning of the answer to the question we asked in 1922; and the energetic or causal nature of the function even assured it a significant role in life. This, in turn, raised the question of how this special ability is distributed. In a word, who actually possesses this parapsychical gift?

WHO HAS PSI?

When the test program began at Duke, there were already some suggestions that the "psychic" individual was not so rare as had been popularly believed. Professor Richet had obtained evidence of clairvoyance in children in the 1880's. A young psychologist, G. H. Estabrooks, had tested a number of student volunteers at Harvard in the mid-1920's. But the idea still prevailed that the gifted individual subject was rare; others might have small traces of the power. Our own research at Duke went along with this expectation at first and the concept was revised only slowly over the years.

During the decade of the 1950's, however, the growing knowledge had its effect, especially as work in the schools was extended into the lower ages; the study of psychological correlates also gave us ideas. For instance, it was found that the subject's success depended greatly on his state of mind, so much so that it became clear that *good subjects were made* instead of being born that way. The working view emerged that probably *everyone had potential psi ability* but that only a few had developed attitudes favorable to its observable use. The evidence for this concept is naturally not from a neatly planned research; but it rests on broad observation and a good rationale and it now has a rather wide acceptance.

At the same time, "gifted subjects" are occasionally found; persons who easily adapt to test conditions and do dependably well in prolonged research. HP is one such already mentioned. The delicate psychological nature of psi is illustrated in the fact that HP rather abruptly lost his exceptional scoring ability and has not as yet recovered it. But there have been others who temporarily lost their high-scoring rate and later recaptured it, at least for a time. Also, a few subjects who began low have been able to build up to high level performance rates in new tests.

The problem of how best to train subjects (so they can stand up under prolonged controlled testing) is only at the beginning stage of solution at present, but enough is known to allow me to say psi test performance certainly can be modified, and latent capacity can be discovered, demonstrated, and sometimes considerably improved. On the other hand, psi can remain hidden and can easily be lost, at least to all practical purposes. So far, only a few psi workers have been busy on this more difficult task of developing the art of psi testing; it seems to depend on an indefinite amount of knowledge that has first to be acquired. Those familiar with the (analogous but much easier) problem of intelligence may appreciate the psi problem best.

PSI IN ANIMALS

As the idea grew that psi was a general gift of the human species, there were suggestions that other animals might also have it. A survey of relevant literature around 1950 revealed that there was enough unexplained (and psi-like) animal behavior to justify a thorough investigation. First, we assembled a large collection of anecdotal case reports, many of them on domestic animals, and most of which suggested the clairvoyant type of ESP. The most impressive cases were of dogs, cats, and birds that, with no conceivable sensory guidance, "trailed" their human friends to a new territory, often over long distances. Such trailing cases, if taken seriously, most definitely suggested a psi factor. Homing behavior and migratory travels, too, although less distinctly, still supported the interest in animal psi, and in 1951 an experimental program was begun with cats, dogs, and pigeons that ran for several years. Then in 1968, after years of neglect of animals as ESP subjects, work was begun by a well known French biologist using the pseudonym Pierre Duval; with the use of automatic methods, Duval and his students tested mice for precognition and obtained significant results. His work was repeated at the Foundation for Research on the Nature of Man (FRNM) in Durham (established to continue the work of the Duke Laboratory) beginning in 1969 and at the University of Utrecht in 1972.

Today the case for ESP in mice and other rodents is very strong, with these three laboratories back of the general finding of precognition. With several findings of first importance as to the conditions (both of the environment and the state of the animals) favoring success, it appears that the "guinea pig" stage in psi research has been reached. In addition, the help of automatic test apparatus and computer control has been added.

One of the first fruits of the "guinea pig" method has been the use of "random behavior" selection. With the animals, certain trials could be designated "nonpsi trials," those in which the animal had no chance to use psi. When these were omitted, the scores went up markedly. W. J. Levy, in charge of these tests at RFNM, adapted the random behavior device to the testing of human subjects and a similarly marked improvement was obtained. The point is that the discovery was made possible by the simpler routine of the animal tests; then, once made, it was adaptable to human test data. It illustrates the enormous advantage of animal testing for some of the psi problems, an advantage well known in many other fields.

Crossing over the species line as we began to do thirty years ago has obviously been slow, but it has been definitely worthwhile. One main benefit has been in the broadening of the biological perspective of the psi function. I confess that I had first thought of psi as probably a human derivative, a sort of incidental emergent in man's own evolution, evident perhaps in only a few individuals. But, as the evidence accumulated and psi appeared to be species-wide, my first guess had to be discarded. Now there promises to be a great project ahead in getting on further with the search for origins, partly through comparative inquiry among existing species.

Still another jump took place more recently that has opened up an exciting block of new psi territory, yet one that is still in the animal psi section. It now seems logical enough, but no one had stopped to reason that, since psi consists of a unity of both ESP and PK, and since we now know some other animal species that have ESP, we should now look for PK in other species, too.

Helmut Schmidt, a physicist at the Boeing Laboratory in Seattle at the time, had developed a sensitive random number generator that depended on radioactivity to keep it random. He had given tests of ESP with this delicate machine, in which his subjects pressed buttons to predict which lamp would light next. But he thought too that a specified lamp (one of two or more) could perhaps be made to light next by means of the subject's PK. If so, that one lamp could be made to light more often than chance if operated randomly on or off at short intervals. He found that it could, and then asked: What else besides human subjects might influence it? Anything, perhaps, that was cold and wanted heat? Among the variety of things he tried was the family cat, with the animal shut in a box "out in the cold" with the warm light coming on or off by pure chance. He found the lamp did turn on more often than the 50 percent expected. It was only suggestive, but that was enough to win encouragement when he later joined the staff at the FRNM. Another area of research had been opened up.

Animal PK has, during the last two years, been tested with a number of animal species, mostly with the need-of-heat as the motivation. The success in these exploratory tests has been quite uneven, yet on the whole, the program adds up to a rather strong case. Chicks have been most consistent, and have proved effective even before hatching. Do I really mean that these embryos influence that random number generator that turn on the light? It does indeed look like that. Yet, the stage of the psi research and the incidental problems to solve as we go, make it wise to suspend conclusions for the present; still more independent confirmation is desirable.

As noted above, animals might be expected to have PK capacity since several species have been shown to have ESP; but different species were involved in ESP testing than have been in PK. At any rate, Dr. Schmidt has at least given us the method, we have the equipment, and a wealth of various types of evidence from a mounting number of experimenters. The research team under Levy has found repetition fairly dependable, and the project is now continuing with automated testing and computerized recording.

By this time, psi seems to be a normal biological function not at all confined to man and perhaps only more hidden in this species. The range of its distribution widens as other species are tested; no limit has so far been met. Some of the farthest out projects lead to the question of its relation to basic life processes; the PK interaction of the animal with the physical environment gives a new idea for consideration by the biologist who is seeking the elements of life's "magic," a possibly distinctive vital agency. Animal ESP has now had extremely good independent confirmation; the many confirmations of animal PK are still from only one institute (the FRNM), but it is time to look for repetition elsewhere.

PSI BEHAVIOR

What I have said in the sections on the distribution of psi ability (in men and animals) has shown that the psi function seems to be a part of the natural evolutionary heritage of man; it seems now to be a part of his own nature derived from points far enough back at least to have been shared with the origin of a number of other families of animal life from which we have some evidence. This makes psi as definitely biological as it has been found not to be recognizably physical. But where does it belong with respect to psychology, the field from which it has received most of its rejection slips?

As I have already indicated, the extrasensorimotor nature of psi agency has an unbroken line of separation (at least on the surface) from the field of academic psychology, presently limited as it is to the sensorimotor basis of behavior. Psi behavior is necessarily defined as a region definitely apart, one not even mediated by any of these specific physical principles essential to the senses and muscles.

Yet, there is common ground, too. Even though nonphysical, the psi process must have some interaction (and of course some way of exchange) with physical systems, directly or indirectly, or else there would be no evidence or experience of its agency. In ESP, the psi message converts to intuitions, dreams, hallucinations, and perhaps many unobservable forms, and in PK, it seems directly to influence physical states and operations, animate and inanimate, moving and static. These interconversions offer great invitations to well prepared researchers to explore, much as the many discoveries of types of energy interconversion did in the past for physics.

Parapsychology's first main contribution to psychology may be that it can yield to quantitative experiments. It thus provides a comparative basis of measurement of the different communication systems, sensory with extrasensory, and motor with extramotor (or PK). This allowed the necessary clear-cut distinctions and similarities to be drawn. Eventually, it may lead to the discovery of the larger organismic unity that permits these functions to dwell in the same creature, man or mouse.

The most valuable psychological finding about psi in the long view may be the fact that it is normally *voluntary.* This makes an enormous difference in what we can think about it both in laboratory and life. Otherwise, a test subject could not (as they all do who succeed) hit a specific target hidden in a given time and place. In fact, one of the better confirmed findings about psi is that the subject's effort or strength of motivation is essential to success. Under certain circumstances, the subject need not even be aware of the motivation for it to be effective.

This brings up the most revealing feature of psi from the psychological viewpoint—the fact that the subject is unconscious of it. He does not generally have even a reliable introspective awareness of the psi experience, either of its occurrence or its truth (evidentiality). The discovery of this lack of assurance of genuineness explained many of the difficulties in psi testing, among which were the extreme irregularities in the level of scoring rate; unconscious resistances could account for some effects such as consistent missing (i.e., making consistent mistakes and thus scoring *below* theoretical chance). Other results attributable to this hidden status of psi were the position effects, such as the diagonal declines of hits on the PK record sheets mentioned earlier.

Knowledge of this unconsciousness of psi gave other helpful illumination on the process. One example is the "psi differential effect"; if there are two conditions in the test (e.g., two types of targets being compared) the subject will usually tend to favor one over the other, even if only unconsciously. He will rather regularly give a positive score on the favored targets but will do approximately as well in *avoiding* the other targets, giving a negative (below chance) score.

More important, however, is the story this differential effect tells on this unconscious psi process. It reveals that the amount of psi is not (or not much, if at all) affected by these conditions that cause the differential effect (with one part going below chance). The negative side may show as much (or more) evidence of psi as the other—in other words, psi-missing is just as truly a psi effect as psi-hitting. But the point I am making here is that two kinds of results emerge from such an experiment; one is the *amount of psi,* best measured by the *size* of the difference between the two sets of scores; this is the primary psi effect. The other finding is the more psychological measure, which indicates which *direction* of deviation from chance is produced by one or the other of the two mental conditions being contrasted.

Many standard mental tests have given this psi differential effect when a class or other group was given both ESP and the mental tests, and the results correlated. Thus, in a psi differential test, the subject makes a sensitive unconscious discrimination between two situations, and the signs of the deviation of the scoring rates register this subtle judgment.

As a result of analyses of mental states, traits, moods, and attitudes in relation to psi test data, the psi process stands out as rather generally unaffected in its efficiency (e.g., as measured by the standard psi quotient, which is independent of the direction of deviation). In fact, the only mental state that affects the amount of psi itself is the subject's drive or motivation; this determines the *extent* of his deviation from chance but does not affect the *direction.* Thus, whether or not the scores will be above or below mean chance expectation depends on the moods, attitudes, and other normal mental states.

The research has given a working view of psi as a delicate, unconscious but, to some extent, voluntarily dirigible process. The subject tries vainly to register the effect consciously and has to let it penetrate the normal stream of mental life in its own still untraceable way (not unlike crossing a broad street in heavy, undisciplined traffic). Much is known or half-suspected about how to help it get through; but this aspect has had to wait for the special studies still lying ahead.

Current studies in unconscious sensory "learning" from the side of experimental psychology may be of help in psi research, but the help could be the other way around if we receive the necessary support. We have long been engaged in testing unconscious cognitive judgments. I suspect there is much general psychology in common here, in spite of the basic difference between psi and the "learning principle" (or intelligence factor).

COMMENT ON CRITICISM

The controversy over psi research has been a long and vigorous one. In looking back over it now, two rather distinct divisions of the criticism of psi research are evident. On the one hand was the ever present need of help in the safeguarding of the research methods and conclusions. On the other hand, there were the efforts made more or less from the outside to discourage and even defeat the whole psi program. I will discuss these separately in this order.

From the beginning, we were, as I have said, severely warned against the hazards of the psychical research field; these warnings came best from well-informed sources, which means from the field itself (i.e., from the McDougalls and the W. F. Princes rather than from the Jastrows). The years of preparation for this venture were consciously devoted more to the dangers (ever present in our minds and discussions) that we might, as many expected, make fools of ourselves in this uncharted undertaking, than they were to the more positive prospect. Thus, we made ourselves hypercritical and invited the critical vigilance of our colleagues. We set up special safeguards on the statistical phase of the work by engaging qualified help in the laboratory and on the staff of the *Journal of Parapsychology*. We raised our standards above the usual practice in psychology both in the criteria of statistical significance and in the requirement of the pilot-confirmation methods of experimenting (essentially a repetition). And there were other special requirements.

There was important help especially welcomed from outside. From time to time, a critical review of psi research by a competent but independent judge could be obtained; for example, Professor E. V. Huntington, the Harvard mathematician, reviewed the ESP statistics in 1938 (*American Scholar*), and Dr. Gardner Murphy, then a psychologist at Columbia, appraised the early Duke research methods in the same issue. Several national scholarly societies held evaluative symposia during the late 1930's, one of these the American Psychological Association. These "hearings" were of great educational value. By far, the most helpful one was a spontaneous development; a group of members of the

American Institute for Mathematical Statistics held a special session at the annual convention in 1937 at Indianapolis and issued a press release approving the mathematical methods of the ESP work at Duke. These had been under attack by a number of psychologists.

Few editors, however, were ready to publish reports of ESP research, although critical articles on the subject were generally acceptable. However, the launching of the *Journal of Parapsychology* in 1937 took care of the flow of research papers that had developed. It also published critical papers and became an open "proving ground" for the setting of standards and the settling of issues.

The more hostile attacks, on the other hand, were something quite different. They were seldom written from a basis of adequate knowledge of the new findings. For example, when in 1940, Dr. Willy Feller of Princeton made a poorly informed attack on the mathematics of ESP research, Professor Huntington assisted our staff in preparing a reply that effectively silenced Feller. Again, when Dr. John L. Kennedy of Stanford criticized the ESP methods before a massed convention of psychologists at Columbus in 1938, Dr. Gardner Murphy answered him so conclusively that he refused to allow his paper to be printed.

These more destructive criticisms were sometimes inferably identifiable with ulterior interests. For example, the most damaging series of attacks and the most numerous came from Stanford University, where there was a large sum of money for parapsychology that was being used instead for the psychology department. I have no doubt the people responsible believed psychology was a better place for the money than parapsychology, so naturally they would have preferred to have the new competition vanish.

When, in 1940, it seemed advisable to organize the contest over ESP, I wrote and (along with four colleagues) published *Extrasensory Perception After Sixty Years* to sum up the evidence, the criticisms and the replies. Seven leading critics were asked to read the text and comment for publication. Only three complied and only one (Dr. Chester Kellogg) was persistently unfavorable. Another, Dr. Robert H. Thouless, later on became a leading contributor to the field.

Following this book, there was no major criticism until Dr. George Price's extraordinary attack in *Science* in 1955. *Science,* then edited by Dr. Dael Wolfle, one of our earlier critics, gave such space and prominence (the leading article) to this lengthy diatribe against the character and sanity of the psi researchers as to make it the high point in all this lower level criticism. The author has had the grace and candor to publish (*Science,* 28 January 1972 Letters) an apology; the editor has not. This curious case best illustrates the distinction between helpful criticism and the attempt merely to destroy something the critics failed to understand.

This is a glimpse into a long and amazing story—the lengths of design to which a few ardent conservatives will go when obsessed with the overconfident urge to discourage an upsetting idea. Parapsychology has had more than its share of this fanatic type of opposition. But this present account is concerned with the story of progress made and not with all the untoward incidents along the way. Fortunately, the experimental controls have thus far been well enough designed to allow small latitude for even the crafty seekers after an exposé story. The fact that psi researchers have been a rather dedicated group has not relaxed the essential vigilance; it is true, the use of automation, and other technology is proving advantageous as well. Animal subjects, too, make for easier control.

The ultimate safety in accepting a scientific fact lies, of course, in independent confirmation. One may wait for as many of these supporting replications as he likes. In this field, the evidence automatically mounts with every well-controlled experiment that yields significant evidence of psi; thus, no excessive weight gets put on a single experiment or an individual researcher. Rather, an even more reassuring cumulative judgment is acquired.

This judgment then, in turn, takes much internal bracing from the way the facts combine and interlock into an organized body of knowledge. The total structure of general types and properties of psi gives the best assurance that a sound science is emerging from the researches. The confirmatory results as they come from the different laboratories add further firmness to the body of findings of the whole. Accordingly, if the psi results do not carry weight, it has to be due to lack of knowledge or lack of an adequate appraisal. Therefore, a few words are in order to consider some aspects of appraisal of the value of the psi research.

THE MEANING OF PSI

Some people will reasonably enough think primarily of the practical importance of psi in extending the range of man's communication with his world. Ignoring for a moment how feeble and uncontrollable psi ability still is, and assuming that the research will go on to verify all the other subtypes of psi abilities suggested by spontaneous cases, there appears to be *no limit to the reach of psi* in space, time, matter, and mind. Clairvoyance, precognition, and PK with moving targets are all three firmly established. (PK of living targets has some fair evidence and may later be found acceptable, and the PK of static targets is making a beginning. Telepathy is only an uncertain "probable" as yet.)

But this roundup includes about *everything that exists* as coming within the reach of the psi process. What in the universe would then be left? It is a truly fantastic concept of the role of mind in nature that emerges from this analysis of the findings about psi. It brings down to earth, to man himself, the concepts of omniscience and omnipotence which the founders of the theologies ascribed to divine agency. One sees, too, the resemblance between the subtypes of psi discovered in man and the specific principles of religious communication. It looks (as I suggested in my article "Parapsychology and Man," *Journal of Parapsychology*, June 1972) as if the founders of western theology must have known a great deal intuitively about the principles of modern parapsychology—and as intelligent observers of spontaneous psi in their everyday lives, they probably did.

But, does such a wide range really matter if the control over psi is so weak? No one can yet confidently say much about the prospect of increasing control over this ability. That it can be controlled to some extent is now well known, and much is even known about the actual conditions that help and hinder the ability. The control of unconscious sensory functions, too, is becoming a major topic of research in psychology and physiology today, and no one would want to rule out the possibility that at least some of the limitations due to the unconsciousness of psi might be removed.

There is good reason, however, to restrain one's optimism regarding unlimited psi control. One needs only to think what an uncontrollable social situation would result if only a few individuals become really able to control their psi capacity at will and without restraint. For example, complete precognition in everyone would seem to require absolute fatalism; no choice would be left. So far as I know, there has never been anything on record to suggest even the likelihood of such psi perfection. Rather, it looks as though in the evolution of the psi process, some limitation of the ability may have had to be built into the balancing system of the organism for survival. This seems to be general biological law; life is an operational equilibrium among many complex factors, most of which could be lethal if not contained and regulated.

However, the greatest meaning of psi, as far as I understand it, does not depend entirely—or perhaps even very much as yet— on how much control over the ability can be developed. But it does matter greatly how the psi process is found to function in the total mental system of a person, where it belongs in the living organism, how it evolved in nature, and what gives it the potential (or energy) to interact with so wide a range of the physical order. These all seem to be great problem areas, and they should yield eventually to continuing psi research with the help of the other branches of science to which they interrelate. The outcome will, in the course of time, reveal more fully where psi belongs in the larger system of nature.

It is reassuring to see this mere inclusive relationship of psi to the rest of nature emerging even when the outlines are still dim and fragmentary. The fact that this ability seemed at first to mankind in his earlier stages so completely mysterious and miraculous as to call for a supernatural explanation, and yet today yields gradually to an elementary lawfulness of its own, is reassuringly typical of the history of science. We can even agree with our remote ancestors that, until it was found by experiment that men themselves (and even their animal subjects) have natural powers beyond the range of the senses and muscles, it was reasonable to consider them supernatural. We could even grant that our more recent forebears and contemporaries, faced as they were with the compelling and inclusive physical explanation for all nature given by the sciences, were rather intellectually forced to deny the existence of these same psychic abilities.

But, so it has been also throughout the nascent stage of the other branches of science as they progressed from the supernatural to the stage of natural physical law. The analogy is much the same with psi except that parapsychology has advanced from the supernatural to the natural as *superphysical.* Unlike the other sciences, as we have seen, it has no physical basis that has been discovered. Yet, even here it discloses, as science has done in many of its branches before, an area of hidden reality no less actual for its invisibility, and, as usual, as "impossible" at first as it is revolutionary.

But let us forget about control over psi ability for the moment, and consider possible social consequences of the mere fact that men have psi ability, however latent, unrecognized or underdeveloped it may presently be. I will assume only that everyone most likely has some psi capacity and take only the present knowledge about the nature of psi.

First, the basic classification of man will have to be relabelled. Most important of all is the fact that he has a mental system that actually exists and works. The psi evidence shows the mind has independent causal efficacy. The psi experiments are going on that make that conclusion increasingly safe.

By refuting the many essentially physical theories of man's nature, the new concept of the parapsychical side of man logically counters all those many rejections of a transcendent or subjective quality in the human individual. Since something distinctly mental is established as part of man's nature, those many values and assumptions based on that idea can now be reexamined and to some extent reactivated. The many practices and institutions in our culture that assume the mind is real, that it influences conduct, and that it is in some measure a subjective, intelligent and volitional self that governs the physical system of the organism—all these are now at least well enough supported by experimental research to warrant the reevaluation mentioned.

I have elsewhere indicated that, for religion, this is somewhat like the role of microbiology in the 19th Century medicine. The discovery of the scientific roots of the miraculous in man's own nature compares with the finding of the causes of disease in the germs of the air instead of in magic or demons. As with medicine and other disciplines have been, in turn, religion may itself conceivably now be "saved," also with the help of science; the time has come for the "Parapsychology of Religion" to become a scientific offshoot from the basic psi principles now taking shape.

Medicine, itself, already half psychosomatic, may again open new windows, this time to psi research and make from the possibly verifiable PK elements of faith healing a beginning science instead of a fast expanding quackery it so easily appears and can very well be. Medical parapsychology would seem a necessary branch at this state if only for the research on which to check the doubtful claims. For the other great disciplines that depend on a theory of man's nature (law, education, psychotherapy, ethics, and such) there is space for only a word: In all these, it is fundamentally important to check the assumed theory of the nature of man against these new psi findings. The practitioner can, of course, act only in accord with what he thinks his client is and is like. Is he a completely physical system (which he certainly is much like)? Or is the common intuitive impression of volitional independence, one that transcends mechanistic causality, a more justifiable conception?

Our social institutions—and not just our temples alone—hinge heavily on the transcendent side of this cultural issue. This derives, of course, from our religious heritage and is declining along with theological authority. The mechanist's theory of man is a product of those sciences that have been restricted to the basic principle of physical determinism. Now, however, that the science of psi has added a new principle and has disproved the exclusive finality of physical agency in nature; each individual and each discipline can weigh the evidence and make an objective scientific judgment instead of a metaphysical one. This is the outcome envisioned by the follower of science.

A PERSONAL VIEW

Growing up as we did in the relatively healthy and sheltered world of the U.S.A., the central problems of life's struggles were moral ones. As a student heading for the ministry, the main question for me was that of how to help myself and fellowmen to seek and achieve a higher degree of self-control. Basic to this character-building ethic was the universally accepted belief in free will. The church, the court, the school, the government all assumed it. I was shocked to discover that my psychology teacher did not, and the textbooks of psychology in the college library agreed with him. I could see for myself that they were consistent with the natural science of the time. Only a few like William James said this freedom issue was a question for philosophy. For me, an eager convert to science, it seemed a good reason for dropping out of the program I was in. For that matter, the psychologists have not only dropped the concept of the will, but for the most part, that of the mind as a useful reality.

Now, as has been related, I have been enabled by the research in parapsychology to join McDougall, Beloff, and others in taking the mind as an actual causal entity. This research has actually made its way partly, as we have seen, by showing that the mind can freely will physical things to happen. Even if it is only a beginning it is great to know this little fact. Previously, the physical order was all science was able to claim for reality; now, it looks as though the mind is able to influence that material system; perhaps even more than we know yet. However small we may regard this finding, it gives firm encouragement to keep on with the search.

Why did not the mere fact of common experience of conscious willing satisfy the psychologist (and me too)? Why does it have to have had a PK demonstration? Briefly, the answer is that without PK, we cannot be sure there is any distinctly mental (nonphysical) action involved. The behaviorist would say it is just the nervous chain of physical events and that the conscious willing is a mere impotent epiphenomenon. The PK experiments show that the mind does have real causal efficacy and can even exert its dominion over the physical world. How so and how much we will strive to learn in time.

Today, the greatest question I see in human life is still this same one we once took so seriously: Have I some free personal choice in what I do—free from the determining forces within me or my organism? These forces are mostly the physical grounds for my appetites, needs, attractions, and distractions. Now, I know from decades of tirelessly objective research by many workers, that I can, with some freedom, exercise my natural power over the physical elements in my own nature, much indeed as I thought (on quite other authority, of course) in my earlier years that I could.

It is not, I confess, all so simple as brevity makes it seem. There is more research to do and much to explore in this parapsychoethical area of problems. But, what a welcome opportunity it should be (as it is for me) in this day when probably nothing is more confused than the world of moral contradictions! If I am right in accepting this help from the science of parapsychology, then it has restored and confirmed my confidence in the reality and the causal influence of my mind, partly at least because of its superphysical function in free volitional agency. In time, it should be expected to bring both psychology and biology back to the study of the nature of the human will as a genuine force in the life of the organism and the personality. They will, of course, carry the search far beyond the realm of moral values. But, for me, and I suspect for much of the world at this stage, the meaning of psi is greatest in its modest indication that, in some small way, "I *am* the master of my fate."

Chapter X

A CASE FOR INTUITION AND COMMON SENSE

Roger J. Williams

Roger J. Williams is the discoverer of pantothenic acid, a key B vitamin required in the machinery of all living organisms, and did pioneer work with folic acid, an anti-anemia vitamin, and gave it its name. From 1941-63, Professor Williams was Director of the Clayton Foundation Biochemical Institute at the University of Texas, where more vitamins and their variants have been discovered than in any other laboratory in the world.

Born in India in 1893, the son of missionary parents, he received his B.S. degree from the University of Redlands and his M.S. and Ph.D. degrees from the University of Chicago. Ever since, at the University of Oregon, Oregon State University, and the University of Texas, he has been exploring in the field of biochemistry.

He is the author of textbooks on organic chemistry and biochemistry and more than two hundred scientific articles. In the last 25 years he has been interested in individuality as it impinges on life and health—physical and mental—as well as its meaning for society. In this area he has written The Human Frontier (Harcourt, Brace), Free and Unequal (Univ. of Texas Press), and Biochemical Individuality (John Wiley & Sons). The latter has been translated into Russian, Italian, and Polish. One of his best known books is perhaps Nutrition in a Nutshell (Doubleday & Co., Inc.), continuously in print for ten years and considered by many to be a classic of its kind. In 1967 he published You Are Extraordinary (Random House). This book, written in simple language, supersedes the earlier popular books and has been heralded as outstanding by leaders in science, medicine, psychology, psychiatry, theology, humanities, and industry, as well as by well-known writers. In 1971 he published Nutrition Against Disease (Pitman Pub. Corp.) which may be his most influential book. Its major thesis is that our internal microenvironment is determined largely by the food we consume—its content of minerals, trace minerals, amino acids, and vitamins. Prevention of noninfective diseases demands improvement in our internal microenvironments.

One result of his publication of this book was Dr. Williams appointment, in May 1972, to President Nixon's Advisory Panel on Heart Disease; another was his appointment as Honorary President of the International Academy of Preventive Medicine. He also became in 1971 (London) a Founding Fellow of the Academy of Orthomolecular Psychiatry.

Long recognized by fellow scientists as a leader, Dr. Williams is a member of numerous scholarly and scientific organizations. In 1946, he was elected to membership in the select National Academy of Sciences. He also received the Mead Johnson Award of the American Institute of Nutrition, and honorary degrees from Redlands, Columbia, and Oregon State University. In 1957, he was made President of the American Chemical Society.

His broad knowledge has been utilized in connection with the medical boards of the National Polio Foundation, the Multiple Sclerosis Society, and the Muscular Dystrophy Association of America, Inc., as a consultant for the American Cancer Society, and as a member of the National Food and Nutrition Board.

IN MANY CIRCUMSTANCES thought appears to be conveyed by what is said, but the full meaning is lost if one misses what is implied. If in sketching the story of my scientific work I dwelt in great detail on the circumstances of my birth and bringing up, this discussion would carry, in our environmentalist culture, the strong implication that these circumstances made me what I am. This implication I strenuously avoid.

If I were to appear to "sum up my life work in science," this would carry the implication that I have completed what I will do. This implication I also avoid. In this respect I feel like the weather-beaten New Englander who was asked "Have you lived in New England all your life?" His reply was "Not yet." I can only tell about my scientific activities up to my present age—79.

If up to now I have made any one substantial dent in people's thinking, it has been because I have called attention many times in many ways to the common sense and easily demonstrable fact that *every baby arrives distinctively equipped.*

At the University of Texas I gave for at least a dozen years a maverick course which had as its central theme the five word telegram italicized above. The course was first given in the Chemistry Department (because I was a Professor of Chemistry), but later because of its interdisciplinary nature was listed also under Comparative Studies. Fortunately, since my retirement from teaching a year ago, the course has been continued under the able leadership of Dr. Charles W. Bode, one of those who was greatly impressed by the contents of the course when I gave it.

This course was never given the same two years in succession because of the constant accumulation of new scientific information. No one who has not taken the course (even if they have read my books *You Are Extraordinary,* and *Biochemical Individuality*) can have an adequate idea of the wealth of material available regarding the kind of equipment a newborn baby has, and how highly distinctive each item of equipment may be for any infant. Among the striking features are those of an anatomical nature—detailed brain structure, the structures of the sense organs, the structure of internal organs, bones, muscles, circulatory systems, nervous systems, etc. Accompanying these anatomical features is distinctiveness in body chemistry, in physiology, endocrinology, psychology and in every other imaginable way. All of this distinctive equipment has a terrific impact on the life of each individual person whether he or she is aware of it or not.

Yet scientists in general are not interested in the subject of individuality no matter how much of an impact it may have. Most of the vast available material bearing on this subject must be gathered from incidental rather than purposeful observations.

The basic reason for resisting information of this sort is because it makes more difficult, not easier, the formulation of generalizations which are considered to be the life-blood of science. This greater concern for the *ease* of making generalizations than for the validity of the generalizations that are made, is in my mind a disease from which scientists suffer. It is furthermore a generalized disease afflicting anatomists, physiologists, endocrinologists, biochemists, molecular biologists, geneticists, psychologists and anthropologists alike. It helps them have a tremendous bias in favor of finding easy answers (worthless or not) and against tackling tough problems which may be of paramount importance. This bias is often rationalized on the basis of a desire to be truly scientific.

One might suppose that the common sense objective of understanding human nature would be uppermost in the minds of hordes of scientifically inclined people, but no, the vast data which throw the most light on human nature tend to be relegated to the trash heap. The desire of scientists to be "truly scientific" is too strong to be overcome. Besides, they have been trained to have a strong bias in favor of environmentalism.

Of course, environmental influences have a great effect on the lives of all of us, but we by no means start out as blank sheets on which environment inscribes our life history. Each of us has his own characteristic conditionabilities.

When the facts of individuality are ignored in the "social sciences," this may lead us to a most disastrous idea—that one's environment determines one's outlook and one's actions and hence no blame can ever be cast on any individual. If this is accepted, there can be no such thing as self-respect, because to respect one's self one must have some kind of standards. If our conduct is environmentally determined, there can be no standards.

I hold it to be a commonsense and wholesome idea that each person is some kind of a captain of some kind of ship traveling through some kind of waters. The ship may have specific limitations and weaknesses, and the waters may be rough indeed, but a great deal still depends upon the captain.

Rejection of this idea leads to the acceptance of a meaningless life, to permissiveness, irresponsibility, lack of standards and eventually to the decay of society. It is most unfortunate in my opinion that current university education has contributed so much to promote this decay. Recognition of individuality might serve as a turn-around point in education.

To make more clear how inborn individuality functions, let us briefly consider, for illustration, the training of cats and dogs. Both respond favorably to the same stimulus—food. A trainer can behave in the same manner toward a dog or cat and give similar rewards, but because the make-up of each of the two species of animals is so different, the results are in strong contrast. It is relatively easy to train a dog to run and fetch a stick or to walk at one's heel or to plunge into the water to retrieve a fallen bird. But imagine trying to teach a cat to do these things! Running to fetch sticks, or plunging into water are most distasteful activities to a cat. Cats do not perceive these activities even as possibilities. Their nervous systems turn out any such suggestions. To these suggestions they are both deaf and blind; they are unaware that the suggestions exist.

There are many kinds of activities to which dogs and cats alike are not conditionable. They are not built so that they can learn to read a newspaper, listen appreciatively to classical music, or enjoy having poetry read to them. To respond to these activities, they would have to have entirely different sense organs, brains and nervous systems.

The same principle holds in connection with the teaching of children. Some are equipped so that music has an immediate appeal. They are readily conditionable. They do not need to be told that music is pleasant and beautiful. If they have to be told, they don't believe it. Some children, after they learn to read, become avid readers. The equipment involved includes not only suitable eyesight characteristics but the complex psychological equipment which makes them enjoy what they read. Those children who have to be told that reading is fun generally know that it isn't. A tremendous range of conditionabilities exists in this regard. Some children are so equipped that arithmetic and later other branches of mathematics "make sense" and give satisfaction. In other words, this perceptual apparatus is part of their make-up, and they are readily conditionable with respect to mathematics. Other children, however, may, in spite of having excellent perceptual apparatus for appreciating language, history and literature, lack the perceptual apparatus necessary for learning mathematics. As a result, complicated mathematical formulas are, and always will remain, as incomprehensible and undesirable to them as fetching a stick is to a cat. A wide range of conditionabilities exist among children as to how well, with comparable effort, they can comprehend mathematics.

Each newborn baby, according to these concepts, arrives with equipment which gives him a distinctive pattern of conditionabilities. Activities, including thinking, tend to develop in accordance with a pattern which is distinctive for each one. Every baby has to learn (at first they are chock full of ignorance), and here the environment (the opportunities to learn) comes into play in a most significant way. Motivation enters into all our activities, but because of the distinctiveness in make-up we all have, it cannot be turned off and on following a simple formula.

Before discussing my own individual conditionabilities, I wish to consider an environmental factor of extreme importance—nutrition— which unfortunately is all too frequently and effectively dismissed as of little consequence. The effects of nutrition (good or poor) begin prenatally and continue through babyhood, youth, middle age and old age.

In my own case I have very few clues as to what kind of nutrition my mother may have received while I was a developing fetus. My mother, even in those days, was somewhat food conscious, and all indications point to the conclusion that her nutrition was passably good but not of the highest quality. If it had been of real high quality, I would probably have had teeth more resistant to decay than mine have been.

It is my opinion, based upon vast evidence, that many difficulties we encounter in later life have their roots in poor prenatal nutrition. In general I have been fortunate in this respect.

As a youngster my food was probably of passable quality. We usually kept chickens and generally had one or two cows. To the extent that milk and eggs were staple parts of my diet, it was good. In California where I spent several formative years, we usually had fresh fruit. There were times when we were not able to afford butter for our bread, but advantageously, neither were we able to afford soft drinks, candy bars and snack foods which often corrupt the nutrition of the overprivileged children of today. I discuss my early nutrition to call attention to the fact that children's brains cannot possibly develop to full potential unless the child is furnished in his or her food a good assortment of about 40 *essential* nutrients—amino acids, minerals, trace minerals and vitamins that are needed to build healthy bodies and brains.

It is now time to discuss some of the distinctive equipment items which influenced my scientific activities the most. My eyesight stands out as particularly important.

For reasons unknown to me—quite possibly poor prenatal nutrition was the basis—my complex eyesight characteristics were such that the mechanics of reading was always a chore for me and became more of a chore as I grew older. While a college student, for example, I had a tremendous liking for literature, but I found I couldn't read like my friends did. I had a close friend, Owen Walker ("Socrates" we used to call him) who was nearsighted and on occasion would sit up all night to read books in the area of economics and sociology. In my case, the maximum duration of my reading spurts was probably about an hour. If I didn't get what I was after in a short time, I didn't get it. Literature nevertheless attracted me greatly. Another friend, Harley MacNair, later a professor at the University of Chicago, introduced me to the *Forsythe Saga.* I read all of this work (aside from my school work) a little at a time with great relish. As I look back now I realize that psychologically I was very well equipped to enjoy reading, and I probably would have been a voluminous reader *if* my eyesight had been such as to make reading easier.

Over the years I have spent considerable time, effort and money trying to overcome my eyesight difficulties. Severe astigmatism was one of my difficulties, but when it was corrected with glasses, reading was still a chore. Muscle imbalance was another difficulty, but extensive exercises followed by an operation failed to bring substantial relief. For several years I did all my reading with one eye at a time. About this time Dr. Adelbert Ames, founder of the Dartmouth Eye Institute, discovered aniseikonia, and a few years later it was determined that I had this affliction. It involves, I was told, supposed differences in the sizes and shapes of the images on the two retinas. Whatever the basic difficulty, my two eyes did not work together well.

When Dr. Ames heard that I had this difficulty, his Institute paid my expenses so I could come from Texas to Dartmouth for a visit. He personally tested my eyes and prescribed for me. These spectacles with warped lens gave some relief, but I never was changed into a voluminous reader. Probably established habits had something to do with this. Eventually it became impractical to get aniseikonic prescriptions made or filled, and I reverted to the more usual spectacles. This reversion was promoted by an ophthomologist in San Francisco who prescribed and furnished me with "aniseikonic" spectacles at an appropriate high price which turned out not to have any aniseikonic correction in them. The subject of aniseikonia and related disorders needs badly, in my opinion, thorough investigation. Dr. Ames is now gone, and unfortunately few men of his caliber have delved into eyesight difficulties. Even the problem of dyslexia may be related.

Strange as it may seem, I now regard my eyesight difficulties as a *blessing* rather than a curse so far as my scientific work is concerned. Here we come to the discussion of another portion of my innate equipment—my intellectual conditionabilities and capabilities. Since I could not spend long hours reading, I had long hours to think; and fortunately I had equipment which made this activity possible and profitable.

Because of limited eyesight capabilities, I established more or less unconsciously a *modus operandi* which is the reverse of that more commonly employed. Many investigators read extensively about what has been done and reported, and from this reading they got ideas about what they wish to do. My method, in many cases, has been the reverse. I first think extensively about problems that interest me, and then go to the library to see if I can find any light. Very often I have found, to my disappointment, that no one has posed the questions which interest me, and that there is a wide open field.

I do not wish to give an appraisal of the quality of my mind, nor do I feel competent to do so. I do not know what my I.Q. is, nor do I care. The measurement of I.Q.'s involves jumbling together apples, oranges, bananas, coconuts, etc. (different facets of people's minds) and coming out with a relatively meaningless numerical answer. A few years ago I was invited to speak to the Annual National Convention of Mensa, all members of which pride themselves (supposedly) on having I.Q.'s above some particular figure which I have forgotten, and which I think others should forget. I did not have the inclination to tell them outright that I thought their mutual admiration society was ill-founded, but I think I did give them some hints.

My mental abilities as measured by traditional methods are not exceptional. If my intellectual abilities are in any way outstanding, it is because of my originality, inventiveness, creativeness, intuition, common sense and catholic interests. These characteristics are not measured when I.Q. tests are made. To develop a good intelligence test, leaving out originality and creativeness is almost like trying to make a good apple pie, leaving out all apples.

My contributions which may seem to merit praise have been made possible in considerable part by the fact that not being able to read with convenience, I have thought extensively and intensively, and my mind has not been excessively cluttered up by what everyone else has thought and written. I would go so far as to recommend to many young prospective scientists the motto "Read less; think more."

Another innate characteristic has influenced my scientific work appreciably. This has to do with my sleep tendencies. I am not unusual with respect to the amount of sleep I need each

24 hours, but since youth I have always much preferred taking my day's sleep in at least two installments. After about forty, my daily sleep as a rule has been taken in three installments.

No one knows why we have to sleep or what is accomplished by long hours of sleeping. The brain is extremely active biochemically and presumably something very interesting is happening there during sleep. It is easy to imagine that something is being built up or is getting reorganized, and that it takes long hours of what we call sleep to do the job. For fun we may call what we gain by sleep "repoz." The problem of what "repoz" is and why we need it is a tough one and is not attractive to those scientists who are looking for easy answers.

Some people have the innate ability to stay awake many hours and then make up for it by extra long periods of sleep when they get a chance. Some are very effective sleepers and get enough "repoz" quickly. In my case, it is as if during sleep I am filling a relatively small container with "repoz," and when it is full my sleep is over for the time being. Correspondingly, when I have been awake for six or seven hours, my "reposite" container begins to run dry, and I need to replenish it. Because of the relatively small size of my "repoz" container, when I go to bed at night I sleep only a few hours and then lie awake for an hour or more until I am ready for more sleep.

Coffee drinking, excitement or unusual activity can alter this pattern, but otherwise the distinctive neurological equipment which I know I possess makes it happen this way day after day and year after year.

The effect of my scientific work was this: I have done by far my best thinking in the middle of the night and my best writing in the earlier morning hours. Hundreds of times, probably thousands, I have gone to bed with a difficult problem unsolved and have arisen the next morning knowing just what to do next. The first time I remember doing this was when I was in college when an unusually difficult problem in calculus stumped me and the rest of the class. The next morning I knew just how to do it. The last time I had such an experience was the night before last when I went to bed with a difficult letter to write, but during my waking hour in the middle of the night I decided just what should be said and just how to phrase it.

There was one environmental factor in my early life which probably contributed toward making me the kind of scientist I have become. This is the fact that I was five to ten years younger than my three brothers and my sister. This age gap tended to make me a "loner," and more inclined toward self-reliance and independence than I might have been if I had brothers more nearly my age. When we lived in Greenwood County, Kansas, twelve miles from Eureka (I was about 4 years old), I had an imaginary friend, "Frank," with whom I conversed and played. About this time my father gave me a small pig to raise. My brothers and sister called this pig "Frank" and distinguished it for my benefit from the other "Frank" by the fact that "Frank" had a tail.

I was born of missionary parents in Ootacumund (Ooty), India, a delightful mountain spot where my parents sometimes went in summers to escape the extreme heat of southern India. My father had a crippling fall when I was about one year old, and the family had to return to the United States the next year. Because of the move, my education was considerably more regular than that of my brothers and sister whose education was partly in India, partly at home, and only partly in regular schools. We were all good students when we applied ourselves. I think my sister who was the eldest probably had the best academic record.

I'm sure that my career in science has been substantially affected by the fact that my beloved brother Bob (known to science as R. R. Williams) chose chemistry for his life work. He in turn was influenced by my mother who encouraged this. She, in turn, was influenced by her father, Harry Mills of Buffalo, New York, who though an organ maker by trade (with only a grade school education) became able through frugal management of his limited funds to buy microscopes and telescopes and became an amateur scientist—all on his own. He explored extensively and wrote articles, particularly about fresh water sponges, on which subject he was a national authority.

Sometimes I have been accused of having a missionary spirit, and people have attributed this to the fact that I came from missionary parents. To think that I have this characteristic because it was instilled into me from my youth is, I believe, a misinterpretation. I have some of the psychological and intellectual characteristics of my father and mother, not so much because I was drilled in following their precepts, as the fact that I inherited from them some of their conditionabilities, capabilities and leanings.

Once I remember reading an autobiographical account of how Arnold Toynbee became a historian. I thought his discussion of this was singularly lacking in discernment. He evidently thought that his mind was like a blank sheet, and that his interest in history happened merely because his mother nurtured him in this direction. He neglected to recognize the fact that when some mothers try to nurture their sons to become bank presidents, they turn out to be bank robbers instead. A really important reason for Arnold Toynbee becoming a historian was because he was born with history-prone equipment. He doubtless inherited from his mother some of the same intellectual leanings that made her interested in history.

Historians and "social scientists" in general need badly, in my opinion, to know something about biology; otherwise how can they possibly understand human nature or study and interpret intelligently human activities? This is a common sense, but not a popular view.

My schooling began when I was four years old in a country school about a mile and a half from our home. I realized at this time that the shortest distance to the school house was a diagonal line across a pasture, but I also knew there were cattle there and that they might be dangerous to a small boy. Sometimes when the cattle were some distance away, I did crawl under the fence and cut the corner.

I think that my schooling was not exceptional. I had some good teachers and my share of poor ones. After reaching college I had three teachers whom I regard as outstanding. Victor L. Duke, who later became President of the University of Redlands in California, was, to my mind, a wonderful teacher of mathematics. The class periods went so rapidly that many times I felt that we had barely become comfortably seated when the hour was over and we *had to* leave. One of the attractive features of his teaching was that we actively *learned* during the class period. It was not a case of coming to recite what we had learned between sessions. I liked mathematics the way he taught it and habitually made A grades.

Another of my excellent teachers was Richard C. Tolman who taught me what I learned about chemical thermodynamics at Berkeley. Later he became Dean of the Graduate School at Caltech. I remember one discussion I had with him in which he admonished me about accepting intuitive ideas. I agree they have to be tested.

The best lecturer I ever listened to, but not the best teacher, was Julius Steiglitz at the University of Chicago. Not everything he said would bear careful scrutiny, but he put on a remarkable performance, and a great deal that he had to say was eminently worth saying. Repeatedly I remember having a feeling that he was winding up the lecture when a look at the clock would show that he had two minutes to go. The serious drawback to Dr. Steiglitz's teaching was the fact that there were no interruptions and no time for embarrassing questions. He taught me, by bad example, to follow the practice in my teaching of *always* allowing time for questions.

The first time in my scientific career when I exhibited what might be thought of as unusual prowess was when I accepted, as a matter of course, in my own mind, the intuitive idea that any chemical which I might discover to have highly favorable effects on growing yeast cells would also prove to be effective for other organisms, including human beings.

This seems to me as rather a common sense idea and not

revolutionary. Yet it was revolutionary. During the 1930's and perhaps 40's it was an idea about which an orthodox scientist would say, "It may be true, but it has not been demonstrated; hence, it belongs in the area of speculation and should be distrusted."

My realization of how other scientists might regard this intuitive idea came as a result of a fatherly and friendly letter from Lafayette B. Mendal of Yale (then editor of the *Journal of Biological Chemistry* and one of the top men in biochemistry) advising me to forget about my yeast work and attack the subject of vitamins in a more realistic way, using experimental animals. I laughed inwardly at his friendly advice when it came, and now after about forty years I'm still laughing, because during this period the use of microorganisms in vitamin research has contributed mightily. Without this approach, many of the vitamins we have known for thirty years or more might well be still undiscovered, and the vast information we have gained about how the B vitamins function would be largely a blank page.

After we had discovered the existence of what we called "pantothenic acid," we worked assiduously to concentrate it. Personally I never had any serious doubts about whether or not it would ultimately fit into the general scheme of living things. We found evidence of its presence in every kind of living cell, animal, plant or bacterium. It was even found in "slime molds" which have no visible cells.

After we had made some progress in concentrating pantothenic acid, I had a surprise visit from Warren Weaver of the Rockefeller Foundation. He expressed an interest in supporting our work and encouraged me to ask for support. "Grantsmanship" as it has come to be called was foreign to my nature and thinking, and I would never have had the nerve to ask a Foundation for support at that time.

At this point it is appropriate to call attention to the fact that I have been almost unbelievably fortunate in gaining financial support for my scientific work, particularly because of my first contact with Mr. Benjamin Clayton in 1940. He has continuously been most generous and most understanding. The Clayton Foundation for Research has put millions of dollars into the support of the Clayton Foundation Biochemical Institute over the years, and this has been an unending cause for rejoicing and satisfaction. It is safe to say that without this help and sympathetic understanding of the importance of common-sense but novel ideas, my scientific work could not have been accomplished.

In the course of attempting to determine the chemical nature of pantothenic acid, several novel approaches were made. Perhaps the most striking of these involved "detective work" relating to its structure, even before it was highly concentrated.

Professor Alexander Todd of Cambridge (now Lord Todd) commended me enthusiastically for this and told me that my papers dealing with this were required reading for his students.

The fact that pantothenic acid was an acid was determined by the electrical behavior (Fractional Electrical Transport) of the active principle, at least ten years before the substance was obtained even at a level of one percent purity. Its approximate ionization constant, its approximate molecular weight, the absence of several functional groups SH, NH_2, $-CHO$,

H H

$-C=C-$, and the fact that it was subject to hydrolytic cleavage, were all determined long before it was obtained in even approximately pure form. The basis for these findings was a highly quantitative and sensitive biological test for the active principle. We *assumed* that any marked change in the structure of the principle would alter (probably destroy) its physiological activity. This unproved assumption (not, however, a wild one) was fully borne out by later experiments. As an example of our reasoning we assumed that if the unknown acid had an unsaturated double bond in its structure, the active principle would be destroyed or at least altered by hydrogenation procedures. The active principle remained unscathed by such treatment, hence we concluded—"no double bond."

I cite these deductions to call attention to the fact that reasonable, common-sense *assumptions* (for which there was no advance scientific proof) played a very prominent role in our investigations. They served as a working basis; proofs came later.

After many years of effort on the part of many able co-workers and myself pantothenic acid was obtained in concentrated form. An important procedure was fractional separation of its brucine salt from other brucine salts using chloroform and water as the solvents. During this time certain new methods of microanalysis were developed, "oxidation equivalent analysis," and micro determination of hydroxyl groups. These proved very helpful.

"Oxidation equivalent analysis" makes possible, if one knows the approximate molecular weight of the unknown, to determine in many cases, particularly highly oxygenated components, the complete empirical formula of the substance from one determination—the amount of oxygen required to burn a known quantity of the compound.

The discovery of this method of analysis is interesting because it illustrated the use of intuitive thinking. I approached the problem in a common-sense way, and though I was told later that I used "Diophantine" equations to accomplish my purpose, I had never heard of such equations before I used them. This demonstrates, I believe, that I had some mathematical *originality* even though I do not have a keen mathematical mind."

One of my early scientific accomplishments was the writing of my first book, *An Introduction to Organic Chemistry*. This was published in 1927 when I was thirty-four, and was used at once in about 300 colleges and universities including Yale, Dartmouth and Princeton. This was particularly noteworthy because the school I was connected with had no particular national standing scientifically.

The virtues of this book were, I believe, its straightforward common sense approach to organic chemistry, and its emphasis on rationality and deemphasis of memory work. This book served to get my name before the scientific public and doubtless helped in attracting the attention of the Rockefeller Foundation several years later.

A minor scientific activity of mine illustrates further how intuitive thinking played a large role in my scientific life. My associate Dr. Alfred Taylor, began to get (about the year 1940) evidence suggesting that viruses are involved in animal (and human) cancers. In spite of the fact that the evidence was not clear-cut and repeatable, it seemed to me, on the basis of *many* considerations, that the etiology of cancer would be found to involve virus-like agents. At a symposium at Atlantic City, I "went out on a limb" to advocate the active pursuit of this hypothesis which was definitely *not accepted* by the leaders in the field of cancer research at the time. The symposium was presided over by Vincent du Vigneaud, since a Nobel Laureate, and I remember his warning the audience that I had been right before when I predicted that pantothenic acid would be a vitamin, and that I might easily be right again. It seems probable in this case as in others that my intuition was based upon extensive circumstantial evidence that could not, however, be tabulated, codified or offered as "proof."

I will discuss next what I believe has been my greatest contribution to science—my explorations into the facts of individuality and the tremendous implications thereof.

My own consuming interest in this subject stems from my *thinking*, certainly not from my *reading*. Furthermore, my thinking was not based upon abstruse or involved concepts derived from specialized knowledge; it was based on commonplace facts which a man on the street can well comprehend.

I remember early in my study of this subject that I received about the same time two letters reacting to the same article. One was James B. Conant, a fellow chemist, President of Harvard University and later U.S. Ambassador to Germany. The other was an unschooled paperhanger from the same state of Massachusetts. Of the two the paperhanger showed a far better grasp of what I was trying to say. Dr. Conant, whose mind was doubtless cluttered with vast learning, could not quite grasp my meaning. I cite this not to downgrade Dr. Conant but to call attention to the existence of widely different patterns of mind, and the impossibility of judging minds on their I.Q. values or on academic degrees.

In 1940 when I began to be interested in the subject of individuality, nothing was to be found on the subject. In the Encyclopedia Brittanica, for example, there was nothing whatever in the way of information about human individuality. This is based, of course, on the innate differences between individual people. I'm sure that many contributors to this encyclopedia knew in a general way that individuality exists, but no discussion could be found of the ways individuals differ.

My *thinking* approach to this subject (it could not be a library approach) was a common sense one. To myself I argued thusly: "To get anywhere in social science and human relations we must obviously understand *people*. Is it enough to understand hypothetical 'man'? Do not social problems arise because people are real and not hypothetical? Don't we need to know what real people are like"?

The common sense answers to these questions are obvious, even if they may appear to fly in the face of time-honored pronouncement generally quoted out of context that "all men are created equal." As pointed out in my book, *Free and Unequal* (1953), the earlier version presumably also written by Thomas Jefferson in the Virginia Bill of Rights, put it his way: "All men are by nature equally free and independent." The "created equal" clause is sometimes explained by saying, "All men are equal in the sight of God." This hardly explains anything, unless we presume God to be blind and unable to see our inequalities.

Actually, the innate individuality we all possess greatly enhances the dignity of human kind, gives meaning to brotherhood, and strengthens the desirability of treating individual human beings with deep appreciation. If human beings were actually as alike as "peas in a pod" are supposed to be, no one of us would deserve any special consideration or admiration.

I have occasionally been jarred when people have commended me for being interested in *the individual*. I want to ask them "which one?" The abstract hypothetical individual is of no interest to me. At times I have been dubbed an "individualist." It seems to me that an individualist is one who has some scheme for dealing with individuals. I propose no scheme.

The *facts* of individuality (everybody arrives distinctively equipped) are of primary concern to me. They are solid and unshakable and must be accepted regardless of what philosophy one chooses to apply.

My first serious contribution along this line was a full length book, *The Human Frontier* (Harcourt, Brace, 1946). This attracted some attention and brought the publisher a reasonable return. I have in my files many highly complimentry comments about this book from prominent people. Perhaps the most significant is a statement of Professor Samuel Stouffer of Harvard, a leading sociologist of his day, who said. "Thirty years from now *The Human Frontier* will be looked upon as an epoch-making book."

My conviction that this was a badly overlooked field was strengthened by such comments as these, and I attempted to interest the National Academy of Science (to which I had recently been elected) in the possibilities by presenting the following common sense resolution:

Proposed Resolution

(National Academy of Sciences)

November 17, 1947

Whereas many of the problems which confront humanity originate within human beings rather than externally, the National Academy of Sciences hereby urges the President of the United States, in connection with plans for future research in America, to call a conference at an early date to consider the potentialities of a concerted long-range scientific attack, involving many natural science disciplines, directed toward a better understanding of human beings, their physical and psychical variabilities and the numerous factors which enter into the creation and propogation of social, economic, governmental and international problems.

This proposed resolution received only superficial consideration, and was tabled (by a committee) or in some other way was rejected. Stouffer's thirty-year period had just begun. Twenty-six years have elapsed, and I am still waiting—not, however, without signs that his estimate may not be too wild.

For example, an anthropologist told me a few months ago that at long last an overdue, and academic book on social anthropology has been published in which my essential point of view has been adopted and pursued throughout the latter discussions. Hurrah!

Another sign—early in 1971 I published, after a hassle with some of the editors, an article, "The Biology of Behavior," which set forth some of the most crucial ideas that I have been plugging for ever since *The Human Frontier* was published. This leading *Saturday Review* article attracted enough attention and interest that I have received seventeen different requests to allow its complete republication in books and periodicals. This must be some kind of record, and indicates how the essential ideas expressed twenty-six years ago are even now considered novel and, to a degree, *appropriate.*

This degree of acceptance of the importance of individuality in all human affairs has not come without further effort on my part. Three more full length books have dealt with expanding facets of this same idea: *Free and Unequal,* University of Texas Press, 1953, paperback; *Biochemical Individuality,* John Wiley & Sons, 1956, paperback 1963, second paperback edition, University of Texas Press, Austin, 1972 (Translated into Russian, Italian and Polish); *You Are Extraordinary,* Random House, 1968, paperback, Pyramid Press, 1971.

By the time *You Are Extraordinary* was published, the evidence regarding the highly distinctive innate make-up of each individual human being had become so compelling that no serious scholar could possibly reject it. There are other ways that intellectuals have, however, of discriminating against ideas they cannot reject. *They simply look the other way.*

Even though there is tremendous pressure to continue this policy of "looking the other way," I do not believe it can continue indefinitely. The pressure stems, of course, from the fact that it is vastly easier to plan for society or make "wise" comments about it if one rules out real people and is only concerned with hypothetical statistical man. It is the easy way out to forget that every citizen is every inch an individual.

After *The Human Frontier* was published, it became increasingly evident to me that it was an entirely impractical, even a ridiculous, strategy to try to *learn everything about everybody*. Instead, as I see it, we should approach each human problem with the question in mind, "How does human individuality impinge on this problem, and what knowledge about individuality will help us eliminate the difficulty?"

Among the human problems that need to be approached with these questions in mind are: alcoholism, accident proneness, learning disabilities, dyslexia, emotional upsets, drug addiction, mental disease, sex perversions, arthritis, obesity, heart disease and all other health problems, family troubles, divorce, hippyism, laziness, unemployment, race hatred, bitchiness and war.

Not one of these problems involves hypothetical "man"; they all involve real people and are greatly affected by individuality. If we are to make progress in solving them, we must take individuality seriously into account. There are no short cuts on a straight road.

Because it seemed probable that it would have clear-cut biochemical parameters, I chose alcoholism as a specific problem on which I personally would direct an attack. After about twenty-five years' study of this subject, I am fully convinced that alcoholism is a manifestation of malnutrition, (which to a surprising degree is an individual matter) coupled with a poisoning effect on appetitive regulatory mechanisms in the brain; and some individuals are peculiarly susceptible to the poisoning.

Alcoholism can be prevented by good nutrition (it usually takes years of nutritional abuse to produce it), and if not too far progressed, it can be treated nutritionally with success—at least in thousands of cases with whom I have become acquainted. In my opinion, it is a disgrace to the medical profession (and particularly the psychiatrist) that they have general and consistently "looked the other way."

The alcoholism story is a long one involving in a crucial way the facts of biochemical individuality. Our body chemistries are *highly* distinctive. I first wrote a book, *Nutrition and Alcoholism* (University of Oklahoma Press, 1951), which was superseded by *Alcoholism: The Nutritional Approach* (University of Texas Press, 1959).

Out of our alcoholism work developed a concept of far-reaching importance. Briefly and simply it is this: A person may develop a disease because he has unusual nutritional needs that are not easily met, especially if one is careless. If, however, these unusual nutritional needs are met, the disease disability disappears. This is the genetotrophic concept. There is no telling how widely this concept is applicable, because medical science has never explored it. Medical science has yet to take nutrition to its bosom and nurture it as a legitimate child. Furthermore, medical science has never given more than lip service to the broad and fundamental problem of how to deal with individuals and individuality.

One relatively important study conducted in our laboratories was concerned with "metabolic patterns" of individuals, as made evident primarily by urine and saliva compositions. "Ascending paper chromatography" was developed in our laboratories with the able help of Helen Kirby Barry and constituted a very practical method of study. We found that the urines and salivas of each individual were highly distinctive but that the patterns of monozygous twins showed close resemblance. We also found that the patterns of "mentally retarded" individuals could easily be distinguished from "normals" and that "imbeciles," for example, could easily be distinguished from "morons." I mention these studies particularly because they were published in a University of Texas bulletin (5109) which is out of print, and the study could easily be overlooked. In the same study, it was found that the "patterns" of schizophrenic patients were characterized by relative instability. They showed wide intraindividual variance with respect to specific parameters.

In the course of our studies of individuality we have dealt with rats, mice, hamsters, guinea pigs and chickens. In all these species we found each specimen to be a distinctive individual in many ways. Not only are they distinctive in their internal biochemistry, but there are many outward manifestations. For each individual animal, the answers to the following questions are liable to be widely different: How will foods be chosen if there is "cafeteria" selection? How long can life be sustained on a particular imperfect food? How much alcohol is required to bring about intoxication? How much alcohol will be consumed voluntarily under comparable conditions? How much exercise will be taken voluntarily?

Often numerical answers to these questions, as derived from one animal, may be ten times that derived from another animal of the same species, breeding and sex.

Particularly surprising to me was the fact that highly inbred animals supposedly with very similar ancestry often showed very wide divergences when studied individually. A common sense view of this problem led me, in effect, to "smell a rat" with respect to current ideas of mammalian heredity.

These observations—always with *strong* evidence of individuality even among inbred strains—led me to suggest and urge upon one of my graduate students, Eleanor Stoors, a study of newborn armadillos with respect to a few anatomical and biochemical parameters. She did an excellent job, and came up with results that "flabbergasted" (and still does to the best of my knowledge) expert geneticists. She found that although the quadruplets, which are commonly born to female armadillos, are monozygous, and supposed to arise from exactly the same nuclear genes, they may differ very materially from each other in organ weights, and even more markedly with respect to biochemical parameters, amino acids in the brain and hormone levels. The presence of highly distinctive patterns in these animals can hardly be accounted for on the basis of differences in intrauterine environments.

It may be presumed, lacking experiments, that monozygous armadillos would show individuality with respect to food choices, exercise, length of life on a specific deficient diet. Translating our findings to human beings, we must conclude that innate individuality exists even within so-called "identical twins." Some monozygous twins resemble each other far more than do others.

This revolutionary finding makes mammalian genetics far more complicated than it would otherwise be. I have detected in many geneticists a strong urge to "look the other way." Whatever the explanation of our findings may be, it is apparent that what we have said of human beings ("every baby arrives distinctively equipped") applies to armadillos as well as all other species.

I suppose my scientific interests could be summed up in the words "chemistry and its applications." I was attracted to biochemistry probably because it promised for me more interesting applications.

Of all the potential applications inherent in biochemistry, probably the most intriguing of all are those concerned with human health. Of all the health applications, the one which stands out is that of nutrition. To this area I turned my serious attention when I wrote (and published in 1962) *Nutrition in a Nutshell* (Doubleday). This was one of my best pieces of writing up to that date, and was characterized by readability for laymen. Many ideas and pieces of information about nutrition that are in it had never been gathered together before. I have in my file letters and comments from many prominent scientists which are more complimentary, I believe, than any made about any other book written on the subject of nutrition. A New York foundation gave 50,000 copies of the paperback edition to medical and dental students all over the world to stimulate their interest in nutrition. In spite of this, some supposedly "authoritative" outfit (in Massachusetts, I believe) put this book on a "not recommended" list, presumably because it was too original in its approach, and failed to say over again the same things that had been said many times before.

When I had written and published *You Are Extraordinary*, I was seventy-five years old and beginning to think that it was time to quit, or at least slow down my operations. I was fortunate, however, to attract the attention of Mr. S. Rodman Thompson who was keenly interested in nutrition, and had done a prodiguous amount of library work, and was willing and anxious to help me by running down hundreds of additional articles. In so doing, he made possible the production of my next book *Nutrition Against Disease,* which was published in 1971.

Actually the writing of this book was self-serving to a degree because in writing it I got new ideas about how to care for my own health, and about the possibility of slowing down my own aging process.

Very fortunately for me, my mental faculties were retained, and my intellectual work became, if anything, easier. Anyway, during the writing of this book, three major new ideas came to me or at least developed to the point of clear expression. The first one is so simple that one doubts that it can be a new idea. It is this: The three outstanding factors in an external physical environment are air, water and food; of these three, the most important to watch, the most complicated and the most subject to alteration is the *food.* The food we eat is the raw material for our internal environment—"milieu interieur" Claude Bernard called it—and the adequacy or inadequacy of the microenvironment of our cells and tissues is determined by the adequacy or inadequacy of the food we consume.

Closely related to this idea is a second one: Suboptimal nutrition is practically universal. Just when this idea became clear to me I cannot say. I am sure it stemmed in part from my early and later experiences with yeast. When I discovered pantothenic acid, it came about through my attempts to improve the nutritional environment of yeast cells; and I found after years of experience that this was a complicated matter. Pantothenic acid was not by any means the only factor involved, and it eventually became possible by the use of various other vitamins (biotin, thiamin, pyridoxine and inositol, for example) and amino acids as well as minerals to make yeast grow incomparably better than it would in a simpler medium. If yeast cells are given *good* nutrition, a half-ounce cake of yeast will produce over a billion tons *in one week,* but yeast cells (even in a yeast factory) never get this kind of nutritional environment.

I first encountered data related to this problem in the animal world when I carried out my first experiments with animals in 1919. At this time it was thought that weanling rats were doing well when they grew and gained weight at the rate of one gram or possibly two grams per day. My rats did this on a grain mixture diet furnished by an animal dealer. I found, however, that diets containing high quality protein promoted growth much better than this. Subsequently increasing knowledge about rat nutrition has made it possible to make weanling rats grow and develop so that they gain five to seven grams a day. Their heredity largely determines their ultimate size, but they arrive much more rapidly if their food is good. Generally in nature, however, their nutrition is suboptimal.

Suboptimal nutrition also applies to plants. Corn growing in a field and producing ten bushels to the acre has a poor nutritional environment. It can be improved, however, so that the production is twenty, fifty, one hundred or more bushels per acre. The upper limit is not known because, practically, corn nutrition is always suboptimal.

Human populations all over the world have commonly lived under conditions of suboptimal nutrition. In particular this must be true of children.

The idea of the ubiquitous occurrence of suboptimal nutrition gives one an entirely new perspective on nutrition (medical profession, please note). It makes the field infinitely more interesting and intriguing because it leads to the conclusion that nutrition as it occurs "naturally" is always subject to improvement. It is also subject to deterioration.

The third outstanding idea which came to me while writing *Nutrition Against Disease* arrived fullblown only when I was writing the last chapter. It is this: No nutrient *by itself* can accomplish anything. Teamwork is always essential. Individual nutrients—minerals, vitamins, amino acids—are like cogs, bolts, spindles or gears in a complicated machine; they operate only in conjunction with other working parts.

This means that nutrition, to be effective, must be *total* nutrition and that individual nutrients by themselves should not be expected to cure or prevent or bring benefit to any diseased condition. When they appear to do so (e.g., thiamin—beriberi, ascorbic acid—scurvy) it is because they fit in, to supplement an otherwise complete team. Nutrients such as riboflavin, calcium, manganese and lysine (to name only a few) cannot *by themselves* cure or prevent or benefit any disease. However, in cooperation with other nutrients, each one can make possible the prevention of practically every type of disease.

When these three ideas are accepted along with the genetotrophic concept developed twenty years earlier, nutrition will have a rebirth, and this will be the best thing that has happened to medicine in a hundred years.

I am reminded of a statement quoted from H. L. Menken who said in effect, "A problem may go unsolved for a million years unless someone stops to think about it for a few minutes." The place of nutrition in medical science is such a problem. When the answer arrives, its soundness and simplicity is so obvious that one wonders, "Where have these ideas been all these years?"

In the spring of 1972 I was appointed by President Nixon on his Advisory Panel on Heart Disease. The Panel was asked the question, "Why is heart disease so prevalent and so menacing, and what can be done about it."

My appointment on this Panel of twenty, as the only non-physician doubtless came about because of my book *Nutrition Against Disease,* and a review which came out about the same time, "Nutrition and Ischemic Heart Disease." I felt it my duty and privilege to try to sell to the other panel members the three ideas above as well as acquaint them with the genetotrophic idea.

To do this I furnished each panel member with copies of the books *Biochemical Individuality, Nutrition in a Nutshell,* and *Nutrition Against Disease,* and three articles, "Nutrition and and Ischemic Heart Disease," "How Can the Climate in Medical Education be Changed," and an article written by my colleagues, Drs. James Heffley, Man L. Yew, Chas. W. Bode and myself entitled, "A Renaissance in Nutritional Science is Imminent."

How much of this material the panel members read I do not know, but to help out the situation, I sent each several pertinent memoranda. The result was that the panel without dissent agreed to incorporate one strong statement giving high priority to the nutritional approach. The document as a whole was far more discursive than I would have wished.

It is difficult for a layman to comprehend how foreign down-to-earth nutritional science is to the thinking of physicians. They much preferred to "look the other way" and talk about other things. Many of them told me very frankly that they knew almost nothing about nutrition, but in the end they were more receptive. In spite of some encouraging signs, I decided to file a Minority Report which is quoted from in the appended self-explanatory open letter I wrote to then Secretary Elliott Richardson:

November 1, 1972

The Honorable Elliot Richardson
Secretary of Health, Education and Welfare
Washington, D. C.
My Dear Mr. Secretary:

On September 15 of this year I wrote you a letter telling you something of the problems I faced as the only nonphysician member of the President's Advisory Panel on Heart Disease, appointed this spring.

You referred this letter to Dr. Theodore Cooper, Director of the Heart and Lung Institute, from whom I received a very friendly, courteous and on the whole encouraging reply.

I wish to call your attention again, however, to the fact that the problem which I face cannot be met by referral to any physician, since it involves vast educational endeavors, embodies concepts not yet accepted by the medical profession generally, and in effect is highly critical of medical education (and the profession) for its short-sighted neglect of nutritional science.

Below are presented excerpts from my Minority Report to President Nixon:

"Most Probable Cause of Heart Disease Prevalence

While no one knows why heart disease is so prevalent, it is highly probable that a primary cause lies in the fact that in our industrialized age the public chooses its food only on the basis of appearance and taste, and has not been educated to choose on the basis of nutritional value. Much of our food is processed, transported long distances and kept a long time, and the purveyors of food cater to those who want attractive and tasty foods and who pay little attention to its nutritional efficacy. Modern scientific prowess has not been utilized as it should have been. Nutritional science has lagged.

"External and Internal Environments

Three things in our 1972 physical environment stand out as requiring the utmost in scientific attention: air, water and food. Of these three, food is by far the most complicated and hence requires by far the most scientific attention. Food contains about 40 nutritional elements that have to be taken into our bodies daily in about the right amounts and proportions. Nature helps us immeasurably in meeting these demands, but we must learn better how to cooperate with nature.

These nutritional elements enter into and become a part of what Claude Bernard, a famous 19th century French physiologist, called the *milieu interieur* of the body. This internal environment should be of crucial concern in connection with heart disease, as I have brought out in chapter 5, "Protecting the Hearts We Have," in my new book *Nutrition Against Disease*. This chapter is documented by about 450 references to the scientific and medical literature.

" 'Sins' of Commission and Omission

Two kinds of "sins" can be committed against our internal environments—those of commission and those of omission. One flagrant sin of commission occurs when we inhale tobacco smoke. This corrupts the environments of cells and tissues and is one of the causes of heart disease, as practically all panel members would agree. But many people have heart attacks who do not smoke, so we must look elsewhere.

The sins of omission occasioned by modern industrialization of food production without adequate regard for nutritional value are many. Among the essential nutrient items likely to be deficient or out of balance in the supermarket produce commonly consumed are vitamin B_6, magnesium, vitamin E, ascorbic acid, folic acid and trace minerals. This is not a complete list, but these items all appear to be involved in the heart disease problem. All these and other nutrient items are needed to keep the cells and tissues of hearts and blood vessels healthy.

"Early 'Sin'

When, particularly in West Germany, thalidomide, used as a medicine, was introduced into the environment of growing fetuses, deformed babies were born. This resulted from a sin of commission. Sins of omission committed in early pregnancy can have similar results. Folic acid is one nutrient that needs to be scrutinized carefully in this context.

It is highly probable that heart and blood vessel defects, which are common in the general population, arise largely because of the poor environments pregnant women furnish their growing fetuses when they eat in a careless and uninformed manner. Many heart problems arise from these defects. One responsible medical dean has

written me that the reproductive record of human beings is "terrible" —much of the difficulty probably arises from poor prenatal nutrition.
"Nutritional Disease Prevention (U.S. Dept. of Agriculture)

In a 1971 two-volume report issued by the United States Department of Agriculture, it is estimated that in the case of 13 common serious diseases, 20-90% relief can be looked for as a result of nutritional research. Some of these estimates would have been increased if the writers had been aware of some of the material contained in my book *Nutrition Against Disease*.
"Remedy: Promote Nutritional Science

The President's second question, "What can be done about it?" can be answered broadly and very simply: promote nutritional science. The air we breathe and the water we use are now receiving substantial scientific attention. The food we eat requires incomparably more scientific attention, and it is not getting it. Nutritional science is underdeveloped and at a low ebb. This is primarily because medical science and education has never accepted and nurtured nutritional science and treated it as though it really belonged. This fact and some of the historical reasons behind it have been discussed in my book *Nutrition Against Disease*.

The situation has become so bad that Senator Schweiker of Pennsylvania has introduced the Nutritional Medical Education Act of 1972 to provide funds for developing nutritional education in medical schools. The low ebb of nutritional education was emphasized in a two-column article on "Nutritional Illiteracy" in the New York *Times* of June 14, 1972, by the industrialist and food producer, Henry J. Heinz II. As one who has spent a lifetime of study in this general area, I would say that the situation is even worse than Mr. Heinz pictures it.

If something is not done soon, our physicians are going to be *far* behind the dentists and the osteopaths in their comprehension of nutritional science. It is good for the dentists and osteopaths to forge ahead, but it is intolerable for the physicians to forge behind. A multidisciplinary approach involving not only biochemistry and physiology but also internal medicine, pathology, microbiology, dentistry, endocrinology, reproduction, and other related areas, is urgently needed.

In my letter of October 9 to Dr. Millis, Chairman of the President's Panel on Heart Disease, I wrote: "I regard it as a national calamity that nutritional science has received so little attention and that physicians and other medical scientists are so inattentive to and ignorant of what might be a tremendous boon for humanity."
"Uncertainty, Confusion, Ignorance

The mere teaching of traditional "nutrition courses" will not by any means meet our needs. The strongest statement regarding nutrition in the majority report of the President's Advisory Panel on Heart Disease is on page 36, Recommendation 1.8: "The Panel endorses creation of Comprehensive Research, Training, and Clinical Cardiovascular Centers. The Panel believes that first priority should be given to support of a Center in Arteriosclerosis, including, as a very important component, studies on nutrition—a conspicuous field of ignorance and one which offers great promise for prevention."

The matter of uncertainty, ignorance and confusion in the field of nutrition cannot be overemphasized. There are, as all of us know, many conflicting ideas about nutrition afloat, and many notions of a faddist nature which gain more or less acceptance. Unfortunately, some of the most "crackpottish" ideas are promoted by licensed physicians who failed to get adequate grounding while in medical school. People's ignorance in this field is being exploited. Millions of people are grasping for help and do not know where to go for sound advice since it is notorious that most physicians know very little about nutrition. Many of them, including panel members, will freely admit that this is so. Typically, the advice patients get when they ask their doctor about their nutrition is, in effect, this: "Forget it. We are the best fed people in the world. If you want to take vitamins, they probably won't hurt you." If the physicians were informed about the intricacies of nutrition and were to give this advice, the situation would be very different from what it is when they speak out of ignorance rather than knowledge.

"Institutes for Nutritional Science

The only way the uncertainties, confusion and ignorance about people's nutrition can be dispelled is through careful, comprehensive and realistic objective research to ascertain the answers to a host of questions. In one of the memoranda which I passed out to the panel, there were thirty-six pressing problems relating nutrition to heart disease. None of these were even discussed, and there are many more. While there is a large amount of research to be done, the picture will clear rapidly as soon as competent scientists, in sufficient numbers, *put their minds to it*. This at present is not being done. Many who are interested in nutrition are concerned with defending time-honored positions which are certain to become obsolete.

The only way I see out of this crippling situation is for the Federal Government to create two or more Institutes for Nutritional Science. This can be done under the *Heart, Blood Vessel and Lung Act of 1972*. One Institute could well be concerned with nutrition as it relates to atherosclerosis; the other to prenatal nutrition as it relates to congenital heart disease and cardiomyopathies.

Manpower for these Institutes for Nutritional Science will present a problem, but not for long if money becomes available; for there are real problems to be solved, and keen interest can be engendered in the minds of thousands of competent scientists once support is assured.

"Impact Much Wider Than Merely on Heart Disease

Once nutritional science gets substantial support, it will become more evident that nutrition can play a tremendous role in the prevention of all types of disease. This is the theme of my book *Nutrition Against Disease* which has been pronounced even by some physicians as "thoroughly sound." Mental retardation, dental disease, arthritis, mental disease, alcoholism, and possibly even cancer, can be blamed on the poor internal environments which the cells and tissues of our bodies have to live with. These environments can be vastly improved by nutritional means.

The basis for wide sweeping hope for prevention of disease lies in the realization that environments are of paramount importance, and nutritional environments have not really been considered seriously. Are environments important to living creatures? The answer is obvious. Are environments important for living cells and tissues? The affirmative answer is also obvious. Do cells and tissues become deranged (diseased) when the environments are inadequate? This too can be answered with certainty. Improvement of internal environments can be accomplished through the application of technical prowess—by developing nutritional science. Creation of Institutes for Nutritional Science would be an important step toward the promotion of better general health for the entire public.

'Economies Involved

In the *Heart, Blood Vessel and Lung Act of 1972* it is estimated that the potential gain from conquering heart disease would be more than 30 billion dollars per year. This figure would certainly more than double if we could conquer other diseases as well. Of course there is no magic formula for eliminating disease entirely, but we are dealing with enormous potential savings not only of money but also in terms of grief and distress. A private citizen would not hesitate to invest ten dollars per year if there were reasonable prospect of getting 30 thousand dollars per year in return. The Federal Government should not hesitate to risk 10 million dollars a year when the return to the public might well be 30 billion dollars per year.

"A Vote for Ignorance?

If we reject the proposal to develop nutritional science, we are voting for ignorance. This is unthinkable in the light of the unexplored gold mine of opportunities for health betterment suggested by the U.S. Department of Agriculture's report. Surely we wish to adhere to the basic philosophy that knowledge is to be preferred to ignorance. In the field of nutritional science we cannot afford to remain ignorant.

"Not a Problem for Routine Referral to a Medical Committee

Because of decades of indoctrination, many physicians will automatically "pooh pooh" the idea that nutrition can be so important for the prevention of disease. This, in my opinion, is because they are so inexpert in the area of nutritional physiology. No physician worthy of the name, however, can take the position that ignorance about nutrition is preferable to understanding.

I therefore respectfully urge that the proposal to develop nutritional science be broadly considered, and that it not be merely referred to some medical committee.

"Popular Demand

Millions of people are keenly interested in exploring the possibilities of attaining better health through nutrition. Many more can be easily led to have such an interest. If you, Mr. President, can in your administration start paving the way to better health through nutritional prevention of disease, many millions more will indeed rise up to call you blessed."

Since this whole matter is very much on my mind and on my conscience, I expect to make my position fully known to the public in every appropriate way.

I sincerely hope you will be interested and will communicate with President Nixon and cooperate in every way with all efforts to bring understanding and action on behalf of nutritional science.

Sincerely yours,
Roger J. Williams

RJW:mj

P.S. For your more complete information, I am sending a copy of my complete Minority Report.

A sidelight on my scientific work has been the coining of a number of new words which appear in dictionaries. Among these are: *nutrilite, pantothenic, folic, lipoic, genetotrophic* and *avidin.* Other new words which may not have appeared in dictionaries yet are: *isotelic, propetology, paragenetics,* and *discomformity.*

The word *nutrilite* resulted from a dream in which I was talking to my brother Bob about scientific matters. The term vitamin, we agreed, is applied only to substances which in small amounts are needed in *animal* nutrition. "There should be," I said in my dream, "a word which is more inclusive to apply to substances which may be needed by nonanimal organisms. How would 'nutrilite' do?" He agreed in my dream that it was a good word. I remembered the dream in the morning, published a short note in *Science,* and that was it.

Pantothenic, the name I gave to the substance which I discovered, was coined after consulting some Greek dictionaries. It means "from everywhere." Actually it was not known at the time that the "from everywhere" designation would eventually appear to apply equally well to many other nutrients which are universal cogs in the machinery of living things.

Folic acid was the name we gave to the substance we concentrated starting with eleven tons of fresh spinach. Since the Latin word for leaf is *folium,* this name seemed appropriate. Leaves are a rich source. The name applied by those who first synthesized it, "pteroylglutamic acid," was too cumbersome for general use. Before the latter name was coined, samples of "folic" acid had been sent, utilizing a government subsidy, to scores of laboratories all over the world, and the name folic acid has stuck.

"Lipoic acid" was the first B-vitamin-like growth factor found to be readily soluble in lipid solvents. Up to this time vitamins had turned out to be *either* fat soluble or water soluble. This substance was both.

The origin of the term *genetotrophic* has already been given. *Avidin* was so named because of its avid attraction for one of the B vitamins—biotin. It is a protein found in raw egg white which combines with biotin and inactivates it. *Isotelic* is an excellent word etymologically, and one for which I know of no synonym. It means "having the same purpose." Some individual scientists have raved over the usefulness of the term, but it seems not to have been used extensively.

Propetology is the potential science which is concerned with determining the "leaning" of individual people toward specific diseases. The term was used in a lead editorial in the *American Journal of Medicine* entitled "Propetology, A New Branch of Medical Science?" The word has a good Greek origin, and has since been used with approval by Sir Julian Huxley, and will probably eventually find its place in dictionaries. The word paragenetic is a term I am coming at the present moment to designate the study of inheritance without presupposing that only the traditional genes are involved. This word has a place because of our work with armadillos. *Discomformity* is a term I have used to designate features which lean toward "abnormalities" but should not be classed as such because of their widespread occurrence in the "normal" population. If a person has one, two, four, five, or six arteries branching from the aortic arch, these are discomformities. About 65 percent of people have three such branching arteries.

To sum up my scientific work, it must be said that my contributions have been of diverse nature. Perhaps I am one of those specialists who specializes on having broad interests. How important my contributions have been will be left to posterity to judge (if it cares to). They have been, in my view, in the fields of biochemistry, genetics, pharmacology, nutrition, psychology, anthropology, and social science and, perhaps above all, in medicine. Anyway you slice it, it has been fun.

In the foregoing discussion of my scientific work I have purposely restricted myself and have said very little or nothing about many things of great importance—my family, my friendships, my colleagues, my students, religion, my enjoyment of music, shows and other recreations, golf, fly fishing and card playing. Each one of these topics by itself could almost be the subject of a book or a separate chapter.

One parting shot: There is one subject which is as much a mystery as it was 2,500 years ago. When Socrates was about to die, Crito asked him, "How shall we bury you?" Socrates laughed gently and said, "Anyway you want to, provided you can catch me, and I do not slip through your fingers." He then went on to say that the Socrates that was talking to him was not what they would bury or burn. *He* (Socrates) would be gone.

I think it is appropriate for a scientist to attempt to understand the whole world. Is not that which "slips through the fingers" when a noble man like Socrates dies a very significant part of the whole world? Is it not the product of millions of years of evolution? Should this slippery "something" be regarded as ephemeral, transient and as inconsequential as a mere shadow, while matter and energy sit on a permanent throne? Is this a "something" that can evaporate without even becoming a vapor?

In past history, important things have slipped through scientists' fingers for decades—the release of atomic energy is one—only to be captured later. Possibly one day scientists will begin to understand why the ancient philosopher said in effect, "You cannot bury Socrates."

Chapter XI

PSYCHOLOGY IN 1972

Paul Thomas Young

Paul Thomas Young was born in Los Angeles, California, in 1892. He attended public schools of that city; received the AB in 1914 from Occidental College; the AM from Princeton University in 1915; the PhD from Cornell University in 1918. At Cornell he was Sage Scholar in Psychology and Teaching Assistant in the Department of Psychology. Subsequently, as National Research Council Fellow, he spent a postdoctoral year, 1926-1927, in Berlin.

Dr. Young's teaching experience included two years, 1919-1921, as Instructor in Psychology at the University of Minnesota. In 1921 he moved to the University of Illinois where he was advanced through the various academic ranks to Professor of Psychology in 1934. In 1960 he became Professor of Psychology Emeritus. Teaching at Illinois was broken by several sabbatical leaves. After the year in Berlin he spent a sabbatical year at Stanford University, 1931-1932; a year at Yale University, 1939-1940, as Visiting Fellow; and a year at Harvard University, 1947-1948, as Research Fellow.

His research has been mainly in the fields of affective psychology and motivation with some work on sound localization and other processes. Young's research has been supported by grants from the American Medical Association, the Quartermaster of the United States Army, The Research Board of the University of Illinois, and the National Science Foundation.

Young is a Fellow of the American Psychological Association and the American Association for the Advancement of Science, a Life Member of the Midwestern Psychological Association and the Illinois Psychological Association. He is a member of the Psychonomic Society, the American Association of University Professors, and Phi Beta Kappa, Sigma Xi, Psi Chi, and Phi Delta Kappa Fraternities.

Dr. Young's Publications include more than a hundred research and theoretical papers, about a dozen encyclopedia articles on motivation and emotion, and three textbooks. His most recent book is Motivation and Emotion: a Survey of the Determinants of Human and Animal Activity (Wiley, 1961).

Following retirement in 1960, Young continued research on affective processes under a grant from the National Science Foundation. In 1963 he moved to Claremont, California, where he continues writing on psychological and related topics.

Dr. Young has received various recognitions. In 1961 his alma mater, Occidental College, honored him with the degree of Doctor of Science. In 1965 the American Psychological Association awarded the Distinguished Scientific Contribution Award, citing a life-long study of hedonic processes, appetitive behavior and preferences. In September, 1967, at the seventy-fifth anniversary celebration of the founding of the American Psychological Association he was included in a group of senior psychologists honored for "a distinguished lifetime's contribution to psychology as a science and as a profession."

THE EDITOR OF THIS BOOK has asked the contributors to present their notions about science and technology today, where it is going, where it should go, their philosophy of science, their biases or research priorities, needs, methods of approach. I have tried to do just that. Ideally one should *learn* from the past, *live* in the present, *plan* for the future. Realistically one difficulty in planning ahead is that the future is unpredictable.

My career has been in college and university teaching, research and writing in experimental psychology. The research has generally been directed toward the solution of some specific problem that seemed important at the time. The teaching has been general and not directly related to the research. The writing has been various, including reports of research, textbooks, encyclopedia articles, theoretical papers.

In the following pages I will consider several questions: What is the present status of science and technology? What is the status of psychology in 1972? What kind of psychology will be needed in the future? Is there a universal psychology? What would I teach if starting a career in 1972? What lines of research would I follow? What philosophical orientation would I maintain?

My comments on these questions and related matters will constitute the bulk of this essay.

THE SITUATION IN 1972

What Is the Present Status of Science and Technology?

We are living in the midst of a scientific and technological revolution. Some have attributed pressing social problems of the day to the growth and influence of science and technology. It is claimed that the applications of science have led to deterioration of the human environment, to destructive weaponry and wars of annihilation, to the population explosion, to undermining of the family as a unit of society, to racial injustice, drug addiction, violence and crime in the streets, and other grave consequences.

Others have pointed to the remarkable achievements of modern science and technology: communication by telephone, radio and TV; transportation by jet airplanes; exploration of space typified by putting a man on the moon; developments in medicine and surgery; scientific agriculture; applications of electricity to the home, and so on. The scientist and technologist are praised for achievements based on science as well as blamed for the evils.

Much current criticism of modern science would disappear if it were realized that the application of science for good or evil are *nonscience* activities. It is the practical consequences of science that are evaluated as good or bad—not the scientific facts and truths. Scientific activity is only part of the total human undertaking. Human beings are involved in various kinds of *nonscience* activities: religious worship, aesthetic expressions in music and other arts, athletic performances in sports and games, political activities, working, eating, sleeping, seeking entertainment, etc.

Specialization in Science and Technology

One important point should be made: In the contemporary physical, biological, social, and behavioral sciences there exists a high degree of specialization. Each scientist is concerned with a specific interest, communicates with a small group of experts, and works in a laboratory or in the field on a rather limited problem. Our educational system is oriented toward producing specialists: high-energy physicists, solid-state physicists, enzyme biochemists, and psychologists who are specialists in information processing, psycholinguistics, brain function, aversive conditioning, and other specialties. With such intensive specialization, it is about all one can do to keep up to date in his chosen field of specialization. There has been an explosion of scientific knowledge.

Much of the same can be said about the applied sciences. The technologist has an urge to solve some special practical problem. In his work he draws support from a variety of sciences but his work is more or less limited by a specific problem in hand. Both the scientist and the technologist are concerned with solving problems and both are specialists.

Weisskopf (1972), considering the significance of science, stated eloquently that a broad understanding of science as a whole goes beyond the specialties. The contemporary scientist, he said, should seek a deep understanding of nature as a whole. The scientist, as citizen and a human being, should consider the social consequences of his work and share the responsibility of solving problems that confront humanity as a consequence of his work.

What Is the Status of Psychology in 1972?

When I attended my first meeting of the American Psychological Association, in Philadelphia, in 1914, the Association could be described as a small learned society. There were a few hundred scholars, mostly associated with educational institutions, and some with a philosophical rather than a scientific outlook. In 1972 the American Psychological Association has about 30,000 members, fellows and associates.

The Association is bifurcated. One branch contains psychologists who are concerned with developing psychology as a basic science. The other branch, which has grown rapidly and proliferated, contains psychologists whose chief concern is with the practical applications of psychology to human welfare.

The objects of the Association are described as follows:

> The objects of the American Psychological Association shall be
> to advance psychology as a science and as a means of promoting

human welfare by the encouragement of psychology in all its branches in the broadest and most liberal manner; by the promotion of research in psychology and the improvement of research methods and conditions; by the improvement of the qualifications and usefulness of psychologists through high standards of professional ethics, conduct, education, and achievement; by the increase and diffusion of psychological knowledge through meetings, professional contacts, reports, papers, discussions, and publications; thereby to advance scientific interests and inquiry, and the application of research findings to the promotion of the public welfare. (Lazo, 1968, p. xii)

The two basic concerns of psychologists today are the advancement of psychology as a science and the applications of psychology to promoting human welfare. One can ask: What kind of research will advance psychology as a science? What kind of psychology is needed to advance human welfare?

Psychology in Transition

Psychology as a science is in a state of transition. The direction of change is fairly clear. In the nineteenth and early twentieth centuries psychology, regarded as mental philosophy, was breaking away from the main-stream of philosophy and becoming established as an independent science closely related to biology and especially to physiology.

The physical sciences, perhaps unfortunately, provided a model for scientific psychology. The physical sciences and technologies were in an enviable position since they had led to remarkable discoveries with applications in the fields of communication, transportation, agriculture and medicine.

In the present situation people are turning increasingly to the behavioral and social "sciences" in the hope of promoting human welfare. The trend in 1972 appears to be away from a purely academic and scholarly discipline toward a psychology that is relevant to the solution of human social and personal problems. *Relevance* is the key word. Is the science of psychology ready for widespread social application?

Psychology as a Natural Science

Eisenberg (1972), a psychiatrist at Harvard Medical School

and Chief of Psychiatry at Massachusetts General Hospital, has questioned whether there can be a genuine science of behavior. In discussing the *human* nature of human nature, he writes:

> The thrust of my argument is that there is no solid foundation to the theoretical extrapolation of the instinctivists, the ethologists, the behaviorists, *or* the psychoanalysts, despite their special pleading that often is so seductive to those eager for a "real science" of behavior. Further, to the point, belief helps shape actuality because of the self-fulfilling character of social prophecy. To believe that man's aggressiveness or territoriality is in the nature of the beast is to mistake some men for all men, contemporary society for all possible societies, and, by a remarkable transformation, to justify what is as what needs must be; social repression becomes a response to rather than a cause of, human violence. Pessimism about man serves to maintain the status quo. . . (p. 124).

The gist of Eisenberg's argument is that *human* nature is something other than the nature of a naked ape, activated by territorial imperatives and impelled by aggressive instincts. Human nature is something more than the nature of uncivilized brutes. It is *human* nature.

History tells us what has been; but history is futile in predicting what can be. The study of man, according to Eisenberg, takes its meaning from involvement in the struggle for human betterment. We cannot avoid the struggle for human welfare. And that is a sound basis for optimism.

James B. Conant (1967) has a slightly different view of the nature of psychology as a natural science. He believes that the *biological* aspects of behavior are part of the science of biology but he doubts that the *social* aspects of behavior can ever constitute a science. Conant writes:

> The social sciences are not yet sciences; no *widely accepted* conceptual scheme with posits other than those of common sense has as yet developed. Perhaps someday it will. So I have been assured by friends in economics, sociology, anthropology, and psychology, for half a century. I am beginning to doubt it. The failure, I have come to think, is to be traced to the fact that the instruments used in the natural sciences cannot talk back. Human beings can and do. On this basis, experimentation with animals, even if performed

by investigators who label themselves "psychologists," is part of a science, namely biology. Psychology, as an examination of human behavior, like sociology, is in quite another category. I am inclined to think the history of psychology will bear out my rather unusual dissection of a field which for practical reasons many professors have in recent years endeavoured to consider as a closely knit unit. (p. 325)

Conant views the problems of human behavior broadly in relation to ethics and values. He postulates three areas of experience: (1) nature and natural science, (2) interpersonal human social relations, (3) religious experience (in the sense of William James). Conant calls these areas "the realm of nature, the realm of human nature, the realm of religious experiences." (p. 321)

As noted above, Conant believes that the study of animal, including human, behavior is part of biology which is a natural science. The study of interpersonal social relations, however, is and will probably remain a nonscience. Conant has thus made a dichotomy between biopsychology (a science) and the disciplines (nonsciences) concerned with interpersonal and social relations and with human welfare.

Now Conant is a chemist and thinks of science in terms of physics, chemistry, astronomy, and related physical sciences, where exact predictions can be made and where precise controls over phenomena are possible. In terms of physical science there appears to be uniformity, stability and order in the universe.

I do not agree with Conant's limitation of natural science to the physical and biological sciences. There is a scientific method of observing, analyzing, and interpreting human phenomena which can be applied in the social and behavioral disciplines. I believe (contrary to Conant) that there is a *science* dealing with interpersonal and social relations and that every social act is a natural event which can be examined scientifically even though precise control and prediction are impossible.

Psychology differs from the physical sciences in that beliefs, attitudes, motives, habits, and similar dispositions, are continually subject to change by influences that cannot always be foreseen and predicted. Statistical prediction in terms of probability is possible in psychology but mathematically exact predictions are often impossible.

LOOKING AHEAD

When the American Psychological Association stated as one of its major aims the promotion of human and public welfare, it committed the Association to a normative goal. Human welfare and social betterment imply evaluative judgments which differ from psychologist to psychologist and with place and time. Psychology and ethics, therefore, are involved in the same tasks.

It is important to consider the kind of psychology that will be required in the years ahead by psychologists concerned with human betterment.

What Kind of Psychology Will Be Needed in the Future?

In an attempt to answer this question it is important to consider the biological nature of man as well as man's social history.

Mayr (1972) pointed out that the Darwinian revolution produced a profound change in man's view concerning his nature and place in the world. Man had long regarded himself as the product of divine creation, master of living things and the world, the most highly developed of all creatures. The doctrine of evolution through natural selection places man in the animal world. Man differs from other animals but is not necessarily Lord and Master. The fate of *Homo sapiens* on the face of the earth is like the fate of other species that have seen their day and vanished. Evolution is not a process that moves toward perfection but rather a process that produces variations and random selection of forms of life that are capable of surviving in a severe struggle for existence. Now it is obvious, as Mayr points out, that man's religion, philosophy, humanism, and outlook on life, have been profoundly affected by the Darwinian revolution.

The Biological Nature of Man

To answer the ancient question "What is man?" one must begin by considering man's biological heritage. Since the day of

Darwin, man has been regarded as an animal living within a natural world and sharing his environment with other living things. Man is part of nature's ecology.

Simpson (1966) has pointed to the many resemblances—anatomical, physiological, psychological—between *Homo sapiens* and living apes as well as between present forms and known human ancestors. He concludes:

> Like other animals, man develops, is born, grows, reproduces, and dies. Like other animals, he eats, digests, eliminates, respires, locomotes. He bends the qualities of nature to his own ends, but he is as fully subject to nature's laws as is any other animal and is more capable of changing them. He lives in biological communities and has a niche and an ecology, just as do robins and earthworms. Let us not forget those aspects of man's nature. But let us also remember that man stands upright, builds and makes as never was built or wrought before, speaks and may speak truth or a lie, worships and may worship honestly or falsely, looks to the stars and into the mud, remembers his past and predicts his future, and writes (perhaps at too great length) about his own nature. (p. 478)

Man differs from other animals in two important respects: in the remarkable development of tools and in the development and use of language. The tools and the language differ greatly from one cultural group to another but despite deviations there are biological constants which rest upon common human needs.

To understand human nature one must understand man's biological background. Simpson is right: Man is an animal living within a sociocultural environment—an environment which is to a considerable extent self-made.

The Anthropological Evidence

The evidence from physical anthropology confirms Darwin's view that man is an animal closely related to living and extinct members of the primate group. The evidence from fossils indicates that the ancestors of *Homo sapiens* were ape-like creatures living perhaps 25 million years ago in Africa and Asia. The ancestors of modern man were also ancestors to chimpanzees and gorillas.

The divergence of man's ancestry from apes was early

marked by bipedalism and upright posture. Our immediate ancestors were fully bipedal, ground-living animals, using hands for manipulations much as we do. The teeth of the Hominids were so like ours as to be hard to distinguish. The brains of these creatures were little larger than those of apes and the intellectual characteristics but all belong to the same species, *Homo sapiens*.

Viewed biologically, there are, indeed, *races* of man, characterized by body form, skin color and behavior, just as there are *races* of dog, cat, horse, poultry, and other animals. The *races* of man differ in anatomical, physiological, and psychological characteristics but all belong to the same species, *Homo sapiens*.

The Influence of Culture: People living in different parts of the world differ greatly in manner of dress, language, religious beliefs and practices, methods of child training, of curing disease, of producing food, and in other respects. Man has adapted to wide variations in his natural environment—from the tropical forests to the polar regions, from the mountains to the deserts, from country to city environments. The adaptations of behavior differ widely with place and time but most adaptations are relevant to survival of the human species. Demography and human history have much of interest to offer the student of cultural differences.

The early development and training within a cultural group leave a permanent stamp on personality, behavior, and traits of character. For example, anthropologist Clyde Kluckhohn (1949, p. 21), describes a young man who arrived in New York City from China. He could not speak a word of English and was obviously bewildered by American ways. His genes had been transplanted from America because his parents had gone from Indiana to China as missionaries. Orphaned in infancy, he was reared by a Chinese family in a remote village. All who met him found him more Chinese than American. He had blue eyes and hair but that was less impressive than a Chinese style of gait, Chinese arm and hand movements, Chinese facial expressions, Chinese modes of thought. His biological heritage was American, but his cultural heritage and background were Chinese. He later returned to China, being unable to adjust to American ways.

Is There a Universal Human Psychology?

The anthropolist, G. P. Mrudock (1945), pointed out that despite wide differences in human activity, language, dress, beliefs and attitudes, there is a common denominator of cultures. Murdock prepared a list of items that are common to all known cultures. He writes:

> The following is a partial list of items, arranged in alphabetical order to emphasize their variety, which occur, so far as the author's knowledge goes, in every culture known to history of ethnography: age-grading, athletic sports, bodily adornment, calendar, cleanliness training, community organization, cooking, cooperative labor, cosmology, courtship, dancing, decorative art, divination, division of labor, dream interpretation, education, eschatology, ethics, ethnobotany, etiquette, faith healing, family, feasting, fire making, folklore, food taboos, funeral rites, games, gestures, gift giving, government, greetings, hair styles, hospitality, housing, hygiene, incest taboos, inheritance rules, joking, kin-groups, kinship nomenclature, language, law, luck, superstitions, magic, marriage, mealtimes, medicine, modesty concerning natural functions, mourning, music, mythology, numerals, obstetrics, penal sanctions, personal names, population policy, postnatal care, pregnancy usages, property rights, propitiation of supernatural beings, puberty customs, religious ritual, residence rules, sexual restrictions, soul concepts, status differentiation, surgery, tool making, trade, visiting, weaning, and weather control.

Rarely, if ever, Murdock points out, do the universal similarities represent identities of specific cultural contents. They are similarities in the *classification* of the cultural elements rather than in actual content. The elements of culture are diverse, but competent observers feel compelled to classify them together. For example, the actual behavior exhibited in acquiring a spouse, teaching a child, or treating a sick person, differs enormously from one group to another; but the divergent acts can be classified under unifying rubrics of marriage, education, and medicine. Early reports of people lacking language or fire or morals or religion or marriage or government, Murdock states, have proved to be erroneous in every instance. Cross-cultural comparisons and classifications reveal many universal, common, features of human groups.

The common features of different cultures can be explained by the fact that *Homo sapiens* can survive only if the individuals of a group obtain food and water, protect themselves against the extremes of heat and cold, exercise, rest and sleep, avoid predators and human enemies, reproduce and rear children, and continue techniques that have proved successful in the past. Murdock's common denominator of cultures is thus a *biological* denominator. The ways in which biological needs for survival and maintaining a group are met vary widely from culture to culture but despite diversity in the contents of cultures, the basic needs for human survival are uniform and are somehow met.

Is there a universal psychology? I believe that a universal psychology is possible because, despite wide differences in behavior within cultural groups, there are common biological requirements for continued existence of the human species. Human animals share common motivations, emotions, perceptual and cognitive reactions. There are common bodily needs for survival and growth.

A universal psychology will not predict specific bodily movements but it can describe specific motives, values, attitudes, habits, frustrations, and the like. Precise prediction is impossible because the environmental situation is always changing and never twice the same. But there are common psychological principles.

The principles of development apply to mankind everywhere as well as to nonhuman animals. Positive and negative effects (rewards and punishments) reinforce patterns of behavior in every social group. And there are common characteristics of perception. Eleanor J. Gibson (1970) pointed out that perception of events in space develops early in the life of individuals. To survive an organism needs information about surfaces, edges, cliffs, distances, objects, the behavior of animals (including human beings), and so on.

Further, human behavior everywhere shows a degree of similarity in emotional reactions. Izard (1971) has described nine fundamental emotional expressions which are quite generally recognized in different cultural groups. In all groups, for example, there are expressions of pleasure and displeasure, of friendliness and hostility. There are uniformities in emotional reactions as well as culture-bound differences in conventional expressions.

A universal human psychology considers functional uniformities of behavior and experience in diverse cultural and social settings. Such a psychology is possible but at present not well formulated.

A STRICTLY PERSONAL VIEW

In the above pages I have reviewed the situation in psychology as it appears in 1972. It is time to turn prophet and view the years ahead: What kind of a career would I plan if I were a graduate student of psychology at age 20 instead of an oldster terminating a career at age 80?

One difficulty with this question is that the details of a career in experimental psychology are rarely planned in advance. From the start I have followed my inclinations and interests. Interests have changed from year to year. [See my autobiography in Krawiec (1972).] This laissez faire philosophy would doubtless continue if it were possible now to start another career. My weltanschauung has changed through the years and would certainly continue to change. Hence any projection into the future is hazardous.

My intellectual career as noted above has been in the fields of teaching, research and writing. The roles of teacher, investigator, and writer would doubtless continue in the future, if I had any choice in the matter. These roles fit together nicely; to some extent they are inter-related.

In the following pages three questions will be considered: (1) What would I teach if starting a career in 1972? (2) What lines of research would I follow? (3) What philosophical orientation would I maintain?

What Would I Teach if Starting a Career in 1972?

In the role of teacher my main interest has always been to present a basic scientific psychology that is factually sound and socially significant. I have taught courses in general psychology, social psychology, experimental psychology, and others. On an advanced level I have repeatedly taught courses dealing with motivation and emotion. If I were starting a teaching career in 1972, I would want to continue these courses.

A citizen who is concerned with human welfare and social betterment needs much more than a course in psychology. He needs a broad orientation in the social disciplines: history, sociology, political science, social psychology, psychiatry, education, economics, law, and others. Education in the humanities as well as in the natural sciences is also desirable. The do-gooder needs a well-rounded education.

If I were teaching courses in general psychology and social psychology, I would keep in mind the two aims of the American Psychological Association. I believe that the best course in psychology for a student interested in human welfare is a basic scientific course that has universal applicability. Such a basic psychology deals with human behavior and experience as it is found in all parts of the world at all times. A basic psychology also includes the findings of the laboratory. Such a course has universal and widespread significance.

My special interest in teaching, however, has long been in the areas of motivation and emotion. In the classroom and in the laboratory I have been concerned with feelings, emotions, moods, beliefs, desires, habits, attitudes, and related determinants of action. If I were teaching in 1972, I would want to continue the development of this specialized line of psychology. I have revised and up-dated my text entitled, *Emotion in Man and Animal; Its Nature and Dynamic Basis* (Young, 1972) and I would like to try out this text in the classroom.

There is a good deal of latitude in teaching with the possibility of changing the content and improving a course each time it is offered. Laboratory research is different. One usually continues on an experiment until a result is reached and then turns to another experiment. It is often impossible to foresee a result and that is why an experiment is made.

What Lines of Research Would I Follow?

My laboratory research, in general, has been concerned with specific problems in motivation, affectivity, perception, learning, conflict of motives, and related problems. The relevance of this work to social welfare may or may not be apparent but it is part of the basic science of psychology. I would like to continue basic research if I had a laboratory in 1972.

I will mention below three rather specific lines of research that I would like to pursue. These are my special interests.

The Capacity to Integrate Discrete Bits of Sensory Information. When I recall the early experiments in my laboratory there is one line of work that stands out as worthy of further research. That is a series of studies on "organic set" and in particular two doctoral studies with Compton (1933) and Thomas (1942).

The reason why this work seems important to me now is that it deals with the basic human capacity to integrate simple bits of sensory information. This kind of sensory integration is a cerebral function that is a universal characteristic of man. Simple "point" stimulations in the field of vision, audition, and touch, are possible with human beings of all races in all cultures. The integration of these "point" stimulations is a function that can be studied within a universal human psychology.

In both doctoral studies successive "point" stimulations were presented at different spatial positions. The temporospatial presentations formed a pattern, or gestalt, which "set" the subject for immediate reproduction of the gestalt. Compton presented brief stimulations in visual, auditory, and cutaneous spatial fields and had the subjects reproduce the patterns immediately by pressing keys. Thomas presented all stimulations visually but had the subjects reproduce the patterns immediately with different motor systems of signalling: pressing keys or pedals or by special head keys.

In a series of studies it was found that performance varied with such factors as age, practice, mode of presenting a pattern, speed of presentation, the gestalt or configuration formed by the stimulations, and other factors. Compton and Thomas found, however, that a major source of difficulty lay in the organization, or integration, of a gestalt. This finding, I believe, is important because it reflects a central capacity to organize sensory content and to react immediately on the basis of a gestalt.

I believe that this kind of work should be pursued. The apparatus, of course, could be greatly simplified by reducing spatial positions to two points (right and left) and limiting responses to two signal keys.

The Hedonic Organization and Regulation Of Behavior. If I were starting a career in experimental psychology in 1972, I would certainly give priority to studies of hedonic processes (Young, 1966 and 1967).

I believe it is important to clarify the relation between hedonic processes and reinforcement. Positive and negative affective arousals organize and direct behavior. A positive affective arousal is shown by tendency to continue the stimulation that elicits it; a negative affective arousal by tendency to terminate conditions that evoke it. These primitive reaction tendencies are basic; they activate the direct behavior and influence the course of learning.

The principles of reinforcement have been amply demonstrated in experiments with laboratory animals but further work is needed to clarify the nature of reinforcement. Modifications of behavior obviously come about through exercise. The relation between exercise and the intensity of affective arousal should be examined quantitatively.

A problem in this area that needs to be investigated is the process of algebraic summation of hedonic processes. Some unpublished data with laboratory rats show that positive and negative affective processes that are simultaneously produced summate algebraically across sense modalities. Thus a positive affective arousal through sweet taste and a simultaneous negative affective arousal through shock on the feet are integrated hedonically so that a single reaction of choice results.

Clearly there is *hedonic* integration. This is only one form of integration, however, since there is integration on the level of reflexes (as Sherrington has shown) and there is also a rational, cognitive, form of integration as noted above in experiments with "point" stimulations.

The Experimental Study of Values. If I were starting a career in 1972, I would certainly continue the study of evaluation.

I have argued that when a rat accepts a food and ingests it he is reacting *as* if that food had a positive value. If he rejects the food, his behavior reveals negative evaluation. Further, in genuine preferential discriminations between test foods, an animal reveals relative evaluations since food A is "better than" food B in some way. It is easy and useful to regard such behavior as evaluative (Young, 1968).

The conditions that determine hedonic values can be studied objectively, experimentally, quantitatively, with animals including humans. The study of human values becomes complicated when speech is involved. There are evaluations in complicated aesthetic judgments, religious beliefs, and decisions in politics, social policies, and in other areas.

It has often been said that science deals with facts and not with values. But there are *facts* of evaluative behavior, *facts* of conflict in evaluating dispositions, *facts* relating to the hierarchy of values, etc. I believe that a limited science of axiology is possible and that such a science can be established on an objective, experimental, matter-of-fact basis. There are values in every culture.

I agree with Conant (discussed above) that much human activity is nonscientific. The philanthropist, the religious worker, the citizen of good will, are commonly engaged in the search for human betterment and social welfare. They deal with values. I believe that evaluative behavior is real and can be studied scientifically.

The above are only three general areas of investigation in which I would like to pursue specific research programs. I have repeatedly found that when one piece of research is finished other problems appear and in the laboratory one does what seems most important at the time.

What Philosophical Orientation Would I Maintain?

Back in 1924 I argued that the systematic approach to psychology should be through phenomenology and I still feel that a realistic phenomenalism is a sound philosophical position (Young, 1924).

The advantage of a phenomenological approach to psychology is that it includes data obtained from all possible points of view. The sum total of raw data on which the objective sciences rest, after all, is composed of observations made by scientists—physicists, chemists, astronomers, and others. These data are accepted realistically. Among the phenomena experienced by individual, however, are the so-called subjective experiences: dreams, mental images, feelings, emotions, sentiments, cognitive beliefs, desires, and others. Such subjective phenomena are of special interest to the psychologist. A psychology that omits the experimental analysis of conscious experiences, I believe, is to that extent limited in scope. The student is losing out if he does not investigate *all* the phenomena, including psychiatric, that are directly related to human activity.

The phenomenological approach makes it possible to examine and compare the subjective and objective facts of human conscious experience. A strict physical positivism and the S-R behaviorism is, I believe, limited and inadequate. For a consistent physicalism the conscious state of organisms is hypothetical, assumed. But the subjective phenomena of dreams, sleeping and waking, of drug states, of psychoses and neuroses, hypnosis, and other conscious states, are *given* and they are of profound scientific and practical significance though not described in physical terms.

In the twentieth century, major advances have been made in the objective studies of the behavior of organisms. The present day student of psychology must understand behavioral and physiological psychology as a basis for any advanced research upon human activities. The contributions of B. F. Skinner in behavioral psychology, Neal Miller in physiological psychology, and the theoretical works of Hull, Tolman, Guthrie, Hebb, and others, are worthy of very careful study by the present-day student.

The approach to psychology through phenomenology does not deny objective science. It goes beyond objectivity to include much else. The phenomenological approach is a comprehensive, multidisciplinary, eclectic approach.

Psychology and Common Sense

Half a century ago Titchener used to say that scientific psychology (his variety) is removed from common sense. As a student I did not like this view. It seemed to me that significant problems of science often arise from the observations of daily life. And starting from the views of common sense a scientist moves beyond the realm of common sense into worlds of theory. Common sense is useful and not to be disparaged.

As a matter of fact, a universal common sense psychology already exists which deals in practical ways with beliefs, attitudes of friendliness and hostility, emotional behavior, motives, expectancies, learning and memory, habits, and other psychological processes. Categories may not be sharply defined by common sense psychology but this everyday psychology is based on the raw stuff of human nature.

In a universal psychology based on common sense there is a principle of relativity of cognitions and attitudes. *If a person believes that something is true, it is true for him and he acts accordingly.* The beliefs of individuals have social consequences since the actions of one influence the behavior of others. But it is obvious that beliefs differ from individual to individual and from group to group. For example, some persons believe that unidentified flying abjects (flying saucers) are visitors from outer space, but scientists find no objective evidence for this belief. Others believe in the reality of extrasensory perception; but the validity of this belief has not been scientifically established. For many centuries men believed that the earth was flat and that sun and stars rotated about it.

The principle of relativity of beliefs and attitudes becomes important in areas of politics, religion, education, and most other areas that involve social interactions and human behavior. A dynamic psychology that starts from common sense can deal with these matters tracing the development and operation of evaluative, including nonrational, processes.

Conclusion

The majority of psychologists today are concerned with psychotechnologies in the fields of health, education, social welfare, government, industry, advertising, military, and others. The minority are concerned with development of psychology as a basic science through laboratory and field research.

There are some who question whether a psychology that deals with interpersonal human relations and social behavior can ever become a natural science. They believe that coping with personal and social problems remains an art which involves moral judgments. I believe that there will always be an art in human relations. My personal feeling, however, is that the soundest and most useful kind of psychology for those who deal with human welfare is a *basic biosocial science*. Such a universal science, biologically grounded, already exists. It is multidisciplinary, eclectic. It needs to be developed by further research and theorizing.

A universal human psychology considers basic determinants of behavior—perception, learning, motivation, emotion, the dynamics of interpersonal relations, and other processes. The methods of a universal psychology are comparative, genetic and experimental. Human behavior in different human groups (primitive and civilized) can be analyzed and studied comparatively and developmentally. Observations can be made in the field and in the laboratory. Critically important problems can be studied intensively.

If I were a young man starting a career in experimental psychology in 1972, I would work toward the development of a basic, scientific, universal psychology of the kind that would be useful to technologists and persons concerned with human welfare. I have indicated several facets of my research that seem worthy of development. These, however, are specific and personal. I realize that each investigator would follow his own inclination.

Compton, R. K.; and Young, P. T.: A study of organic set; Immediate reproduction of spatial patterns presented by successive points to different senses. *J Exp Psychol, 16*:775-797, 1933.

Conant, J. B.: Scientific principles and moral conduct. *Am Sci, 55*:311-328, 1967.

Eisenberg, L.: The human nature of human nature. *Science, 176*:123-128, 1972.

Gibson, E. J.: The development of perception as an adaptive process. *Am Sci, 58*:98-107, 1970.

Izard, C. E.: *The Face of Emotion*. New York, Appleton-Century-Crofts, 1971.

Kluckhohn, C.: *Mirror for Man; the Relation of Anthropology to Modern Life*. New York, McGraw-Hill, 1949.

Krawiec, T. S. (Ed.): *The Psychologists* (I). New York, Oxford University Press, 1972, pp. 325-355.

Lazo, J. A. (Ed.): *American Psychological Association; 1968 Directory*. Washington, D. C., American Psychological Association, 1968, p. xii.

Mayr, E.: The nature of the Darwinian revolution. *Science, 176*:981-989, 1972.

Murdock, G. P.: The common denominator of cultures. In Linton, R. (Ed.): *The Science of Man in the World Crisis*. New York, Columbia University Press, 1945.

Simpson, G. G.: The biological nature of man. *Science, 152*:472-478, 1966.

Thomas, W. F.; and Young, P. T.: A study of organic set; Immediate reproduction, by different muscle groups, of patterns presented by successive visual flashes. *J Exp Psychol, 30*:347-367, 1942.

Weisskopf, V. F.: The significance of science. *Science, 176*:138-146, 1972.

Young, P. T.: The phenomenological point of view. *Psychol Rev, 31*:288-296, 1924.

Young, P. T.: Hedonic organization and regulation of behavior. *Psychol Rev, 73*:59-86, 1966.

Young, P. T.: Palatability, the hedonic response to foodstuffs. In Code, C. F., et al., (Eds.): *Handbook of Physiology; Section 6, Volume I*. Baltimore, Williams and Wilkins, 1967, pp. 353-366.

Young, P. T.: Evaluation and preference in behavioral development. *Psychol Rev*, 75:222-241, 1968.
Young, P. T.: *Emotion in Man and Animal; Its Nature and Dynamic Basis.* Huntington, New York, Robert E. Krieger, 1972.